Margaret Atwood's Textual Assassinations

Margaret Atwood's Textual Assassinations:

Recent Poetry and Fiction

Edited by
SHARON ROSE WILSON

 THE OHIO STATE UNIVERSITY PRESS
Columbus

Copyright © 2003 by The Ohio State University

Library of Congress Cataloging-in-Publication Data
Margaret Atwood's textual assassinations : recent poetry and fiction /
edited by Sharon Rose Wilson.
        p. cm.
Includes bibliographical references and index.
    ISBN 0-8142-0929-7 (Cloth : alk. paper) — ISBN 0-8142-9012-4 (CD-ROM)

1. Atwood, Margaret Eleanor, 1939—Criticism and interpretation. 2. Women and lit-
erature—Canada—History—20th century. 3. Postmodernism
(Literature)—Canada. 4. Postcolonialism in literature. I. Wilson,
Sharon Rose.
    PR9199.3.A8 Z775 2003
    818'.5409–dc21

                                2002151545

Cover design by Janna Thompson Chordas.
Text design by Jennifer Shoffey Carr.
Type set in Sabon by Adobe.
Printed by Thomson-Shore, Inc.

The paper used in this publication meets the minimum requirements of the American National Standard for information Sciences—Permanence of Paper for Printed
Library Materials. ANSI Z39.48-1992.

9 8 7 6 5 4 3 2 1

Contents

Contents

Acknowledgment

I am grateful to Margaret Atwood and the Thomas Fisher Rare Book Library at the University of Toronto for use of the Margaret Atwood papers.

List of Abbreviations

AG	Alias Grace
BA	The Blind Assassin
BH	Bodily Harm
CE	Cat's Eye
EW	The Edible Woman
GB	Good Bones
GBSM	Good Bones and Simple Murders
LBM	Life before Man
LO	Lady Oracle
MBH	Morning in the Burned House
MD	Murder in the Dark
PP	Power Politics
PU	Procedures for Underground
RB	The Robber Bride
SP	Selected Poems
SPII	Selected Poems II
THP	Two-Headed Poems
WT	Wilderness Tips
YAH	You Are Happy

. . . .

Introduction

SHARON R. WILSON

For most readers today, Margaret Atwood no longer needs an introduction. A Canadian writer of novels, short fiction, poems, and essays, she is one of the foremost writers in the world. Her works are taught in nearly every English department and in many women's studies, Canadian studies, postcolonial studies, and even economics, political science, communications, sociology, business, and other courses around the world (Wilson, Friedman, and Hengen, *Approaches,* 1). Her books are both best-sellers and the subjects of thousands of reviews and scholarly studies, written by scholars from China to Italy to Belgium to New Zealand, England, France, Canada, and the United States. Atwood texts are anthologized in most introduction to literature texts and collections of twentieth-century literature, adapted for films, and even performed as plays (*Good Bones*) or operas (2000 Danish production of *The Handmaid's Tale*). Although Atwood is a popular writer whose works are easily understandable on a surface level, she is also a difficult writer whose texts are multilayered, filled with literary, political, and historical allusions, and subtle in their use of symbolism, parody, and satire.

Atwood's standing in both Canadian and international literature also no longer needs defending. Atwood has received countless literary prizes, including her country's Governor General Award for *The Circle Game* and *The Handmaid's Tale,* the Booker and Dashiell Hammett Awards for *The Blind Assassin,* the Trillium Book Award for *Wilderness*

Tips, and the Giller and Premio Mondello Prizes for *Alias Grace.* She has been president of both the Canadian Writer's Guild and PEN International. Her work is the focus of over forty books from several continents, thousands of articles, numerous dissertations, and a number of books and articles comparing her to one or several authors. Two biographies have also recently appeared.

Margaret Atwood's Textual Assassinations: Recent Poetry and Fiction focuses on recent Atwood: her work of the eighties and nineties and also that which is either new or the culmination of a development over preceding years. Although Atwood's novels, especially *The Handmaid's Tale,* are popular and the subject of numerous reading groups and critical studies, her recent poetry and short fiction, especially her experimental prose pieces and flash fiction responsible for many of the "assassinations," have been largely ignored. This collection also focuses on feminist, postcolonial, postmodern, and formal issues in Atwood's art. It is no accident that the words *strange* and *stranger,* along with *alien* and *alienation, murder* or *assassination, survival,* and *trickster* recur in the article titles or the essays themselves. The issues of power and sexual politics that mark Atwood's earliest work have evolved. Recent texts not only feature self-divided and oppositional alienated characters and character pairs but, despite Atwood's earlier assurance that she doesn't kill off characters (Lee film interview), actual murder and possibly a real split personality. As a quick look at *The Edible Woman* (1969) and *Alias Grace* (1996) indicates, by the eighties and nineties, Atwood's characters and readers are more aware of the multicultural, colonized, racist, and classist as well as patriarchal, sexist, and hypocritical nature of the worlds they occupy. If anything, their alienation is more complex, with multiple causes. Not only is the Canadian experience itself still perceived as "strange" and sometimes estranging, as Atwood discusses in *Strange Things: The Malevolent North in Canadian Literature* (1995), but despite some critics' labeling them dated oversimplifications, the victim positions that may result from some kinds of this alienation still apply. Atwood's recent essay, "Survival, Then and Now" (1999), and several of the essays in this book attest to that. Increasingly, Atwood's survivors are trickster creators, using their verbal "magic" to transform their worlds. The "assassinations," foregrounded not only in *Murder in the Dark* (1983), *Good Bones and Simple Murders* (1994), and the recent novel, *The Blind Assassin* (2000), occur, ironically, both in form and content. The violence, including actual assassinations, that underlies every societal function has been recognized in *The Handmaid's Tale* (1985) but ignored in less discussed texts, especially Atwood's recent poetry, short fiction, and flash fictions or prose pieces. Similarly, the formal brilliance of the recent texts, "assassinations" of traditional genres, plots, narrative voices, structure, techniques, and reader expectations, deserves far more attention. Both the notions that literature is detached or amoral and that it necessarily takes a clearly defined position or presents a "moral" are deconstructed, along with the characters' and readers' comfort, self-satisfaction, or placidity.

Margaret Atwood's Textual Assassinations: Recent Poetry and Fiction, featuring essays by many of the best-known international Atwood and Canadian studies scholars, most of whom have written books on Atwood, is distinctive in its focus on recent texts, including poetry, prose pieces, short stories, and novels, and on postcolonial, cultural, and postmodern issues, as well as feminist ones, in Atwood's texts. For readers either new to Atwood or engaged in comprehensive study, essays by Reingard M. Nischik, Sharon R. Wilson, Mary K. Kirtz, and Karen F. Stein consider the focus text in reference to all of Atwood's work. So far, few critical studies of *The Robber Bride* (1993), perhaps Atwood's most intriguing novel, have appeared. Apart from a number of reviews when these works were published, *Murder in the Dark* (1983), *Interlunar* (1984), *Good Bones* (1992), *Good Bones and Simple Murders* (1994), *Wilderness Tips* (1991), *Morning in the Burned House* (1995), *Alias Grace* (1996), and Atwood's most recent novel, *The Blind Assassin* (2000), have received virtually no scholarly comment.

Reingard M. Nischik's "Murder in the Dark: Margaret Atwood's Inverse Poetics of Intertextual Minuteness" uses some of Atwood's published and unpublished cartoons, including cultural implications of their dichotomy of *large* and *small,* to trace this size motif throughout Atwood's work and approach aspects of the brevity, generic hybridity, and intertextual impact of *Murder in the Dark.* She explores how Atwood's satire and parody connect to her "poetics of inversion: her techniques of undermining conventional thought-patterns, attitudes, values, or textual norms by turning them on their heads."

In "Fiction Flashes: Genre and Intertexts in *Good Bones,*" Sharon Wilson maintains that apart from differences of genre, style, tone, and a growing use of postmodern techniques and postcolonial themes, Atwood uses some of the same myths and other folklore intertexts, particularly goddess and trickster ones, in fairly consistent ways throughout her career. *Good Bones* is again metafiction, about storytelling, tricking, and surviving in a patriarchal, colonizing, environmentally ruined world. Ironically, Atwood uses postmodern techniques to uncover a traditional subtext—the survival theme—that has been evident throughout her career and is discussed in *Survival* as the main theme in Canadian literature. Despite its subversions, in *Good Bones,* Atwood's tricksters are often ironic culture heroes in tales that, together, are about saving, transforming, global human culture. Wilson also connects the cover designs of both texts and the illustrations for *Good Bones and Simple Murders* to this volume's use of borderline genre: flash fictions or fictions that are not only over in a flash but that also precipitate flashes of insight in readers.

Shannon Hengen's "Strange Visions: *Interlunar* and Technopoetics" suggests that *Interlunar* marks a conclusion to the poetry volumes preceding it but still presents a changed perspective, "a stranger vision." Making fruitful references to Donna Haraway's discussions of technoscience, Hengen asserts that *Interlunar* presents a technopoetic view, whereby images and the inarticulate join with the "data of nature."

In "(Dis)unified Field Theories: The Clarendon Lectures Seen through (a) *Cat's Eye,*" Mary Kirtz examines both Atwood's representation and transformation of the myth of the malevolent north. Using the Clarendon lectures Margaret Atwood gave at Oxford University in 1991 as a lens for reading *Cat's Eye,* Kirtz shows how the four "cliché-images" and stories about the "malevolent North" that Atwood considers to be identifiably Canadian are, in *Cat's Eye,* transformed onto a southern, urban landscape. In revealing the instability of these categories within the continually changing sense of identity held by Anglophone Canadians, the novel is not only about a girl growing up; it is about Canada and Canadian identity following World War II.

Initially using the perspectives Atwood tempts critics to impose on the stories, in "Strangers within the Gates: *Wilderness Tips,*" Carol Beran examines how Atwood's strangers in *Wilderness Tips* push readers toward becoming the creative nonvictims of *Survival.* She reveals how Atwood satirizes not only the myth of the polite Canadian, but also critics who fit the stories into their own categories of belief.

Reading *The Robber Bride* as a postcolonial novel, Coral Ann Howells suggests in *"The Robber Bride*; or, Who is a True Canadian?" that the novel is part of Atwood's ongoing inquiry into Canadian identity, a means of "narrating the nation." Addressing English Canadian anxieties about changing representations of national identity, the novel exorcises ghosts.

Kathryn Van Spanckeren, in "Humanizing the Fox: Atwood's Poetic Tricksters and *Morning in the Burned House,*" offers a meditation on death in this most recent poetry volume, suggesting that the book moves from a foxlike cynical vision of survival in the body through imaginative experiences of death to a transformed appreciation of life and vulnerability. This essay compares Atwood's poetry with seminal poems of the twentieth century that bid farewell to myth and embrace painful individual experience. Atwood's changing use of the fox image reveals her attempt to move toward greater feeling while preserving important elements of myth, seen in the figure of the trickster fox.

In "Quilting as Narrative Art: Metafictional Construction in *Alias Grace*," Sharon Wilson argues that, like many of Atwood's previous novels, *Alias Grace* is again a feminist, postmodern, and postcolonial metafiction, exposing all of our "truths" as theories or speculations, constructions over the abyss. Making use of letters, notes, and manuscripts in the Margaret Atwood Papers (Thomas Fisher Rare Book Library), she offers evidence of Atwood's concern with class, gender, and cultural issues while researching and writing the novel. She examines the contribution of the novel's "metaquilts" (the ten quilt patterns that mark and title each section of the novel) and the quilting of intertexts to the book's metafiction, including the novel's involvement of the reader in the construction of both murder and text.

Next, in "A Left-Handed Story: *The Blind Assassin*," Karen Stein reads Atwood's most recent novel as a Gothic text, with the central theme of hiding and revealing. Atwood works within and against the tradition of Gothic fiction to tell the story of Iris Chase Griffen, who is able to resist the Gothic codes and to transform herself from an "angel in the house" in a position of subservient domesticity to an active agent. Finally, in "Talking Back to Bluebeard," Stein examines how storytelling contributes to the power that Atwood's female protagonists gain in *Bluebeard's Egg* and throughout her work. As they grow more self-aware, they move from victimization to approach the role of trickster—they talk back to Bluebeard. In this book we see how Margaret Atwood's recent texts not only continue genres and themes evident in her earliest work, but also intertextually advance innovative, genre-bending variations on these patterns.

. . . .

Murder in the Dark:
Margaret Atwood's Inverse Poetics of
Intertextual Minuteness

REINGARD M. NISCHIK

The distortion of a text is not unlike a murder.
  Sigmund Freud

The lake, vast and dimensionless,
doubles everything, the stars,
the boulders, itself, even the darkness
that you can walk so long in
it becomes light.
  Margaret Atwood, *Interlunar*

The dichotomy between *large* and *small* is a motif that recurs frequently in the works of Margaret Atwood. This can clearly be seen in
Atwood's various cartoons, in which the main themes of her works—
for example, the status of the author or artist in her/his social surroundings, or the national/cultural relations between the United States
and Canada—reemerge in a deliberately exaggerated form. With iron-
ical self-deprecation, a characteristic that Linda Hutcheon sees as epitomizing Canadian culture (Hutcheon, *Splitting Images*), Atwood
associates her own position in these comic strips (as author, Canadian,
woman) with the characteristic of smallness. An early example of this
method is provided by her comic "Portrait of the Artist as a Young
Cipher"—even in the title, reminiscent of Joyce's *A Portrait of the*

Chapter 1

Artist as a Young Man, the expected noun, *woman,* is replaced by *cipher,* an irrelevant entity. Similarly, the text and pictures portray an up-and-coming author who is impressed, not to say intimidated, by the confrontation with real or imaginary forces of dominating power.

A look at four episodes from this comic strip in Figure 1 will serve to illustrate my point; among other things, they also highlight the biographical elements contained in this humorous series.[1]

FIGURE 1

Margaret Atwood, "Portrait of the Artist as a Young Cipher" (1977).

(1) "I entered the University in 1957."

(2) "I was not happy as a freshperson." (Northrop Frye)

(3) ". . . the sight of Jay Macpherson whisking around corners . . ."

The closing picture in the sequence depicts the established author of 1977, once again with self-deprecating irony and understatement: She is overwhelmed not by professional success, but rather by pet cats (cf. Nathalie Cooke in Nischik, *Margaret Atwood: Works and Impact*, 15–27).

(4) "Buttons fall from my clothes."

After completing *Survival: A Thematic Guide to Canadian Literature* (1972), Atwood, under the pseudonym Bart Gerrard, published a series of "Survivalwoman" comics, which appeared in the Canadian *This Magazine* under the rubric *Kanadian Kultchur Komix* (see Figure 2, page 4).

As can be seen from Survivalwoman's elegant cape, she is a Canadian counterpart to America's Superman (or "Superham" as Atwood prefers to call him). In every other respect, however, Survivalwoman, as her very name suggests, is Superman's polar opposite: She is diminutive, exudes cheerfulness and intelligence, and wears typical northern-Canadian snow boots, indicating a connection with nature and an earthbound quality contrasting strongly with the power and provocativeness evoked by Superman's leather boots. A popular icon of American imperialist megalomania is thus recreated,[2] in Atwood's inverted Canadian representation, as a survival-orientated and dwarfish yet fearless champion of independence ("the FIGHTING FAILURE exerts her utmost powers").

Finally, a more recent comic strip shown in Figure 3, page 4, dating from the mid-nineties, in which the semiotics of small and large remain basically unchanged.

In "The Radio Interview" from "Book Tour Comics," we see Atwood's stylized version of herself, elegantly dressed and with characteristic curly locks, yet so tiny that she seemingly can keep her balance only by holding on to the table. This comic strip is a particularly clear example of Atwood's inversion of conventional large-small hierarchies; here, it is the minuscule author who, with her sparing yet

FIGURE 2
"Kanadian Kulture Komix" by Margaret Atwood under the pseudonym Bart Gerrard.

FIGURE 3
"The Radio Interview" by Margaret Atwood for *Book Tour Comics.*

pointed use of language, triumphs over an interviewer more than three times her size.[3]

Atwood also makes repeated use of the small-large dichotomy in her literary texts, once again inverting norms to significant effect. In *The Robber Bride* (1994), the novel to which "The Radio Interview" refers, the importance of physical size, as in the comic strip, is reduced, thus implicitly increasing the value of smallness: "Tall people's heads are too far from the ground, their center of gravity is too high. One shock and they topple" (39). In "Weight," from Atwood's short story collection *Wilderness Tips,* the reader is told that "Molly was pushy. Or you could call it determined. She had to be, she was so short. . . . She'd made it on brains" (182). Here again, nonphysical qualities can be seen to compensate, or more than compensate, for a small physique. A similar point is made in the following fictional interview, which surely touches upon Atwood's diverse experiences, both active and passive, in the media circus of literature:[4]

> "I thought you would be different," says Andrea as we settle.
> "Different how?" I ask.
> "Bigger," she says.
> I smile at her. "I am bigger."

This quotation from *Cat's Eye* (92) indeed suggests that Atwood's preoccupation with the small-large dichotomy may also have an autobiographical basis.[5] Yet her own small stature is only a superficial explanation for the inverse relationships present in her work. Rather, they are part of a general tendency in Atwood's work to expose conventions (see note 3 below), that is to say the social, psychological, linguistic, and mythical structures that underpin everyday perceptions and judgments, and to question their value and function.

Since the eighties, Atwood has been using a new medium for her challenging redefinitions and inversions: a type of short text that is hard to categorize and has few real ancestors in Canadian literature. Works in this hybrid genre appeared in the collections *Murder in the Dark: Short Fictions and Prose Poems* and *Good Bones,* published in 1983 and 1992, respectively.[6] The originality of their form and modes of representation, combined with a possible confusion of smallness/shortness with insignificance,[7] meant that these Atwood texts were neglected by critics for a long time.[8] However, it has now been recognized that with these two collections Atwood introduced a hitherto unfamiliar genre into Anglo-Canadian literature: the Baudelairean prose poem. In addition, the short texts in these collections constitute a radical contribution to the development of genre hybridization.[9] A closer evaluation of many of the texts in *Murder in the Dark* and *Good Bones* reveals Atwood's literary art at work in the smallest of spaces. The highly intertextual nature of these works is immediately noticeable,[10] creating networks of meaning and significance despite their limited scope. This frequently goes hand in hand with what I would like to call Atwood's "poetics of inversion": her technique of undermining conventional thought patterns, attitudes, values, or textual norms by turning them on their heads. This leads to a multifaceted interplay between explicit and implicit meaning or, to put it another way, a prismatic multiplication of sense. Since this technique is used in a very restricted space, it almost inevitably results in strongly delineated, suggestive, and highly intensified representations, thus providing a possible explanation for the satirical and parodic tendencies discernible in many of the texts.[11]

One of Atwood's drawings, which was included in the American edition of *Good Bones and Simple Murders* (a compilation of selected texts from *Murder in the Dark* and *Good Bones*),[12] perfectly illustrates Atwood's technique of inverse portrayal. This drawing appears within the text of the heavyweight prose poem "Good Bones."[13]

FIGURE 4
Margaret Atwood drawing appearing within the poem "Good Bones."

Due to its elaborate composition, it is possible to interpret this drawing in many ways, depending on perspective and focus of perception: an undulating moonlit lake or river landscape at twilight;[14] or two sets of two female profiles looking at one another, different from each other (light/dark), yet very similar; or, looking at it the other way round, two female profiles turned away from each other while still constituting two complementary halves of the same figure; or a side view of two dissimilar women (one larger, one smaller), who are nevertheless harmoniously looking in the same direction at the same time; or silhouettes of female physical forms (to put it plainly: stylized female sexual characteristics); or even a stylized bone—a "good bone" indeed! If we were to cover up the lower half of this partly mirroring inverse portrayal, the spectrum of possible interpretations would be reduced by more than half.

Although Atwood's inverse poetics of intertextual minuteness can be seen at work even more clearly and pithily in a number of texts in *Good Bones*,[15] it nevertheless constitutes an underlying principle in the conception of *Murder in the Dark*, too. The collection opens with a series of eight vignettes, grouped together as Part I, which are linked by their presentation of epiphanic events from the childhood of the lyrical "I." The first text, "Autobiography," introduces not only this background situation, but also Atwood's technique of inversion. As Christl Verduyn rightly says of this text, which is no more than half a page long: "As in subsequent texts, the form of 'Autobiography' is in itself unsettling; this must be the world's shortest, not to say oddest, autobiography!" (125)

Atwood's use here of the first-person singular and the past tense are redolent of the genre of autobiography. What is being evoked, however, is a fragmentary epiphanic situation that undermines the sequence of events encountered in traditional autobiographies: a mental painting—the almost static description of a landscape as seen and felt—is used to demonstrate the power of artistic perception and representation to alter and, indeed, create reality. This highly concentrated "Autobiography" refers to no human beings other than the "I" (only the products of their civilization: "dam, covered bridge, houses, white church, sawed-off trunks of huge trees," etc.). Far more important are the relationship of this "I" to its perception of the almost lifeless landscape, as well as the reconstruction and mental working-over of this perception on another, artistic level of reality:

> Once, on the rock island, there was the half-eaten carcass of a deer, which smelled like iron, like rust rubbed into your hands so that it

> mixes with sweat. This smell is the point at which the landscape dissolves, ceases to be a landscape and becomes something else. (9)

This directly articulated change of perspective sweeps aside the inherently static nature of the landscape description, just as on a linguistic level the mental painting was lent an added dynamism by the use of verbs of motion, which convey the process of perceiving and the transforming power of artistic perception and representation ("the lake disappeared into the sky," "trunks of huge trees coming up through the water," "a path running back into the forest," "the landscape dissolves . . . and becomes something else"). The traditionally diachronic sequence of events in autobiographies is replaced, in "Autobiography," by a synchronically located metamorphosis, which is developed within the artistic conscience through its powers of transformation (note the two similes introduced by "like"). And indeed the development of this ability to transform (the perception of) reality is the basic hinge for the (auto-)biographies of artists (see the concept of the "Third Eye" in the final text of this collection, "Instructions for the Third Eye," which is in many ways an extension of the opening text discussed above, with which it forms a frame for the entire collection). Atwood's provocatively titled "Autobiography" takes as its theme the individual point of view ("there was a white sand cliff, although you couldn't see it from where I was standing," "the entrance to another path which cannot be seen from where I was standing but was there anyway"), and implies that even autobiographical texts are quasi-fictional constructs, though this does not make them less important or "true." This reductive, condensed inversion of the genre of autobiography at the beginning of *Murder in the Dark* is therefore a metapoetical commentary on the genre to which it alludes, but also on the collection of "Short Fictions and Prose Poems" that it starts off.

Any author writing in the genre of the prose poem is heavily indebted to the work of Charles Baudelaire, all the more so in the case of an Anglo-Canadian writer working in a literary tradition in which the genre is unfamiliar (see Merivale, "From 'Bad News' to 'Good Bones,'" 268).[16] Concrete proof of Atwood's reception of Baudelaire's poems and prose poems can be found in the highly ironic ending of "Let Us Now Praise Stupid Women" in *Good Bones*: "*Hypocrite lecteuse! Ma semblable! Ma soeur*! / Let us now praise stupid women, / who have given us Literature" (37). The French quotation modifies Baudelaire's famous closing gambit in "Au lecteur," the introductory poem to *Les Fleurs du mal* ("—Hypocrite lecteur,—mon semblable,—mon frère!"

8), and, not without a certain linguistic irreverence (e.g., "lecteuse" instead of the correct form "lectrice"), places the emphasis firmly on the female gender. This reversal ironically highlights a tradition of misogynist representations of women (cf. Clack, *Misogyny*, 1–9), a tradition in which Baudelaire plays a central part. Indeed, Atwood's revisionist attitude to this tradition, her exposing and rewriting of such misogynist portrayals, constitutes, as Patricia Merivale has succinctly suggested in relation to *Murder in the Dark*, one of Atwood's fundamental approaches to Baudelaire's texts:

> Atwood's prose poems of the sex wars invert or subvert the misogyny, bordering on highbrow pornography, of Baudelaire's prose poems, while maintaining, but recontextualizing, in her lyrical transvestism, the irony of the Baudelairean . . . voice. In that whole misogynist repertory, whose most powerfully intelligent exponent is Charles Baudelaire, woman, reified and dangerously idealized, is seen as perfect only insofar as she reflects the man to himself. . . . These are neat inversions of the misogynist patterns in Baudelaire's poems of Woman reified by the Poet; in Atwood the Poet watches the man reify her. (Merivale, "Hypocrite Lecteuse!" 105, 102)

I would like to develop Merivale's excellent analysis in two ways. First, with reference to two texts from *Murder in the Dark*, I will examine more closely Atwood's revisionist approach to gender, and particularly to its portrayal in intertexts by Baudelaire. Second, I will differentiate between Atwood's subversions and inversions, with *subversion* here taken to be the more inclusive concept.

Merivale's observation that the poet watches man reifying woman holds true for Atwood's prose poems "Worship" and "Iconography," from Part IV of *Murder in the Dark*. Such texts can be seen as radically critical continuations of Baudelaire texts such as his poems "*Le serpent qui danse*" and "*Le chat,*" both from *Les Fleurs du mal*, or his prose poems "*Un hémisphère dans une chevelure*" and "*Un cheval de race*" from *Le Spleen de Paris*. In these Baudelaire texts, Woman, as perceived by the lyrical "I," is reduced to a physical level, and is reified by ostensibly flattering comparisons to animals and objects, for example:

> *A te voir marcher en cadence,*
> *Belle d'abandon,*
> *On dirait un serpent qui danse*
> *Au bout d'un bâton.*

("*Le serpent qui danse,*" 50)
[When you walk in rhythm, lovely
    With abandonment,
You seem to be swayed by a wand,
    A dancing serpent.]
("The Dancing Serpent," 37)

Usée peut-être, mais non fatiguée, et toujours héroïque, elle fait penser à ces chevaux de grande race que l'oeil du véritable amateur reconnaît, même attelés à un carrosse de louage ou à un lourd chariot. ("Un cheval de race," 370)

[Deteriorated perhaps, but not wearied, and still heroic, she reminds you of those horses of pure breed recognized by a true connoisseur's eye, even when hitched to a hired coach or a heavy wagon.]
("A Thoroughbred," 99)

In "Worship," Atwood, through a strongly ambivalent use of language, subtly highlights and lays bare the sexuality hinted at in Baudelaire texts such as "*Le serpent qui danse.*" She furthermore subjects Baudelaire's attitude to sexual gender roles to a radical critique from a female point of view. Indeed, the beginning of "Worship" ("You have these sores in your mouth that will not heal. It's from eating too much sugar, you tell yourself," 51) seems to act as a retort to these lines from "*Le serpent qui danse*": "*Comme un flot grossi par la fonte / Des glaciers grondants, / Quand l'eau de ta bouche remonte / Au bord de tes dents*" (50, 52) ["When, like a stream by thawing of / Glaciers made replete, / The water of your mouth rises / Up to your teeth" (37)]. "Worship" is based on two fundamental themes, which are related to each other within the text and mingle in a strettolike combination: religious veneration and physical unification. The admiring, not to say worshipping, attitude of the man to the woman is compared to religious veneration, and its deficiencies and compensatory function are subjected to a complex and pointed analysis (cf. "Madonna syndrome"), for example:

Thanksgiving. That's why he brings you roses, on occasion, and chocolates when he can't think of anything else. . . . Prayer is wanting. . . . You aren't really a god but despite that you are silent. When you're being worshipped there isn't much to say. (51)

The worshipping attitude is ruthlessly exposed, by means of vaginal imagery, as reifying self-reflection, not to say selfishness:

> Jesus, Jesus, he says, but he's not praying to Jesus, he's praying to you, not to your body or your face but to that space you hold at the centre, which is the shape of the universe. Empty. He wants response, an answer from that dark sphere and its red stars, which he can touch but not see. (51)

(Cf. Baudelaire: *"Un ciel liquide qui parsème / D'étoiles mon coeur!"* *"Le serpent qui danse,"* 52 ["A liquid sky that sows its stars / Within my heart!" "The Dancing Serpent," 37])

The reification of women, sexuality, and religious veneration are inextricably intertwined at the close of "Worship," where words like "use/d" and "service/d" take on a kaleidoscopic range of meaning, and a phrase such as "like a chalice, burnished," in the context evoked by Atwood, has a manifold sense, with woman being an instrument in the ceremony of sexual love (cf. e.g. "to burnish": "to polish by friction with something hard and smooth"):

> [T]hat's you up there, shining, burning, like a candle, like a chalice, burnished; with use and service. After you've been serviced, after you've been used, you'll be put away again until needed. (51)

The term *service*, correlating with the religious conceit of the text in its possible reference to religious service, may have yet another, even more radical meaning here. *Service* also refers to the insemination of animals, and this meaning here would imply that human sexual love, in spite of its pretensions, may be based on a primitive need to dominate and control. The couching of this idea in religious ritual and imagery renders the representation of woman as an object of, rather than a mutual participant in, sexual love all the more shocking.[17] The suppressed implications of Baudelaire's strategy in portraying women are thus brought to the fore by Atwood in a subtle act of deliberate subversion. Whereas the Baudelaire text is written exclusively from a male perspective, denying female subjectivity and agency, Atwood also takes account of and assesses the female role in gender relations; her use of the second person ("you") illustrates a universalizing, and in a way even didactic, tendency.

This rearrangement of perspectives, which nevertheless leaves room for the male point of view as an ironic accompaniment, both within Atwood's prose poems and in the intertextual dialogue with texts by Baudelaire, becomes a full-fledged inverse portrayal in Atwood's "Liking

Men" from *Murder in the Dark* (cf. also "Simmering" in the same collection). In the case of "Liking Men," Merivale's observation that "in Atwood the poet watches the man reifying her [woman]" is no longer valid. In this text, in which an ironic reversal takes place, with woman portrayed as reifying man, an undercurrent of irony is present from the outset: "It's time to like men again. Where shall we begin?" (53) With Baudelairean symmetry,[18] the text is divided through the middle into two halves by the crucial phrase, "You don't want to go on but you can't stop yourself" (53). After various parts of the male body have been rejected as too problematic, the seemingly harmless feet of the man are ironically reified and singled out as objects for the action of "liking men." But a positive approach ("You think of kissing those feet, . . . you like to give pleasure," 53) proves almost impossible to maintain: the associations called up by footwear, benign at first ("Rubber boots, for wading out to the barn in the rain in order to save the baby calf. . . . Knowing what to do, doing it well. Sexy," 53), lead inexorably, from "dance shoes," "golf shoes," and "rubber boots," via "riding boots," "cowboy boots," and "jackboots," to war and rape scenes in which men are portrayed in brutally aggressive roles. Going beyond Baudelaire, the "I" in "Liking Men" attempts to differentiate between Man as a category, which includes warmongers and rapists, and men as individuals: "[J]ust because all rapists are men it doesn't follow that all men are rapists, . . . you try desperately to retain the image of the man you love and also like" (54). This attempt takes the "I" back to the birth of the man and, therefore, back to the social conditions that influence him: "Maybe that's what you have to go back to, in order to trace him here, the journey he took, step by step" (54). "Liking Men," then, points both intratextually and intertextually to the constructedness and therefore mutability of gender roles and images. Atwood's inversion technique—as we have already seen in the apparently reflected double moonscape in her drawing—goes beyond mere mirroring and, indeed, in its intertextual double coding reaches beyond Baudelaire's self-reflective portrayal of women; as Margery Evans says of Baudelaire:

> In *Le Spleen de Paris* . . . the descriptions of women are, quite self-consciously, a series of fictions which may help to give the poet a sense of his own existence ("*à sentir que je suis et ce que je suis*") but which in no way purport to be an objective rendering of a common, shared reality. (56f.)

In contrast to this, Atwood's inverse portrayal of women and gender relations has a fundamentally political aim, as can be seen even more clearly in her later collection *Good Bones* (e.g. "Making a Man" with the humorous indirect attacks on the reification of women, often as commercial commodity, in popular culture). In fact, Atwood's acute awareness of gender differences may simply be seen as an integral part of her humanitarianism, her being a champion for human rights in her literary just as well as in her nonliterary public roles (for example, her membership in Amnesty International).

In bringing the genre of the prose poem to the Anglo-Canadian literary scene, Atwood enters into an intertextual dialogue with Baudelaire in a number of ways: in her choice of genre, thematically (notably in her representation of gender), and as regards specific intertextual cross-fertilizations. In this respect, Atwood's "A Beggar" from Part II ("Raw Materials") of *Murder in the Dark* can be interpreted as a rewriting of Baudelaire's "*Assomons les pauvres*" from *Le Spleen de Paris*; and "Bad News," the opening text of *Good Bones*, can be seen as a brilliant new version of Baudelaire's "*Au lecteur*" from *Les Fleurs du mal* (see also the aforementioned direct reference to Baudelaire in "Let Us Now Praise Stupid Women" from *Good Bones*). It is nevertheless Baudelaire's self-reflective, discriminatory gender representations (cf. e.g. Baudelaire's "*L'Homme et la mer*" with his "*Le chat*," "*Le serpent qui danse*," or "*Un cheval de race*") that act as the greatest spur to Atwood, and that, as she progresses from *Murder in the Dark* to *Good Bones*, lead her to increasingly inverted counter-representations (for example, "Men at Sea" from *Good Bones* as an inverse rewriting of "*L'Homme et la mer*"). The development of Atwood's inversion technique, as well as her increasing radicalness (based also on her increasing injection of playful and comic, facetious elements into her short fictions and prose poems), become clear in a comparison of, for example, "Worship" and "Liking Men" from *Murder in the Dark* with "Making a Man" from *Good Bones*, or indeed "Iconography" (*MD*) with "Gertrude Talks Back" (*GB*).

In her contributions to the genre of the prose poem, Atwood documents the fact that, as Umberto Eco puts it in his afterword to *The Name of the Rose*, "the postmodern discourse . . . demands, in order to be understood, not the negation of the already said, but its ironic rethinking. . . . The past, since it cannot be destroyed, . . . must be revisited; but with irony."[19] Atwood's subversive textual assassinations, her "Murder in the Dark" (see Freud: "The distortion of a text is not

unlike a murder"[20]) seek to question the basis, justification, and consequences of traditional judgments and prejudices and call the singular,
one-sided point of view into question without, however, seeking to
negate it. Atwood's subversive poetics of inversion defamiliarizes, irri-
tates, disturbs, and amuses, opening up explanatory chasms as soon as
it closes them. The author as murderer of the conventional, "daylight"
stories, to take up the playful symbolism of the title story, "Murder in
the Dark," teaches us the meaning of fear in order to uncover for us
new and often uncomfortable views (see the end of "Iconography":
"Watch yourself. That's what the mirrors are for, this story is a mirror
story which rhymes with horror story, almost but not quite. We fall
back into these rhythms as if into safe hands," 52). In Atwood's prose
poems this is rendered in language that is closer to poetry than to
prose. As she herself puts it in an interview on the differences between
prose, prose poetry, and poetry: "The difference between a prose poem
and a short story for me is that the prose poem is still concerned with
that rhythmical syllabic structure. You're as meticulous about the syl-
lables in a prose poem as you are in a poem."[21]

And in order to demonstrate the range of Atwood's inverse poetics,
I will indeed conclude with a lasting image from one of Atwood's poems,
"Woman Skating," taken from her 1970 poetry collection *Procedures for
Underground.*[22] In this poem, *woman* can be seen to stand for all human
beings, especially those with a creative or artistic bent. The poem, which
may be linked to the aforementioned inverse landscape portrayal,
evokes a pastoral, northern lakeland landscape on a late afternoon:

> A lake sunken among
> cedar and black spruce hills;
> late afternoon.
>
> On the ice a woman skating,
> jacket sudden
> red against the white,
>
> concentrating on moving
> in perfect circles.
> (96)

The middle section of the poem, which offers in itself a specifying
inverted perspective on the rest of the poem, leads up to this wonderful
closing image:

With arms wide the skater
turns, leaving her breath like a diver's
trail of bubbles.
Seeing the ice
as what it is, water:
seeing the months
as they are, the years
in sequence occurring
underfoot, watching
the miniature human
figure balanced on steel
needles (those compasses
floated in saucers) on time
sustained, above
time circling: miracle

Over all I place
A glass bell.
(96–97)

Here, we can see Atwood's inverse poetics at work once again. Her way of looking at things from a different perspective opens up whole new vistas of meaning, in this case generating an unusual, metapoetic synthesis of stasis and movement ("ice/water," "balanced/floated," "time sustained/time circling"), and elevating the seemingly tiny ("miniature human figure, steel needles, glass bell") to a higher sphere of meaning. Drops of water freeze into a sheet of ice; individual months link together to form a year; a human figure is visible, apparently so tiny set against the enormous natural backdrop, yet whose skill creates an epiphanic moment for the observer in the poem and the reader, in which T. S. Eliot's "still point of the turning world" seems for an instant to be tangible: "the miniature human figure balanced . . . on time sustained, above time circling: miracle." In an everyday context (compare the contrasting, realistic parenthetical insertion in the middle section of the poem, omitted in my quotation), such visionary moments are all too rare. In art, particularly in Atwood's art, they can be achieved more often, even, as demonstrated, in the most restricted of spaces: "Over all I place / A glass bell."

NOTES

1. I am grateful to Margaret Atwood for permission to reprint the comics included in this text.

2. See Atwood's "Afterword" in her poetry collection, *The Journals of Susanna Moodie* (1970): "If the national mental illness of the United States is megalomania, that of Canada is paranoid schizophrenia," 62.

3. For details of conventional concepts such as "bigger is better" or "significant is big," which influence thought as well as language, see George Lakoff and Mark Johnson, *Metaphors We Live By,* e.g. 22 and 50.

4. For further details see Susanne Becker, "Celebrity, or a Disneyland of the Soul: Margaret Atwood and the Media," in Reingard M. Nischik, ed., *Margaret Atwood: Works and Impact.*

5. Pertinent references can also be found repeatedly in Atwood's nonfictional texts, e.g. "where there is a David in Canadian literature there is usually a Goliath, . . . the evil giant (or giantess)," in *Survival, 58*; or in numerous interviews, e.g. in Earl G. Ingersoll, ed., *Margaret Atwood: Conversations.*

6. The idea, hinted at by some Atwood critics, that such a prose-lyric hybrid could eventually replace Atwood's purely poetical work, has been disproved by the more recent publication of Atwood's superb collection of poems, *Morning in the Burned House* (1995). Such a suggestion was in any case hardly plausible, considering the versatility of the author.

7. See William French's summing up in his 1983 review of *Murder in the Dark*: "not quite a major work but hardly minor as its length might indicate," n.p.

8. As late as 1996, Patricia Merivale could still refer to *Murder in the Dark* as "Atwood's most critically neglected text," yet also as "one of her most difficult, challenging, and rewarding" (99). Twenty years after the first publication of the earlier collection, relevant literary studies of *Murder in the Dark* and *Good Bones* can still be counted almost on the fingers of one hand: Christl Verduyn, "*Murder in the Dark*"; Lorna Irvine, "Murder and Mayhem"; Pierre Spriet, "Margaret Atwood's Post-modernism"; Patricia Merivale, "From 'Bad News' to 'Good Bones'" and "Hypocrite Lecteuse!"; and Michel Delville, "Murdering the Text."

9. See especially Merivale, "Hypocrite Lecteuse!" and "From 'Bad News' to 'Good Bones,'" e.g.: "Atwood has, for the moment, the Baudelairean mode almost to herself in Canadian poetry, as she quite brilliantly demonstrates in *Murder in the Dark. Good Bones* consolidates her generic monopoly in such prose poems, while extending her range" (Merivale, "From 'Bad News' to 'Good Bones,'" 268). For genre hybridization in general, and specifically in Atwood's novels, see Coral Ann Howells in Nischik, ed., 139–56.

10. Referring to Baudelaire's prose poetry in particular, critics have recently pointed out the highly intertextual nature of the prose poem. See Merivale, "Hypocrite Lecteuse!" especially page 100: "a multiplicity of generic allusions, to different kinds of prose narratives, seems characteristic of the prose poem."

11. For a general overview of parody in Atwood's works see chapter 5 in Martin Kuester, "Atwood: Parodies from a Feminist Point of View."

12. This book was published by Doubleday, the publishing house of Atwood's American publisher, Nan A. Talese, in 1994; the only text in this book not included in the earlier collections is the murder-mystery parody "Simple Murders."

13. See Merivale, "From 'Bad News' to 'Good Bones,'" 266–69.

14. The portrayal of the moon (here as crescent) suggests a wealth of additional allusions (cf. Horst S. Daemmrich and Ingrid Daemmrich 1987, or Elisabeth Frenzel

1992, under the heading "moon"/"*Mond*"). The most important are: the moon as symbol of the divine and source of inspiration; the moon as ruler over the element water controls the tides and is the source of life; its reflection in the water at night doubles its brightness; the moon god was regarded as being female or androgynous; connection to fertility, creation, imagination; to emotions, passions, especially love. Concerning the crescent moon: a conventional representation is a female figure on the crescent, as source of life; the crescent moon is traditionally associated with good weather or luck; Archibald MacLeish put it poetologically, "A poem ought to be like a crescent moon" (Frenzel, 539).

15. See an article of mine, "Von guten Knochen und Mord im Dunkeln: Margaret Atwoods inverse Poetik intertexteller Winzigkeit," published in German in 2002, which bases its argument, in contrast to the present article, exclusively on examples from *Good Bones*.

16. Although Aloysius Bertrand's *Gaspard de la nuit* (1842) is generally considered to be the first sequence of prose poems, its influence was minor in comparison to that of Baudelaire's *Le Spleen de Paris: Petits Poèmes en prose* (1862) (see Margery A. Evans, *Baudelaire and Intertextuality*), which became the template for the genre as a whole.

17. I am indebted to my former student Ellen McCarthy for the formulation of this further potential meaning of "service."

18. Merivale, "Hypocrite Lecteuse!" 102; Evans, *Baudelaire and Intertextuality.*

19. Quoted in Spriet, 29.

20. Quoted in Irvine, 265.

21. Interview with Karla Hammond, 79.

22. Reprinted in Atwood, *Eating Fire: Selected Poetry 1965–1995*, 96–97.

2

. . . .

Fiction Flashes:
Genre and Intertexts in *Good Bones*

SHARON R. WILSON

Although its performance possibilities have been recently recognized,[1]
Good Bones (1992) has been perhaps Margaret Atwood's most neglected volume. Apart from a number of reviews when it was initially
published in Canada and the United Kingdom,[2] and some on the American and British editions, *Good Bones and Simple Murders* (1994,
1995)[3] and *Bones and Murder* (1995), that combine pieces from *Murder in the Dark* (1983) and *Good Bones,* scholars have nearly ignored
these innovative collections of what can be described either as prose
poems or short-short, sudden, or flash fiction.[4] As I mentioned in this
volume's "Introduction," critics have never given Atwood's short fiction
as much attention as her novels; and recently, even Atwood's poetry,
which first attracted Canadian readers and made her famous, is slight-
ed. In reference to *Good Bones and Simple Murders,* one reviewer
thinks that Atwood "is always at her worst when her acerbic sneer over-
whelms other elements" and that the volume not only "has more to do
with brevity than quality" but demonstrates the "laundry-list mentality
usually reserved for dead authors" (Review, *Kirkus*). Others mistakenly consider it either lacking in structure or "free from the structural
demands of novels, short stories, and poetry"; call the collections "odd-
ities and fragments"; and "feel pity for the author's victims—men in
particular" (Review, *Kirkus*; Seaman; Review, *The Atlantic*).
   Good Bones and its interrelated volumes, *Good Bones and Simple
Murders* and *Murder in the Dark,* all again postmodern metatexts, are

primary evidence of Atwood's innovations of form: her often parodic and satiric remaking of traditional genres, plots, characters, and intertexts. In 1991, at the same time as she began to put together *Good Bones,* "another *Murder in the Dark* type book—short, weird prose and prose-poetr[y] pieces," Atwood conceived of a combination of the best of *Murder* and *Good Bones* for the United States (Atwood fax to Phoebe Larmore, 7 Aug. 1991). Before copyright considerations necessitated a smaller number,[5] she decided in conference with Nan Talese that twenty-one out of twenty-seven selections would come from *Murder in the Dark.* Phoebe Larmore, Atwood's U.S. agent, speaks of the planned volume as a "gift" inviting illustration (Letter to Atwood, 20 Sept. 1993); and James Adams of McClelland and Stewart suggests a "flipper edition," with the *Murder* cover on one side and the *Good Bones* cover on the other, a "packaging" that would give the volumes new life (Letter 1994, Margaret Atwood Papers). While the volume changed over time—eventually including twenty-three selections from *Good Bones,* eleven from *Murder in the Dark,* and one new piece, "Simple Murders," with ten illustrations—its genre and form are interwoven with those of its "parent" volumes.

Good Bones is one of the best examples of Atwood's transgressive and subversive genre bending evident in early work but more radical in recent texts. Consideration of Atwood's flash fictions in the contexts of the authors and texts with which they are anthologized—including Julio Cortazar's "Continuity of Parks," Jorge Luis Borges's "Argentina," Jamaica Kincaid's "Girl," and works by Gabriel García Márquez, Patricia Grace, Richard Brautigan, Italo Calvino, and Clarice Lispector (J. Thomas; Shapard and Thomas)—should make her affinity with international writers and movements more recognizable, if no less controversial, to Canadian scholars. In addition, investigation of *Good Bones,* particularly Atwood's Medusa and Snake Goddess imagery and trickster characters, indicates that, apart from differences of genre, style, tone, and a growing use of postmodern techniques and postcolonial themes (Wilson, "Mythological"), Atwood uses some of the same myths and other folklore intertexts in fairly consistent ways throughout her career. From early works such as *Double Persephone* (1961) to recent ones such as *The Robber Bride* (1993) and *Alias Grace* (1996), Atwood's play with genres and intertexts is metaformal, metacritical, and thereby profoundly political.

Readers have focused more attention on Atwood's themes than her extraordinary manipulation of genre, including its accompanying language, characterization, structure, costumes, and furniture. Few writers so astutely mimic and parody forms, only to turn them inside out and deconstruct them. *Murder in the Dark* (1983) uses a subtitle that calls attention to the genres of short or flash fiction and the prose poem or epiphany (Myers) that seem to fuse in *Good Bones*. Atwood uses the prose poem earlier in "Marrying the Hangman" (*Two-Headed Poems*, 1978, 48–51) and "True Romances" (*True Stories*, 1981, 40–44) and even in sections of "Circe/Mud Poems" (*You Are Happy*, 1974); but on close examination, these and other Atwood poems and prose poems, like the later, long-lined "Machine. Gun. Nest" (*Selected Poems II*, 137–38), share the narrative movement usually associated with fiction. *For the Birds* (1990) features some very short children's stories, but the fairly new genre of the short-short story involves more than simply being very short. Although it is impossible to differentiate precisely between the prose poem and flash fiction, or among flash fiction, sudden fiction, and Allen's name for the Canadian prose poem, the lyric paragraph (13–15), flash fiction has been defined as a 750-word story (instead of sudden fiction's 1,750 words) that can be apprehended in a flash, with "no enforced pause in the reader's concentration, no break in the field of vision. [It] would be apprehended 'all at once,'" ideally on a two-page spread (J. Thomas, 11–12). Flash fiction offers at least the outlines of story plot (including temporal movement that may or may not be chronological), scene, and characterization. In such short shorts, all of these features are likely to be "archetypal," as in the game in which Bill, Louise, a nameless boy, a detective or critic, the book, the reader, and the narrator/author in "Murder in the Dark" shift roles as murderers, detectives, or murder victims (*GBSM*, 1–3; *MD*, 29–30) or the ways that John, Mary, and friends in "Happy Endings" would eventually end up dying in every conceivable plot, no matter how faked (*GBSM*, 50–56; *MD*, 37–40). On the other hand, prose poems, like other poems, highlight language and are often defined by their lyricism, their calling attention to the signifier rather than the signified, or their foregrounding of the relationship between form and content (Delville, *The American*, 97–103; Gerlach, 82; Monroe, 12).[6] Other defining features might include the author's previous identification with a particular genre and the presentation of the text, including whether it uses the line breaks, stanzas, capitalization, and rhymes or rhythms identified with poetry. But Atwood is among the many writers noted for varied genres; and the majority of pieces in some collections of prose poems (Myers) are written continuously or in paragraphs, like short stories. Flash fiction, however, may also be lyrical, and it often seems to resemble the prose poem more than an "ordinary" short story (whatever that is) in its use of language, imagery, and rhythm. Many prose poems, such as Carolyn Forche's "The Colonel" (792), also anthologized as flash fiction (Thomas, Thomas, and Hazuka, 84–85), are at least as narrative as lyrical. Some of the pieces in *Good Bones,* including "Bad News," are shorter than the specified length of flash fiction; and because of its line form, "Let Us Now Praise Stupid Women" would be an excellent candidate for the prose poem label. If flash fictions may be as short as 250 words (J. Thomas, 11–12), length an arbitrary feature of writing (Baxter, 18), fiction poetic, and poetry narrative, however, then rigidly proclaiming that some of Atwood's prose pieces are prose poems, some "flash," and others "sudden" is not only hairsplitting but also an obvious invitation for Atwood's famous satirical scrutiny of the academic scene. Apart from its pleasing alliteration and openness to puns, *flash fiction* appropriately describes the structural buildup to the ending "flash," the operation of Atwood's verbal brilliance and satirical wit, and the verbal play about fiction versus reality in *Good Bones.* In addition, *flash* suggests the reader's flashes of insight or epiphanies while reading these fictions.

Increasingly, at a time when the word *text* displaces language specifying a single genre, the essay may also be a lyrical prose poem (see Neuman and Kambourali, for example); and prose poems/flash fictions may not only be performed as plays but also serve as highly metaphysical or theoretical arguments. One critic refers to the title piece of *Murder in the Dark* as an essay (Irvine, "Murder," 268), another to the volume's six "essay-fictions" (Gadpaille, 96), a third to the collection itself as *"fiction théorique"* (Verduyn, 124), and a fourth to it as a Baudelairean prose poem sequence (Merivale, 254). Atwood found it necessary to tell Larry Goldstein of *Michigan Quarterly Review* that the Male Body piece ("Alien Territory") "is not an essay—better call it a piece" (Letter, 19 Feb. 1992); and Philip Marchand quotes her as saying much the same of the whole volume (Review 1992). In justifying her punctuation in *Good Bones,* however, "the rock on which the editing process always founders," she tells an editor that "these are prose poems and they are punctuated for the ear" (Letter, 20 Sept. 1993 to Atwood; Letter, 7 Apr. 1994 to Jessie). Draper refers to "Making a Man" (*Good Bones*) as a five-part essay (40), and Phoebe Larmore speaks of the pieces in *Good Bones and Simple Murders* as essays (see also Campbell). Atwood, like fellow Canadians Diane Schoemperlen and Michael Ondaatje and Québecois writers of *l'écriture féminine,* including Lola Lemire Tostevin and Marie-Claire Blais, seems to write from the space in between—the Cartesian universe and the wilderness, forms and genres—what Hutcheon calls the "interzone" (Foreword, *Likely Stories,* 12–13). Many of the one hundred chapters in Schoemperlen's *In the Language of Love,* each based upon one of the stimulus words from the Standard Word Association Test, read like prose poems or word collages; and form in Ondaatje's *In the Skin of a Lion* is cinematic, poetic, cubist, surreal, or circular, anything but what might be expected in a realistic novel. Tostevin's *'Sophie* (1988) could be described as a collection of poems, a long poem, or theory; and Blais's apocalyptic "The Forsaken" strips away character identity and definiteness of scene (354–56). Along with Atwood, such writers raise questions of genre that can best be understood in reference to postmodernism. In a comment prepared for James Thomas of *Sudden Fiction International,* Atwood says of "Happy Endings" (*MD, GBSM*), described in the introduction to this volume as a "permutational fiction" in the "'If . . .then' mode" (Baxter, 22), that she "did not know what sort of creature" the piece was—not a poem, short story, or prose poem, not quite a condensation, proverb, or paradox. "It was a mutation," like a white frog.

> This is the way such a mutant literary form unsettles us. We know what is expected, in a given arrangement of words; we know what is supposed to come next. And then it doesn't.
>
> It was a little disappointing to learn that other people had a name for such aberrations, and had already made up rules. (Letter, 5 Sept. 1988; Shapard and Thomas, "Afternotes," 298–99).

In what Michel Delville calls genre theory's "crisis of legitimization" when "generic instability" and its exposure of "the arbitrariness and undecidability of generic boundaries" ("Murdering," 57) is a fact of poststructuralism, terms such as "boundary works," "prose pieces," and "borderline literature" highlight the foolishness of insisting on rigid classifications of genre.

Despite Atwood's overt efforts to revive female villains and refute claims of her "male-bashing" ("Spotty-Handed"; *CE, RB*), some critics of *Good Bones* also continue to misinterpret Atwood's regendering of genre in her critique of patriarchal oppression. Much as Frank Davey does in speaking of "male and female space" in Atwood's poetry (16–36), Delville oversimplifies both *Good Bones* and *Murder in the Dark* by suggesting that a "penchant for binary and, ultimately, essentialist thought models," an opposition between the male and female brain, may limit Atwood's art. Missing her postmodernism and misinterpreting the fourth victim position in *Survival* as determinism, Delville refers to "Atwood's apparent lack of belief in the oppressed individual's capacity for agency within a given socio-cultural dominant" ("Murdering," 62–63, 66–67).

Through the interweaving, regendering, and parodying of varied genres and subgenres—including antifiction, metafiction, revisioned folk and fairy tales, myths, and other canonical texts; fables; parables; monologues; popular romance; biography; autobiography; theology; speculative, science or revenant fiction; recipes; advice; thriller, and adventure stories—Atwood's intertextual play in *Good Bones* undercuts cultural determinism. The flash fictions in *Good Bones* use and parody such traditional intertexts as Great Goddess stories, including ones about Diana of Ephesus, Pandora, harpies, and sirens; Genesis and other Bible and creation myths; *The Aeneid,* "Bluebeard," "Rapunzel," "Cinderella," and "Hansel and Gretel" fairy tales; nursery rhymes; Dracula, stump, and housewife folklore; war rituals; stories of alien invasion; and literary classics. As Merivale notes, *Good Bones* even intertextually echoes *Murder in the Dark* (255). Often evoked through the cover of this volume and the visual art of *Good Bones and Simple Murders* as well, these folkloric and literary references deconstruct stereotypical conceptions of men, women, nature, stories, literary tradition, and reader expectations.

The Great Goddess intertext in Atwood's earlier visual art, including the female crescent moon (*Moon,* 1958, figure 2), *Termite Queen* (undated, plate 12), two harpies—*Mother Harpy and Chics* (1974, plate 13), *Male Harpy* (1970, plate 10)—(published in Wilson, *Margaret,* n.p.), and a spiral (*Circle Game* cover, 1966), sets the stage for the cover art of both *Good Bones* and *Good Bones and Simple Murders* as well as illustrations for the latter text. Most of these art works are parodies of, or associated with, the Great Goddess of earth, sea, sky, and seasons, whose importance in Canadian literature Atwood discusses in *Survival* (1972). Like *Murder in the Dark*'s cover collage of a woman seeking "cover," the collage of the harpy on the cover of *Good Bones,* also constructed from magazine ads and once briefly lost in the mail from France (Wilson, *Margaret,* 63, 71; Cooke, 309), again highlights the mock gothic tone of both volumes. Sporting "a beribboned hat, grape-cluster hair, sun-glass breasts, a tail of mascaraed human eyes, a wing of lipsticked" smiling mouths, a grassy lower body, and a female head (Wilson, *Margaret,* 63) and perched on a female leg, the *Good Bones* harpy is the muse (Sullivan, "Afterword," 113), messenger, and trickster creator of the volume. She is also a parody of human fashion "goddesses" as well as mythical ones. Harpies or Valkyries, originally represented as beautiful winged maidens from the cave of the Cretan goddess, became associated with sirens and furies. As children of Electra, they avenged her father's murder. As "the robbers" who carry off souls of those who disappear without a trace, harpies again represent vengeance: the consequences of evil or irresponsible actions. Although they could also suggest Atwood's many serious or parodic Robber Brides and Grooms (See Wilson, *Margaret,* 63, 199–200), here they are also assertive women, tricksters unafraid to defy convention, and often morality, to get what they want.

In addition, a number of Atwood's provocative illustrations for *Good Bones and Simple Murders* (1994), all but two accompanying stories also published in *Good Bones,* are associated with Goddess intertexts and enhance the meaning of the stories in both volumes. Both the Talese/Doubleday and Wheeler covers of *Good Bones and Simple Murders* depict goddess-queens, one debased and one revisioned. The ten illustrations in *Good Bones and Simple Murders,* originally designed to be watercolors and limited to five or six, go with the mood rather than specific details of the pieces (Atwood letters to Lennie at Virago, 1995, and Nan Talese, 7 Jan. 1994). They were given titles not used in the published volume (U.S. edition drawings, Table of Contents; Atwood letter to Nan [Talese], 28 Feb. 1994). The drawings include another harpy ("The Goddess of Rumour"), a punk-haired and breasted hen on an egg ("Hen Brooding on Cosmic Egg"), a fluid female appearing to blow across a landscape with crescent moon ("Fleeing Heroine"), a toothed stump awaiting a fish and possibly the fisherman ("Fishing"), and a female Medusa snake holding an apple in one hand and the letter *a* in the other ("Invention of the Alphabet"). Other goddess images are a Pumpkin Woman pregnant with an image of herself pregnant with a pumpkin ("Pumpkin Shell"), a trilobite and two cephalopods with female heads ("Life in the Burgess Shales"), a double face enclosed in a free-standing womb ("Double Heads"), an angel of death or suicide hatching an egg surrounded by flames ("Angel of Suicide Incubating Her Egg"), a flower with a face in its bulb ("Tulip/Woman"), and an earth/sea goddess whose body is the land ("Waterscape"; see figure 4, p. 6, in this volume and Nischik's discussion). The snake body and hair of the woman in "Invention of the Alphabet" identify the Snake Goddess,[7] and the Goddess of Rumour and an earth/sea goddess are also easily identifiable. Each of the illustrations for *Good Bones and Simple Murders,* however, not only mythologizes females in the manner Atwood identifies as characteristic of Canadian literature in *Survival* (1972) and *Strange Things* (1995), but also highlights or connects to an image or theme in the fiction it accompanies. For example, the queen on the cover of the 1994 edition of *Good Bones and Simple Murders* is a variation on Atwood's earlier *Termite Queen* (Wilson, *Margaret*, plate 12), a parodic goddess wearing a gas mask. Although the later queen, whom Nan Talese refers to as "the Termite Queen—transfigured" (Letter to Atwood, 17 Feb. 1994), may have a Medusa hairdo more evident in preliminary drawings (Atwood Papers), she is still the socialized prom queen, or a Queen for a Day, as on the old radio and television quiz show that selected queens based on the sadness of their life stories. Reminding us of the captured photograph trophies in *The Edible Woman, Surfacing,* and other novels (Wilson, "Camera Images," 29–57), she is one of this volume's many static, trussed-up snivelers who make perfect victims for the simple murders. Inexplicably, the lesser-known 1995 large-print edition features a quite different cover, uncredited like all of the art in this edition. Contrasting to and even revisioning both *The Termite Queen* and later posing queen, the cover of this edition depicts a much more dynamic figure: a running woman fleeing the "death" of both role and Hecate moon, a better candidate for the prepublication title, "Fleeing Woman," later "Fleeing Heroine," than the illustration that Atwood designed to accompany "Women's Novels" (Table of Contents, U.S. edition drawings; Letter to Nan Talese, 28 Feb. 1994). Although she is not the trickster of the *Good Bones* cover, she is one of these volumes' sassy women—the opposite of the victim archetype. Her hands are extended; and her face, hands, and feet, like the crescent moons on her dress, are the dark purple of royalty. This figure, more woman than queen, has active hands and feet and is a much more positive image than either of the passive-looking, eternally pregnant Termite Queens and Atwood's many initially "handless" subjects (See Wilson, *Margaret*, 61–62, 47–48, 313).

Foregrounded by the visual art, the intertexts in *Good Bones* are evident in plot, characters, point of view, motifs, and themes. Characters in *Good Bones* are mostly parodic versions of ones already familiar to us from popular culture, mythology, and literature: the harpy, the red hen, Gertrude, the ugly stepsister, the witch, the stepmother, Eve, Pandora, Red Cap, the Muse, the Pumpkin Woman, Rapunzel, an angel of suicide, created Gingerbread and biblical men, Bluebeard, and Dracula. But here we often get to hear the story from the usually submerged points of view of "shadow" or Medusa selves, including the sometimes nameless, unlucky, and unloved "unpopular gals." Animals disguised as stumps, airheads whose ignorance causes harm, male and female bodies, alien moths, and bats all have their say ("Mythological," 211). The Goddess harpy underlying all the pieces, on the cover of *Good Bones* and opposite the first page of *Good Bones and Simple Murders* (also rpt. Wilson, Friedman, and Hengen, *Approaches*), is kin to the running woman on the alternative cover of *Good Bones and Simple Murders*. As deceptive as Persephone in *Double Persephone*, both dancing girl and withered crone, whose own breath, rather than that of Hades or his horses, is "impatient for her death," she is still a survivor, both Goddess and trickster ("Persephone Departing," "Double Persephone"; see Wilson, *Margaret*, 61).

· · ·

By recognizing Atwood's many folklore intertexts, we can begin to see that most of Atwood's main characters—including Circe, Joan, Zenia, and Grace—are tricksters; and Atwood herself sometimes enjoys playing this role (Wilson, *Margaret*, 135; "Mythological," 208–9). Tricksters in *The Robber Bride, Alias Grace,* and *Good Bones,* like those in *The Odyssey* and Native American mythology, however, cannot simply be equated with Jung's shadow selves, themselves more complex than the "dark sides," or the evil aspects of the human personality, that Barbara Zimmerman opposes to "light" sides (71–72). Atwood does present the shadow selves of both Zenia and Grace, but she also deconstructs oversimplified binary oppositions. As she points out in her review of Lewis Hyde's *Trickster Makes This World,* tricksters are imaginative artists, often culture heroes. They may lie, like Odysseus; or steal, like Prometheus; or be cunning, like Daedalus, but they are the ones who are subversive and transgressive—they are the ones responsible for change (2, 3). Like the Hecate phase of the goddess cycle (*Survival,* 199), shadow selves are also not "negative" in themselves. As true doubles of the hero in myths, shadow selves may also have good qualities and, in order to triumph (i.e., overcome the dragon), the ego must assimilate the shadow (Henderson, 110, 112, 117). By using tricksters and shadows, in *Good Bones* as elsewhere, however, Atwood parodies not only a traditional story, in this case the hero myth, but even traditional archetypal analysis by reversing the usual hidden gender assumptions enacted in [male] heroes (Perseus) becoming heroic by decapitating or dismembering female monsters (Medusa) in order to rescue a [socialized] female: the anima (Andromeda) (Wilson, *Margaret*, 17–19).

Where she suggests archetypes, Atwood generally shifts characters or perspectives so that we conceive of both female and male playing hero, shadow or villain, victor, victim, trickster, and tricked. Tricksters in *Good Bones* are usually either genderless or female; and they contrast to the "good daughters," such as Ophelia and the queen of the *Good Bones and Simple Murders* cover, who are "so *good*. Obedient and passive. Snivelling" (29), paper dolls consigned to housework who can easily end up drowned or thrown out of a tower. As we shall explore, preeminent tricksters in *Good Bones* include Gertrude of "Gertrude Talks Back" and both the evil stepsister and witch of "Unpopular Gals." Atwood's tricksters in *Good Bones* again fill their traditional role as storytellers or Scheherazades, resembling the ones throughout Atwood's work, including *Life before Man, Interlunar, The Handmaid's Tale,* and recent novels (Wilson, *Margaret,* 175, 248, n. 14; Stein, 86–109). Thus, *Good Bones* is again metafiction, about storytelling, tricking, and surviving in a patriarchal, colonizing, environmentally ruined world. As in many folktales, her tricksters create oral epic situations to involve what here often fails to be a community. Ironically, Atwood uses postmodern techniques to uncover a traditional subtext— the survival theme—that has been evident throughout her career, introduced in *The Edible Woman* and *Surfacing* and discussed in *Survival* as the main theme in Canadian literature. Despite its subversions, in *Good Bones* Atwood's tricksters are often ironic culture heroes in tales that, together, are about saving, transforming, global human culture.

Good Bones opens with both reader and the Medusa-Snake Goddess harpy of "Bad News" awaiting a violent event—"a slip of the knife, a dropped wineglass or bomb," decapitation (9–10)—much as *Good Bones and Simple Murders* begins with the expectation of murder, signified by the harpy drawing ("The Goddess of Rumour") preceding the first fiction, "Murder in the Dark." In both cases, Atwood parodies readers who relish thrillers, ironically including such Atwood characters as Joan Foster and Rennie Wilford and, judging from her comments on John Le Carré and fiction about Raymond Chandler (*GB,* 47–48), Atwood herself. "[B]loodlessness puts her to sleep," says the harpy of "Bad News" (*GB,* 9), introducing the blood and red motifs running throughout the volume and implying the many kinds of "hunger" and "war" that threaten human survival. "Howling like a siren," the pun suggesting both another mythological female bird and an ambulance siren, this reconfigured Goddess of Rumour from Virgil's *Aeneid* (Merivale, 258) does trick readers into paying attention. Again ironically, however, the reader who relishes "bad news" in this "metagossip" text (Merivale, 256), the "you" who "settle[s] back in your chair, folding the rustling paper" and wishing to remain detached (*GB*, 10), is also the reader of this book who cannot resist becoming involved. This and the following "flash" nicely illustrate "the often anecdotal, tightly organized, refrain-shaped . . . short prose pieces, turning on a point at the end." Merivale sees the structure as an "inside-out sandwich," with the fifteen middle poems framed between six opening ones about Woman and Story and six elegiac closing ones (Merivale, 254, 256). Not everyone would agree about what constitutes "the meat" of the book, however, and the volume as a whole, rather than just some pieces (Merivale, 261), is both feminist fabulation and metafiction.

The second flash fiction in the volume, "The Little Red Hen Tells All," is based on the well-known folktale and children's story. Hens appear in many other folktales, such as "Jack and the Beanstalk" and "The Death of the Little Hen," and generally "are emblematical of God's providence" (*Funk and Wagnall's*, 490). Hens do, of course, lay eggs and thus are also associated with the female fertility that marks folktale victims such as Fitcher's "Birds" before transformation. The accompanying illustration in *Good Bones and Simple Murders,* the full-breasted hen on a gigantic egg whose yoke contains letters of the alphabet, foregrounds not only femininity and fertility, but also the hen's ability to hatch a story. In the numerous retellings and updatings, the red hen usually teaches lessons about the benefits of hard work and individuality, the importance of sharing work as well as rewards, and the consequences of laziness. More subliminally, the folktale may teach wifely virtue. But it has always been possible to see the hen as smug, selfish, self-righteous, and unforgiving, an Auntie Muriel clone (*LBM*). Characteristically, in Atwood's version, we get the first-person hen's side of the story and hear her resentment about being an advertisement for capitalism: the pattern of individual effort, capital investment, then collection. "It's not easy, being a hen," being rejected by her friends, denying herself gratification, constantly smiling despite her beak, being blamed for others' problems (11). Much as Circe in "The Circe/Mud Poems" defies the written story that denies individual choice and dictates her words and actions, the red hen essentially "swallows" the story rather than the bread. Apologizing for her ideas, luck, qualities, actions, words, and identity as a hen, she gives even her own portion away. Atwood thus satirizes the North American penchant for Horatio Alger stories of pulling oneself up by the bootstraps and cleverly parodies associated adages: "A grain of wheat saved is a grain of wheat earned" (12). Unless the hen is lying about her renunciations (interesting thought!), however, she also satirizes the hollowness of societal conditioning, especially of the female type, to be humble, giving, meek, and "good." Unlike the harpies who satisfy their "tastes" and give us the news we may not want to hear, unlike the creators who open new stories and identities and plots, the hen stays red: She chooses the role of female martyr, a variation of the willing victim role also played by the good Ophelias of this volume, and chooses to complain or "cluck" rather than to claim "telling all" as an identity. Although some reviewers of the book consider these fictions fables or parables, thus suggesting a heavy-handed moralizing Atwood usually shuns, "The Little Red Hen Talks Back" is clearly a parody of a fable rather than a fable or parable.

Gertrude of "Gertrude Talks Back" also calmly gives Hamlet "bad news": She, not Claudius, killed his priggish father. Like the harpy and the red hen, Gertrude revisions Shakespeare's *Hamlet* and, in a sense true for other fictions here, too, "murders" the intertext by finally not only talking, but talking back. Introducing the bone motif and elaborating on the murder motif before she makes her shocking revelation at the end, she tells the prudish Hamlet that he needs a roll in the hay with someone who is not, like Ophelia, "trussed up like a prize turkey." Ironically, her speaking about sex is, in her straight-laced society, also a kind of murder that precipitates the actual one: Every time she suggested sex to the King, "just to warm up my ageing bones, it was like I'd suggested murder" (17–18). As Gertrude demonstrates here, women in literature may become survivors who take care of their bones and, indeed, Lady Macbeths, acting rather than being acted upon (Atwood, "Spotty-Handed"); but within this volume, the transformative "murder" is verbal. Unlike the legless, hand-wringing "stupid women," Gertrude is a trickster-creator.[8]

Although "There Was Once" may be viewed as a parody of political correctness, this story is one of several texts here and elsewhere that ironically demonstrates the survival of storytelling through antilanguage, anticharacter, antiplot, and antistructure characteristic of Beckett's antifiction and drama (see Wilson, "Deconstructing," 65). The story is a comic flash of the self-conscious narrator's quest for the word as it slips away and erases. The second voice could be internal as well as that of an external reader or critic, and the third, a male voice, known by his "oar," ironically resembles the second in inappropriately expecting a literary work to satisfy personal biases. Resembling voices in the fiction of Conrad, Cortazar, Borges, and especially Beckett, whose verbal echo closes the volume, those in "There Was Once" struggle not only to say, to speak against the silence, but to speak in a world that censors speech as it is uttered and questions or dictates each element of the storyteller's craft, including setting, description, characterization, and plot. Confusing the author with the character and assuming that authors deliberately and consciously present messages in literature—two annoyances Atwood frequently addresses ("Me," 7)—the second voice paradoxically both succeeds and fails, as does the first. Beckett's *The Unnamable* tragicomically ends at the beginning of the Unnamable's story:

> [Y]ou must go on, I'll go on, you must say words, as long as there are any, until they find me, until they say me, . . .you must go on, perhaps it's done already, perhaps they have said me already, perhaps they have carried me to the threshold of my story, before the door that opens on my story, that would surprise me, if it opens, it will be I, it will be the silence, where I am. . . . (414)

More comically in Atwood's story, although the first voice finally anticipates the second by questioning the word *there,* thus erasing it, this story, too—the story of storytelling—does get told. Despite interruptions and deconstructions, it does paradoxically survive in silence.

"In Love with Raymond Chandler" and "Four Small Paragraphs," appearing later in the volume between "Death Scenes" and "We Want It All," also focus on language; and "Four Small Paragraphs" is one of many of this volume's fictions depicting the generation of life out of death. Both are tributes to two well-known writers, Raymond Chandler and Albert Camus. Atwood has previously admired Chandler's humanization of furniture, his knowledge that "furniture could breathe, could feel, not as we do but in a way more muffled, like the word *upholstery,* with its overtones of mustiness and dust" (47). In "Four Small Paragraphs" Atwood plays with the literal translation of Camus's name, *Flat,* as well as his pseudonym, Monsieur *Terrasse* or, in English, *Mr. Patio.* The landscape that Camus loved and where he was buried symbolizes the life cycle, regeneration, "the ochre and rust, that has been used and reused, passed through mouth and stomach and gut and bone, and out again into earth and then into stem and bud and ripe fruit" (137). Thus, it is appropriate that we get more—or less, depending upon outlook—than we expected, real roses left on the grave of one who says, "*This is what there is. . . . You are what you do. Don't expect mercy*" (139).

"Stump Hunting" is a joke "how to" advice column, in this case guiding gullible readers in seeing through stumps' disguises as wild animals in order to kill them. The story resembles a northern Ontario tall tale, a form that is often about hunters, fishermen, and weather (Fowke, *Tales,* 74) and features disguise, another kind of folklore deception predominant among tricksters. Like the illustration accompanying it in *Good Bones and Simple Murders,* showing a toothed stump awaiting a fish and possibly the fisherman (34), this piece is a parody of the malicious nature theme, Atwood's Nature the Monster of *Survival,* so prevalent in Canadian literature before 1970, including Sinclair Ross's "Lamp at Noon" and "The Painted Door," Joyce Marshall's "The Old Woman," and E. J. Pratt's "Toward the Last Spike."

"Unpopular Gals" and "Let Us Now Praise Stupid Women" are again metafictions told by deceptive unreliable narrators. The evil sister or stepsister and stepmother/witch of "Unpopular Gals," never even given names in well-known fairy tales such as "Cinderella" and "Snow White," now "get a turn" to assume subject rather than object positions (25). Illustrating the cruel sister and stepmother folk motifs, subcategories of unnatural cruelty (Thompson), these women wish to overcome prejudice against their trickery. Like the stepsisters of "Cinderella" and many other fairy-tale false brides, the sister is in virtually the same situation as the False Bride in the second section of Atwood's unpublished story "Three Jokes" (*PP* manuscripts, Margaret Atwood Papers). The sister disguised and amputated her foot, and both ugly women used magic to deceive the prince in unsuccessful attempts to get him; but they came to the same kind of bad end as the maid of "Little Goose Girl" and the bad mothers and witches of "The Juniper Tree" and "Snow White." Like Circe of *You Are Happy,* the witch of the second and third sections of "Unpopular Gals" is characteristically double or even multiple: not only the witch of the Grimms' "Hansel and Gretel" and "Rapunzel," she is the many-breasted Diana of Ephesus and other earth or fertility goddesses and, in section three, the stepmother who often doubles with the witch. Like the harpy of "Bad News" and the stupid women of the following story, however, these tricky "unpopular gals" would have us believe that they are the ones who "stir things up, get things moving"; as the witch explains, "I'm the plot, babe, and don't ever forget it" (29–30). Similarly, in "Let Us Now Praise Stupid Women," a poetic joke, the flippant narrator invites "stupid" readers to believe that the Foolish, rather than Wise Virgins and Eve of the Bible, Pandora of myth, and Red-Cap of the fairy tale, "have given us Literature" and deserve praise. The Wise and the Foolish is another of Thompson's folk-motif categories; and although Eve, Pandora, and Red-Cap, connected to numerous folk motifs, are also associated with the Great Goddess and matriarchal power, this fiction presents them as the airheads and bubble-brains of patriarchal versions (e.g., Wilson, *Margaret,* 277–78). The illustration accompanying this fiction in *Good Bones and Simple Murders* appropriately pictures a female Medusa/Eve snake holding an apple in one hand and the letter *a* in the other (58). In addition to talking with snakes and wolves, wishing to please, and uselessly wringing their hands, stupid women seem legless: "running involves legs, and is graceless" (35–36). As Atwood has said, innocence may be equivalent not only to stupidity but to evil (cited in Wilson, *Margaret,* 279). Although the running woman cover of *Good Bones and Simple Murders'* large-print edition and the fates of the good daughters and dutiful wives directly refute any stupid need to praise stupid women, the trickster narrator charmingly traps our attention.

"The Female Body," an especially rhythmical and clever flash, beginning in first person and shifting to an impersonal third, uses a number of familiar Atwood images, motifs, and themes. Atwood's work is full of power politics linked to eating and being eaten; and here is the hungry female body, equipped with fichu (also *LO*), modesty panel (also *BH*), and a head as accessories. A doll, here a Barbie, is thrown down the stairs (40–42, also *EW*), and the illustration in *Good Bones and Simple Murders* even features a Pumpkin Woman (also *EW*), here pregnant with an image of herself pregnant with a pumpkin (70). "The Female Body" is the companion piece to "Alien Territory," both written for Female and Male Body issues of *Michigan Quarterly Review*; and both satirize societal dehumanization and gender scripts inherited from fairy tales, myth, ("Rapunzel," "Fitcher's Bird," the Bible, Aphrodite myth), literature, and our new mythology—advertising: "Is this the face that launched a thousand products?" The female body can be a door knocker or something to hold up lampshades (also *BH*); it sells and is sold (43). If the connections between the two halves of the female brain mean that women listen in to their internal conversations, then the brains of men contribute to their "objectivity," "Aloneness," and mythologizing of the female body, which thus must be trapped, leashed, chained.

"Making a Man," "Men at Sea," and "Alien Territory," later in the volume, focus on male conditioning. "Making a Man," which might remind some readers of Susan Swann's "The Man Doll" (1985)(Hutcheon and Bowering), is a wonderfully funny parody of creation myths, including the Genesis story; of making men (but not women) from dust; of the English folktale "The Gingerbread Man"; and of media "how to" programs and columns. Charlotte Sturgess suggests that "Making a Man" also overturns "the cultural/sexual practice of 'making' women" (91). Reminding us of cannibalistic fairy tales and myths that frequently figure as Atwood intertexts, the flippant narrator turns a pun on female "ribs" into a joke about eating women and adds four other methods, some similarly cannibalistic, for making men: gingerbread, clothes, marzipan or wedding cake, and folk art. In addition, although many readers will miss the irony, this story parallels "The Female Body" in blatantly revealing dehumanization for what it is. Men, too, can be reduced to utilitarian or decorative function, serving as doorstops or figures on a wedding cake. They, too, can become "food" or plaster of Paris statues. Epitomizing Atwood's preference for open-endedness, as in *Bodily Harm*, "Circe/Mud Poems," and "Book of Ancestors" (*YAH*), "Making a Man" offers no period at its ending.[9] Again, form cancels or "cracks" the constructed mold.

"Men at Sea" and "Alien Territory" are about male dis(ease), the male body, male conditioning, and men's alienation. "Men at Sea" is an extended pun. Language in this wonderfully rhythmical flash is "bracing" in its effort to show "Something more definite, more outward then, some action to drain the inner swamp, sweep the inner fluff from under the inner bed, harden the edges" before we return to the men now socially rather than adventurously adrift at the "eternal table" (71). The illustration for "Alien Territory" in *Good Bones and Simple Murders* shows an optical illusion: two interlocking faces—twins exchanging dominance—enclosed in a furry, free-standing womb (96), the not-to-be borne origin of the man (76). Thus, an exile and explorer with a body both undependable and detachable, he is afraid of the bodies of other men; as in "Epaulettes," he kills them in war. Like Bluebeard, he may kill the bodies of the females who adore him in "love." Bluebeard has been a central concern of Atwood's writing, evident in the *Fitcher's Bird* watercolor (Wilson, *Margaret*, plate 3), *Power Politics*, and *Bluebeard's Egg*; and the Bluebeard section here resembles both "Hesitations outside the Door" (*PP*) and the third section of Atwood's unpublished story "Three Jokes" (Wilson, *Margaret*, 257–70; Margaret Atwood Papers, *PP* Manuscripts). In the three texts, the real secret behind the door of the forbidden room is not the chopped-up bodies of previous wives, which in "Alien Territory" are ironed flat and folded in the linen closet (83), but the secret self of the man. In "Three Jokes" this self is empty, and in "Alien Territory" it is the dead "child" to which he gave birth. Illustrating the mirror imagery and narcissism evident in early works such as "The Circle Game," *Power Politics,* and "Tricks with Mirrors"(*SP*), in "Three Jokes" the man exists only in a mirror, in this case the eyes of the woman. As the Bluebeard of "Three Jokes" says,

> I don't exist and never
> have, it's one of my problems,
> I'm only a curved surface
> highly polished, I
> will reflect anything.
> (Margaret Atwood Papers, *PP* Manuscripts)

While offering nothing, however, some men are creators, able to verbalize their bodies so that they have weight. Reminding readers of early Atwood love poems and of the end of *Interlunar,* the end of "Alien Bodies" paradoxically offers hope: "[I]f they can say their own bodies, they could say yours also. . . . they could put their empty hands . . . on your body, and bless it, and tell you it is made of light" (88).

"Adventure Story," resembling John Barth's "Night-Sea Journey" in a volume meant to be "received all at once" (Barth, ix), revisions what seems to be the story of conception as a distillation of the archetypal adventure in myth, fairy tale, literature, and history. "Adventure Story" is supposedly told by "our ancestors, and those before them," and as the narrator admits, it could also be a memory; but at the same time it is apocalyptic, one of the futuristic flash fictions. It begins with the "intrepid band" shooting through a dark tunnel into, again, "alien territory," where magic turns the gate to jelly and one enters the "pink paradise" of the garden to cast "the imprisoning skin of self" while the world "explodes, doubles, revolves, changes forever" (90–91). Whereas Barth's story is narrated from a gendered perspective, by a sperm, this narrator of undisclosed gender assures us that half of the adventurers are females, who swim and help and sacrifice the same as the rest. The adventure ends in a new beginning very unlike the toxic world of "Hardball" and wars of "Alien Territory": "a fresh-laid star . . . harbinger of a new order, a new birth, possibly holy; and the animals will be named again" (92).

Other futuristic fantasies in *Good Bones* also contrast creators and destroyers in the struggle for survival that marks human existence. "Epaulettes" and "Hardball," earlier published with "Cold-Blooded" as "Three Chronicles" (1990), are all about the possible extermination

of the earth, through war, pollution, or the sneaky takeover of a supposedly inferior species. In satirizing the societal predilection for wars
that no one can win, "Epaulettes" humorously uses another folk
motif, the creation of a substitute, in this case for war once it becomes
too dangerous and expensive. According to the male reporter-narrator,
the world leaders consider various sports, including the Mayan ball
game with decapitated losers' heads, and finally select bird-display
play-offs, featuring especially strutting and dancing. Displacing
megadeaths and genocides and serving the same purposes as war,
including clear winners and losers, two days of rape and pillage, modified looting, and ritual drunkenness, bird display not only creates a
new kind of world leader—funnier, more musical, wearing epic
epaulettes—but it positively revises history and cultural values, pre-
venting the disasters predicted in "Hardball." Rather than rolling our
strength and sweetness into a ball, as in this fiction's allusion to
Andrew Marvell's "To His Coy Mistress," in "Hardball" the future
rolls toward us like "a giant iron snowball" of death. This world, also
without Kubla Khan's stately pleasure dome surrounded with "gardens
bright," lacks any possibility of making our sun either run hedonisti-
cally or stand still (326–27; Coleridge, 683). Ironically, "Hardball"
also realizes the latent menace of the lifeless ocean and caves of ice in
"Kubla Khan." As the speaker in the poem does, this whole fiction
cries "Beware!" Like *The Handmaid's Tale*, "Hardball" parodies
adages, biblical texts ("by their fruits ye shall know them"), and
canonical literature by supplying horrifying contexts and effects for
heedless actions. This man-made world recycles and cannibalizes the
dead, and the only "fruits" are those that can be grown in the little
breathable air, in the small amount of "living," as opposed to dead,
space. Atwood's characters, as in *Life before Man*, often play survival
games in which they must rescue themselves, but here the survival is
literal and global: We are invited to "[t]hink of the earth as an eighteenth-century ship, with stowaways but no destination," "as a nineteenth-century lifeboat, adrift in the open sea, with castaways but no
rescuers," and, finally, "as a hard stone ball, scraped clean of life"
rather than packed with joy. The narrator, more reliable and with a
much more explicit message than is usual with Atwood, is indeed blunt
in calling for readers' action: "You don't like this future? Switch it off"
(93–95).

"Cold-Blooded" and "Homelanding" both use alien, female, first-
person narrators and the device of defamiliarization, common in science fiction, to examine, once again, "home ground, foreign territory"

(*Surfacing,* 14). The narrator from the all-female planet of prospective colonizers in "Cold-Blooded" is cold-blooded in a double sense: She predicts the eventual extinction of the blood creatures (human beings) on the Planet of the Moths (earth) when they "have succeeded at last in overbreeding themselves, as it seems their intention to do, or in exterminating one another" (69). Also, the references to patterned carapaces, diaphanous wings, pupation, and cocoons suggest that she has become a butterfly and is thus symbolic of the metamorphosis foolish human beings should seek. In *Good Bones and Simple Murders,* however, "Cold-Blooded" is accompanied by an illustration of other cold-blooded females, including a trilobite and two cephalopods with female heads (78). By contrast, the apparent ambassador of "Home-landing" represents a nation of metamorphs who assimilate and change parts of their surroundings into themselves when they eat. In order to establish some common ground, which turns out to be the knowledge of death, she tells someone not on earth—or perhaps not from Canada!—about her country and people. Resembling early Atwood poems that use the extended metaphor of "that country" as an ironic distancing device (e.g., *AC;* "True Romances," *SP II*),"Home-landing" ironically reverses the ideas of "home" and "away," making "here" "there" and withholding the landing at home suggested by the title (see also *BH*). Several features of this country, such as the small population despite its largeness, are identifiably Canadian; and the images of reflections, dissolutions, and rockiness are prevalent in other Canadian literature as well as in Atwood's works. Deconstructing the many science fiction films that assume hierarchy in any civilization ("take me to your leaders") and hostility between different cultures, this fiction also reduces gender politics between prong (male) and cavern (female) people to the absurd (122–23). As in many of Atwood's poems, including "Against Still Life" and "You Begin" (*SP,* 37–39, *SP II,* 54), this fiction ends with images of the concrete and important, including the life cycle with its hope for survival: the red of leaves (rather than of the violence elsewhere in this volume), trees, breakfast, sunsets, dreams, shoes, nouns, fingers, and deaths.

Regeneration or rebirth and the deconstruction of unquestioned ideas are also themes in the rest of *Good Bones.* "My Life as a Bat" again shifts point of view, offering another unpopular first-person narrator to puncture absolutist religious and cultural mythologies, including the beliefs that reincarnation as an animal is either silly or a punishment, that sanity is a general consensus about the content of reality, that light is life and darkness nothing, that God appears in our form (in this case, as a bat), that we must loathe skin and flesh unlike our own, and even that vampires suck neck blood. The trickster narrator of "My Life as a Bat," who says she was a bat in a previous life, educates about bats in the same way as the narrator of "Snake Poems" does about snakes. She points out that money can be made from believing in reincarnation and that, unlike human beings, bats kill without hate or gloating. "My Life as a Bat" turns on reversal of expectation and parody of both popular conceptions and portrayals of bats, including Bram Stoker's *Dracula* and Dracula films. It is the former bat, not the person, who has nightmares and prays to the Goddess to be "delivered from evil" and the person, not the bat, who is the monster with unseeing cyclops eye, as blind as his or her flashlight. Recalling the mock romanticism of vampires and other projected masks in *Power Politics* and *Lady Oracle,* the narrator engages in an orgy of mock-heroic, mock-gothic rhetoric concerning the main intertext of this piece:

> O Dracula, unlikely hero! O flying leukemia, in your cloak like a living umbrella, a membrane of black leather which you unwind from within yourself and lift like a stripteaser's fan as you bend with emaciated lust over the neck, flawless and bland, of whatever woman is longing for obliteration, here and now in her best negligee. (101)

"Theology" also deconstructs unreasoning absolutism and both conservative and liberal Christian intertexts, questioning whether murdering good people can be bad if it causes them to get to heaven earlier and whether, if God is the good in people, God would cease to exist if everyone died.

"Third Handed" extends folk beliefs that a hand can be a charm, a means of healing, or "bad"—taboo or unclean for certain activities—to create a cause or scapegoat for otherwise unexplained events. In folklore and societal practice, hands are severed as a punishment for breaking a taboo or a law. Hands may also be used for sign language and, as I have discussed previously, hands signify wholeness in Atwood's work (see *Margaret,* 136–228). Ordering, performing magic, and writing—as in E. Fitzgerald's translation of "The Rubaiyat of Omar Khayyam"—the third hand not only can help save us in a blizzard and lead us onward, but is one of the means of "dissolving boundaries" (131) necessary to survival.

"An Angel," "Poppies: Three Variations," and "Death Scenes" all deal explicitly with death and, in some cases, possible rebirth. Again paradoxically, the faceless angel of suicide that illustrates "An Angel" in *Good Bones and Simple Murders* is another of this volume's many "birds" and is coupled with two images of birth: it is hatching an egg, akin to her "face of a grey egg" (*GB*, 110). The flames that surround it can also suggest those from which a phoenix rises: mythic rebirth or eternal life (*GBSM*, 144). Depending upon the reader, the death skull inside the egg may undercut the possibility of a rebirth, enforce the ironic hatching of death, show the life cycle, or serve as another warning. This voice of suicide, here "a rebellious waitress" believed only because of her wings (110–11), is a messenger who appears in *Cat's Eye* and elsewhere in Atwood's work and one of the many messengers in this collection. Offering only rebellion, she illustrates the folklore motif of the rebel angel. "Poppies: Three Variations" varies its epigraph words from its intertext, the well-known Canadian poem "In Flanders Fields" (1915), by John McCrae, to rework images and ideas so familiar that they no longer provoke thought. By the end of this flash, written without paragraph indentations in three sections, however, the sound of the guns—one kind of destruction that threatens human survival—becomes part of the undertone in the volume as a whole, "below thought, below memory, below everything" (120). "Death Scenes" offers several perspectives on a woman's death, that of the woman who thinks about planting rose bushes as she lies in a coma and wants her friend to talk about normal things, of the medical establishment, and of the friend who weeds the dying woman's garden. Like the illustration for "An Angel," the one accompanying "Death Scenes" in *Good Bones and Simple Murders* also appropriately joins death and birth or rebirth in picturing a tulip with a female face (presumably of death) in its bulb (144).

Along with the immediately preceding flash fictions, "We Want It All" and "Dance of the Lepers" prepare for the volume's concluding and title story, "Good Bones."[10] As its trickster narrator says, calling attention to her story of story-telling, although we insist that we love the earth, "We Want It All" is still "the same old story" of human greed: irresponsibility concerning overpopulation, pollution, and disappearing species. We seem to hear the voice of the harpy from "Bad News" and the volume's cover as she warns us about cannibalism of the eye, the colonizing gaze suggested by the harpy's tail of eyes on the cover, and the consequent danger of being cannibalized ourselves, evident in the harpy's wing of mouths. Although the dancers in "Dance of the Lepers" are not lepers and are wrapped like mummies, their dance is nevertheless real and something the rest of us should emulate. It is "a continuation, a dance of going on despite everything, a stubborn dance" (147).

The central image of "Good Bones," the title story, and of the whole volume brings together the twin themes of death and life evident in the book's focus on survival. Bones are what's left when an animal dies and its flesh shrivels, but, like Atwood's own facial "good bones," bones are also the "bedrock. Structural principles," that "come out like flowers" in the right light. The narrator pours ashes of her friend, including dissolved bones, under the tulips so that other things "can grow" (152), recalling the dying gardener in "Death Scenes" and the illustration for that story in *Good Bones and Simple Murders*. In that volume, "Good Bones" is accompanied by an illustration of an earth/sea goddess whose body is the land, the structure reflected in the sky (160), and, as Nischik suggests in this volume (figure 4, pps. 6–7), part of the "bone" that is good. Neither the narrator of this flash fiction nor the goddess of the drawing is just a paper-doll dupe, the kind that the stepmother of "Unpopular Gals" tricks (29) or that Atwood satirizes in her self-portrait of author as paper doll ("Me," 6). Nor are they this volume's destroyers of life. Speaking to her bones as to a dog, the trickster narrator tricks her bones into performing yet another trick. While alluding to *The Unnamable* in the final lines of both story and volume, she demonstrates the flashes of insight and open structure that move both readers and book from murder to survival: "*Good bones! Good bones! Keep on going.*"

NOTES

1. One recent performance, also including selections from *Murder in the Dark*, was directed by Urjo Kareda and featured Claire Coulter at the Tarragon Theatre in Toronto on 28 Nov. 1999 (Laframboise). Atwood herself read from *Murder in the Dark* and *Good Bones* in the BamBoo nightclub; and, judging from Donna Lypchuk's review (1992), she gives quite a performance of these pieces. Neta Gordon adapted *Good Bones* as a play, "Loud Skirts," and directed a 1995 Toronto performance (Crew). Ensemble 9's adaptation, "*Gute Knochen*," was performed in Germany in 1996, and a compilation, "*Alla Tiders Kvinnor*," including material based on *Good Bones* with selections from Euripides, Aristophanes, Brecht, and other writers, was performed in Stockholm (Atwood Papers, Collection 335, *GB* Theatrical Adaptations). *Murder in the Dark* has also been performed, once by the Rotterdam Theatre Company (Independent Theatre Company) in Toronto in 1987, and Claudia Shaffer and Curtis Brown of Haymarket House produced "Strange Fish," later called "Once Upon a Time," a dramatic adaptation of *Murder in the Dark* and *Good Bones* (Letter

from Shelley Noble, Larmore's assistant, to Claudia Shaffer and Curtis Brown, May 1996, Atwood Papers, *GB*).

2. See reviews by John Bemrose, Eve Drobot, and Nancy Wigston. Rejecting "Good Bones and a Little Bit of Murder" and fearing "being twee'd and cutie-pied out of existance" [*sic*], Atwood proposed "Good Bones and Little Murders" as a possible title and wrote "Little Murders" to be the thirty-fifth piece (Letter to Nan Talese, 7 Feb. 1994). That title was abandoned and "Simple" substituted when "Steve" pointed out that Jules Feiffer has a book of that name (Atwood Letter to Nan Talese, 28 Feb. 1994). The 1992 Bloomsbury and 1993 Virago editions are identical to the first Toronto one; and the New Canadian Library 1997 edition, with an introduction by Rosemary Sullivan, has the same cover and stories in a smaller-print, shorter layout.

3. The 1994 Talese/Doubleday edition of *Good Bones and Simple Murders* was also published in London, Toronto, Sydney, and Auckland. Surprisingly, as described in the text, where I also discuss the covers of *Good Bones* and *Good Bones and Simple Murders,* although Atwood's other visual art is the same in the 1994 editions, Wheeler's 1995 large-print edition features a different cover from the Talese/Doubleday one, a fleeing woman illustration. The 1995 Virago edition, *Bones and Murder,* also has a different cover, a photograph of another "goddess." Showing only the upper part of Atwood's face and head in a sophisticated hat, it highlights her eyes and suggests mystery and intrigue. Before publication, the 1994 edition of *Good Bones and Simple Murders* had been titled *Good Bones and Small Murders,* also expected in l994, and a few Web sites still reference this title even though a book of this name was not published. A table of contents for *Good Bones and Small Murders* appears in the *Locus Index to Science Fiction* but is identical with both the 1994 Wheeler and Talese/Doubleday editions of *Good Bones and Simple Murders.* This description incorrectly states that most of these pieces were published in "two small-press collections in Canada." Book reviews slated for *Good Bones and Small Murders,* including those in *The Atlanta Journal* and *The Atlantic,* became, upon publication, reviews of *Good Bones and Simple Murders.*

4. Only Patricia Merivale (253–70) and Michel Delville ("Murdering," 57–67; slightly different version in *The American,* 140–49), analyze *Good Bones* in detail. Karen F. Stein (143–44); Rosemary Sullivan, "Afterword"; Cristina Bacchilega (116–19); and Charlotte Sturgess, and my article and book ("Mythological," 210–11; *Margaret,* 42, 51, 63–64) briefly discuss the volume. Bacchilega suggests that in "The Alien Body" and "The Female Body," "Atwood exposes Bluebeard's plot as a ritual of masculine self-conception which feeds on a denial of the human body" (117). Sturgess suggests that "The Female Body" subverts stereotypes (91). Nathalie Cooke mentions only the problems associated with writing and mailing the volume from France (309), and Coral Ann Howells discusses only one story, "The Female Body." Possibly because her book focuses on Atwood's life up to motherhood, Sullivan's recent biography does not mention *Good Bones.*

5. See Letter from Phoebe (Larmore) to Atwood, 25 Aug. 1993; Letter to Phoebe from Atwood, 29 Aug. 1993; Letter to Nan, 14 Aug. 1993; and Letter from Phoebe (Larmore) to Atwood, 11 Mar. 1994.

6. Although John Gerlach says that "demarcations between modes of narrative, and between genres themselves, are not firm," and admits that the form of prose poems is "virtually indistinguishable from that of a very short story," he goes on to discuss how fascination with language "interferes with the progression of story," how development of story causes poems to become unlyrical, and how stories, but not poems, must have a point (74, 80, 83–84). Presumably, however, the prose poems

collected in Myers's *Epiphanies* all have points, too. More reasonably, Delville discusses degrees of lyricism or narrativity. See him for an overview of critical discussion on prose poems and short fictions (*The American*, 97–149).

7. A drawing of a female dragon with breasts and a long tail, not used in the book, also suggests the Snake Goddess, associated with dragons killed by mythic heroes such as St. George. Her claws seem to write *ano*, nearly a part of her tail, and the word *but* also forms part of the composition. Atwood also did rough sketches of women wearing sea-creature hats, probably for "Cold-Blooded," and an unfinished one labeled "Diana of Ephesus" (Margaret Atwood Papers, *Good Bones and Simple Murders*).

8. Nan Talese suggested that Gertrude could be the Termite Queen-transfigured (Letter to Peggy [Atwood], 17 Feb. 1994).

9. In examining the galleys, Sarah Evans of Coach House Press wrote to Atwood that "Making a Man" ends abruptly (Letter, 3 June 1992, Atwood Papers), something that Phoebe Larmore had previously questioned. Atwood says that "yes, it is supposed to end that way" (Fax to Phoebe, 7 Aug. 1991).

10. Other projected stories for *Good Bones* were "Bearfeet," "Bondage," "Grunnugs," and "Freeforall." When Atwood decided that the latter didn't fit the book's format, she added "Third Handed" as the twenty-seventh piece since she has a preference for odd numbers (Margaret Atwood Papers, *Good Bones*; faxes to Joan [Sheppard], 5 and 6 Feb. 1992).

3

. . . .

Strange Visions:
Atwood's *Interlunar* and Technopoetics

SHANNON HENGEN

But this is Canada, land of contrasts.
  Margaret Atwood, "Survival, Then and Now"

[Nature is] a living process which includes opposites: life and death. . . .
[M]an himself is seen as part of the process.
  Margaret Atwood, *Survival*

[T]he Coyote . . . brings in another set of story cycles, where there is a
resistance and a trickster, producing the opposite of—or something other
than—what you thought you meant.
  Donna Haraway, "Cyborgs at Large"

Atwood's volume of poems published in 1984, *Interlunar,* has received
little critical attention, although its place in Atwood's work is significant. Divided into two sections, "Snake Poems" and "Interlunar," the
volume revisits familiar Atwoodian perspectives and imagery but with
what might be called a stranger vision. And the volume marks the end
of a fairly regular flow of books of poetry beginning in 1967 with *The
Circle Game* and including eight other books whose titles are all familiar to Atwoodian scholars (for example, *The Journals of Susanna
Moodie, Power Politics,* and *True Stories*). Eleven years then pass
before the appearance of the latest poems, *Morning in the Burned
House,* in 1995. Because of the somewhat changed perspective in *Interlunar,* a perspective that could be seen as a kind of conclusion to the

42

books of poems that precede it, more sustained readings of it are called for, despite its oddity. This chapter, suggestive rather than definitive, will outline both the familiar and the strange.

In *Interlunar* we see the play of contrasts and contrasting imagery that identifies Atwood's poetry: Stone, tree, moon, and silence, for example, describe a world apart from the human field of language, lust, murder, love, and free will. Figures from classical and popular mythology appear intermittently and interchangeably and attempt to cross between the two worlds. In terms of vision, we see human inability to understand the natural world as both different from and constitutive of humanity, a misunderstanding that results in destruction of both the natural and human worlds. Another way of stating the theme is that human culture, particularly technoscience but also poetry at times, errs in viewing nature from a dominant vantage point, willing culture to overcome. Nature, however, retains its own power. What creeps into Atwood's poems in *Interlunar* is a sustained suggestion that technoscience represents currently the most obvious cultural activity determined to overcome nature, to eradicate human frailty and loss. These poems become a unique counter-statement to that ideology.

In "Snake Poems," for example—originally published in a discrete volume in 1983 (by Toronto's Salamander Press)—the speaker invites us to reconsider the many human values that have been attributed to snakes. They are "the devil in your garden," she notes ironically (9), including in the poem that follows a list of other "Lies about Snakes": "that they cause thunder / that they won't cross ropes, / that they travel in pairs" (10). Alternatively, the most striking feature of snakes to this speaker is precisely that they are "not human": She muses that "it's hard to believe in snakes loving" (12). How to describe a nonhuman, a snake, in human language? How to find the trickster's subject position between apparent opposites?

A figure in another poem, noted below, attempts to learn "the languages of the animals" by eating snake, and by so eating, the figure loses human speech (15–16). In "Psalm to Snake" the speaker intones, "O snake, you are an argument / for poetry" (17), specifically for a poetry that would not impose its culture's dominant values. We have inadequately understood our natural milieu; poetry in its study of nature should form an argument against false claims of perfectibility made by technoscience. Other books of Atwood's poems echo and reecho this theme, but in *Interlunar* the commentary moves at times beyond the earth into space, and at those times the poems seem futuristic, linked perhaps to her dystopic fiction of this same time (as other critics have noted, below). A poem entitled "Valediction: Intergalatic" from the "Interlunar" section sets out a dominant image pattern and its corresponding frame of mind:

> [S]o at the end I could see only
> the shift between light and dark, and you were
> light at first and then dark
> and then light and then dark, and I wanted it
> to be light all the time . . .
>
> . . . .
>
> Is this intolerance? Am I
> non-human? . . .
>
> . . . .
>
> . . . Do I prefer
> the airless blaze of outer
> space to men, even
> the beautiful ones?
> (43)

Light and dark establish a distinction between human and nonhuman, a distinction that becomes increasingly complicated throughout *Interlunar* as a poetic vision attempts to inform the clarity of scientific achievement and advancement such as that which took humans into space. Therein lies the strangeness of Atwood's vision here, for the discourses of science and poetry are ordinarily kept apart. How would poetry and science change were the discourses to mix? How to mix the language of human limitation with that of mastery?

In what can at best be a preliminary comment on the larger issues raised in *Interlunar,* I will briefly review what critics have said about the volume, and I will discuss some of the poems. Finally, I will make a gesture toward describing what Atwood's vision entails, and to do so I will draw on the theories of U.S. cultural critic Donna Haraway, who, like Atwood, breaks down arbitrary and entrenched distinctions, particularly those between nature and culture, science and literature. This essay cannot critique the progressivist ideology of technoscience, nor can it reclaim poetry as the muted twin, but can only show that such critique and reclamation seem to form Atwood's strange vision in these poems of the mid-1980s.

Commentators have noted the play of contrasts in these poems. Sharon Wilson names "the darkness of interlunar—the period between old and new moons" (*Margaret Atwood's Fairy-Tale,* 230); she continues that "death makes possible the persona's descent and ultimate rebirth" (243), which becomes a "full sun phoenix rebirth" (255). Lawrence W. Norfolk writes: "'Dark' and 'light' are a positive recipe for closure . . . but it is the betweenness . . . which Atwood describes with accuracy and sympathy" (903). Anne Blott defines the book in terms of its title as "a period of waiting that bridges the sinister and demonic waning moon and the regenerative and creative waxing moon. Thus the moon is both constant and changing." She further refers to Heraclitus, discussed below, and the idea of "acceptance of unacknowledged contraries" (276).

Both Linda Wagner-Martin and Jill LeBihan discuss *Interlunar* in terms of Atwood's novel that appeared in the mid-1980s, *The Handmaid's Tale,* and both conclude that the poems are more despairing. Wagner-Martin calls them a "stark testimony to disaster" (81), and yet, LeBihan reminds us, in Atwood's work we must remember the "impossibility of a clear division between the light and dark" (105). Dinah Birch links *Interlunar* with the novel *Cat's Eye,* which she describes as making "closer contact with Atwood's gift as a poet than any of the six earlier novels." Connecting poems and novel explicitly by means of the recurring image of light, Birch continues that "like cats, we need to make the most of the limited light we have. 'It's old light, and there's not much of it. But it's enough to see by'" (3)—the concluding lines of *Cat's Eye.*

Karen F. Stein directs us helpfully to the book's cover: "Atwood's watercolor for the cover represents light rather than darkness; it is a reflection of a red sun (or moon) in the still water of a pale blue-gray lake" (120). About the "Interlunar" section, she writes that its three parts "delineate a journey from darkness to light and explore poetry's power to heal or console" (120). "Poetry may provide a momentary solace," she explains further, "but it is grounded in knowledge of suffering and death" (121). That very grounding, I would argue, assures us of our humanity and if it does not give solace, it at least reminds us that we are not machines.

Concerning Atwood's latest volume of poems, *Morning in the Burned House,* Coral Ann Howells writes: "[J]ust as the light of morning at the beginning of the poem emerges from the mourning process, so the ending focusses not on the ashes of a fire's aftermath but on 'incandescence'" (144). Inclusion in *Interlunar* of the poem entitled "The Burned House," cited below, links the two volumes explicitly. Writing about Atwood's early poetry, Colin Nicholson comments on the absolute faith in science of many of the early, male poetic personae: "In language that drily accepts technological mastery as in some ways superior to human aptitudes, Atwood presents her male figure as blind not only to his own motivation but necessarily refusing to interrogate those attitudes to the natural world which produced his maimed state" (16). The speaker in *Interlunar* would understand clearly this failure of the discourses of technoscience and poetry to address one another. Eli Mandel and George Woodcock both note a discourse that Atwood's poetry seems to posit in opposition to technoscience. Mandel writes: "Scarcely a poem of Atwood's does not in some way allude to magic or sorcery" (60). And he asks: "Does Atwood use magic as a means of political comment?" (63). Woodcock notes Atwood's speakers' "intuitive wisdom that in the last resort we will accept the irrational as truer than the rational" (141).

The critics thus establish a method of reading *Interlunar* by inviting us to look for contrasts of light and dark; hints of disaster and despair; magic, sorcery, and the irrational alongside dreams of technological mastery of the natural world. Canadianist literary critic Diana M. A. Relke has argued that Canadian women poets overall, and Atwood in particular, have consistently opposed the view of nature promoted by Northrop Frye and described as the "'deep terror' myth" (31). Relke writes that "Canada may well have produced an environment conducive to the development of alternative myths of nature, myths informed by self-reflexivity and a sensitivity to the feminine. . . . I . . . suggest that these alternative myths constitute an epistemology of knowledge which operates as a corrective to the hierarchical and oppositional model of nature identified by Frye" (31–32). Atwood's cultural heritage posits nature as monster, but her own sensibility and that of other female Canadian poets, Relke argues, takes other views. In the closing lines of "Snake Poems" the speaker advises following "The Blue Snake," who will ask you "why you are here" and will then direct you to "a river / you know you must follow home" (23). Some reconciliation occurs with the darkness that is nature.

The natural world would seem to hold promise for both poets and scientists as repository of necessary knowledge, but the two perspectives bring such contrasting methods to the study of nature that their observations are certain to clash. For science to acknowledge its ultimate powerlessness over suffering, loss, and death would seriously challenge its project. To do so, science would need to ally itself with poetic thinking, and that would be strange indeed, rather along the lines of seeing this essay published in a biology journal. But poetry too must not abandon science, and must resist merely overturning the hierarchy by placing itself above crass technoscientific ideology and its popular values.

Consider light and dark, central images in *Interlunar*, as presumed opposites linked to more and less satisfying claims about nature. Light carries significance for us in unaccountable ways; we talk about its quality in certain seasons, certain places as though our perceptions of those seasons and places were molded by it. The dark holds similar powers. Light and dark could be understood technoscientifically rather than associatively. In *The Concise Oxford Dictionary*, light is described as "the natural agent (electromagnetic radiation of wavelength between about 390 and 740 mm) that stimulates sight and makes things visible" (685); dark, not surprisingly, is defined as "absence of light" (293). But was Emily Dickinson imagining light as electromagnetic radiation when she wrote "There's a certain Slant of light, / Winter Afternoons— / That oppresses" (118)? More to the point, do Atwood's personae in *Interlunar* consider only the technoscientific properties of light and its absence when discerning their own humanity?

The discourse of poetry can seem as meaningful as that of science when studying Atwood's uses of light and dark. At a time when technoscientific ways of thinking dominate, reading poetry about natural phenomena through what might be called poetic rather than scientific methodology appears necessary, for explanations of how a certain slant of light might oppress do not come entirely from technoscience. Something like wisdom is also at work, at least as consistent and meaningful over time as the discourse of science, and Atwood's speakers point toward it. Darkness may not in fact imply the absence of light, and light may not always make things visible, as the dictionary definitions would have us believe. Such a perspective sees the poetic and the scientific properties of things simultaneously.

In "After Heraclitus," Atwood's speaker refers to what we might call the technopoetics informing this volume—"All nature is a fire / we burn in and are / renewed" (*Interlunar*, 20)—deriving from the thought of Heraclitus of Ephesus (ca. 500 B.C.), who founded a school of philosophy based in the concept that "the world had its origin in fire and would end in fire" (*Norton Anthology*, 430). The writing of Gerard Manley Hopkins is brought to mind by Atwood's title, particularly his "That Nature is a Heraclitean Fire and of the comfort of the Resurrection," where he asserts that "nature's bonfire burns on" (l. 9, *Norton Anthology*, 430). In "God's Grandeur," Hopkins writes, "And for all this, nature is never spent" (*Norton Anthology*, 427). Such thinking is not entirely systematized observation of a phenomenon, but more nearly imagistic rendering of an intuition that cannot be fully expressed. Images and the inarticulate join with data of nature to form a technopoetic view; thus the irrational and felt are given words, speaking to basic human need.

Consider now the varied appearances of light and dark and their interconnections in *Interlunar*. In one of the volume's last poems, the speaker recalls a poetics of nature whereby fire continues to burn when not seen. "The Burned House" describes the fire that consumed the place to which the speaker has returned many years later and where

> I stretch my new hands into the flames
> which burned here and are still burning
> slowly and unseen: that hesitation
> which passes over the flesh
> like breath riffling water,
> that withering,
> that shimmer.
> (93)

Unseen flame turns to a visible "shimmer," and the burned house, which seems destroyed, becomes instead part of a continual process of decay and renewal that persists beyond ordinary human acknowledgement. In such a poetics of nature, darkness itself is reclaimed. The volume ends with the title poem, "Interlunar," which in turn closes:

> I wish to show you the darkness
> you are so afraid of.
>
> Trust me. This darkness
> is a place you can enter and be
> as safe in as you are anywhere;
>
> . . . .
>
> The lake . . .
> doubles everything, . . .
> . . . even the darkness
> that you can walk so long in
> it becomes light.
> (102–3)

Darkness figures slightly differently as the abode of gods in the first section of the book, "Snake Poems." In "Eating Snake," the speaker supposes that

> All peoples are driven
> to the point of eating their gods
> after a time; it's the old greed
> for a plateful of outer space, that craving for darkness.
> (13)

The white snake is believed to appear "at the dark of the moon" and bring on human craving for it.

> There was a man who tried it. . . .
>
> He went blind in an instant.
> Light rose in him . . .
>
> Human speech left him. . . .
>
> Beware of the white snake, says the story.
> Choose ignorance.
> (15–16)

While part of nature, humans are also defined by a culture that cannot simply be abandoned. And the moon itself does the work of this wise thinking as white against black, and white in black at "the dark of the moon." *Interlunar*, the book's title, suggests those changes between and within.

In "Quattrocento," also in the first section of poems, the Garden is set in "still unending noon" (19) from which the Tempter offers release and "the possibility of death" (18). The Fall implies specifically that "you / must learn to see in darkness" (19). Once banished from paradise,

> Here you can praise the light,
> having so little of it:
>
> it's the death you carry in you
> . . . that makes the world

shine for you
as it never did before.
(19)

Light is praised on earth because it is not "unending noon" here, because dark comes with its intimations of death (perhaps explaining why Dickinson's weak light of a winter afternoon can oppress). In the volume's next section, the three-part "Interlunar," a healer can see in goldenrod and purple asters "the light spilling out . . . / unasked for and unused" (39), as though the powers of light were misunderstood. In "Valediction, Intergalactic," the speaker admits, as quoted above, that "I wanted it / to be light all the time" (43). Not knowing how to value light, not acknowledging its link to darkness, diminishes our humanity; to understand the play of light and dark is to begin to see how culture and nature interact.

The moon appears again in a culminating poem of section 1 of "Interlunar," "A Sunday Drive," set in Bombay, India, a city appearing to be in a state of living decay to the onlooker who avers that "The moon is responsible for all this, / goddess of increase / and death" (51). Moonlight's mysterious netherworld must somehow be accounted for amid praise for the bright clarities of day; both shape nature. The broken figure in "Letter from the House of Questions," a torture prison, prays by writing in the dust of the prison floor: "I would spend the rest of my life / in a house corner, in the sun" (76) simply. In the final poem of section 2 of "Interlunar," entitled "Reading a Political Thriller beside a Remote Lake in the Canadian Shield," the speaker sees sunset and moonrise as motiveless, enduring, and pure in comparison with the plot of the political thriller, although the "lake is dying" in the last stanza because of the greed and "viciousness" that inform the "real world" of the thriller (79–80). We see that just as technoscience has not redeemed the greed, violence, and destitution that comprise much of the human world, poetry has been unable to make such proclamations effectively.

The piece "The Words Continue Their Journey" in the volume's final section treats poets and poetry, reminding us that poets have "the sort of thing / we think of as a voice," which they use to define being human (82). Their journey has taken a wrong turn; they are stranded in "the full glare / of the sun" and also, simultaneously, on "this moon terrain / where everything is dry and perishing and so / vivid, . . . vanishing out of sight" (83). A conflation of sun and moonlight is tied imagistically in this poem with the disappearance of poetry itself. Yet we are assured, as in an earlier poem, that

each thing
burns over and over and we will
too, even the lake's
on fire now.
("The Sidewalk," 88)

Another kind of offering, like prayer, comes in "The White Cup," where "This is the one thing I wanted to give you, / this quiet shining / which is a constant entering, a going into" (89). In "The Light," the poet asks:

Where does the light go when the door closes? . . .

Nowhere, you say. And that is
where the light shines endlessly, full
and inexhaustible. It shines nowhere.
(92)

In this volume, whose predominant color setting is the half-light of the moon, darkness pervades while somehow, inexplicably in terms of technoscientific discourse, the light also "shines nowhere," "inexhaustible" and "full." To allow light to imply only power and darkness only the irrational and inarticulate is to misunderstand both. It is as though in our historical phase, the predominance of the discourse of science prevents expression of its other side, its poetry. But both can be renewed by their interconnections, were a voice to appear to articulate them.

Such a bridging figure might be U.S. cultural critic Donna Haraway, professor of science studies, feminist theory, and women's studies, through such works as *Simians, Cyborgs, and Women: The Reinvention of Nature,* should she discuss women's poetry rather than feminist science fiction. Haraway explains how nature has come to be described as a product of culture:

In the 1940s there was quite a revolution in the science of ecology. The new ecosystem biology basically argued that the ecological object of knowledge was not the community of plants and animals, that the ecosystem meant both the living and the *nonliving* components of the system. . . . So you would watch the nitrogen cycle, you would watch the heat budget. That was an epistemological revolution in ecology. . . .

> [T]he ecological object of knowledge can no longer rely on the silent structured division between nature and culture. The ecological object of knowledge also includes human history and actions. . . . The nature/culture division has broken down for political reasons—because of decolonization, because of the intensity of the ecological crisis, because of the threats of destruction from technoscience. ("Overhauling," 81)

To repeat: "The nature/culture division has broken down." And now, Haraway asks, is a new sense of community possible beyond Darwinian thinking, in which nonhuman beings can be granted agency, and in which no subject is privileged as innocent? "Margaret Atwood's project," writes Diana Relke in the article noted above, is "to bridge the gap between . . . culture and nature" (44). The ground between human and nonhuman, occupied by cyborgs and coyotes in Haraway's view and by revisionist, trickster poets in Atwood's, describes the most likely place for wisdom to emerge, strange as it may seem. Dominant ideologies such as technoscience in our time oversimplify and so diminish what they attempt to explain, inhibiting agency.

In an essay that makes direct reference to Atwood's fiction (307), Haraway describes why new articulations and communities of meaning are crucial:

> Real women and real animals cannot escape their complex relations to the signifying systems and histories of domination that constructed Woman, the Primitive, Race, Nature, Animal, the Other to Man. But not being able to escape these histories does not make real women of all colors unable to reinvent and to relive the stories on other terms. Knowing that we are embedded in inherited fields of knowledge and power does not disqualify any of us from working to construct other, more liberatory, conditions for our loves. ("Monkeys," 296)

Restricting herself to the study of science fiction when she turns to literature, Haraway has not yet speculated on how a cyborg feminist critic might conjoin imagistic and systematic thought. But about her own notorious essay "Manifesto for Cyborgs: Science, Technology, and Socialist Feminism in the 1980s," Haraway says: "I think it's an example of how writing itself is a collective, often unconscious process. . . . Many readings are possible, many readings included within it. I often find the essay being used to carry on other agendas" ("Overhauling,"

66–67). That Haraway describes writing as unconscious distances her somewhat from conventional technoscientific discourse and inches her toward the poetic, and on this uncommon cultural terrain where technoscience gives way to poetry, Atwood and Haraway meet. In such areas of "betweenness," gestured toward by Lawrence W. Norfolk in his review of *Interlunar,* quoted above, we find real meaning. When the future of poetry itself is the issue, as it seems to be in *Interlunar,* alongside the ability of any discourse conventionally seen as outside of technoscience to address technoscience, the writing seems timely and significant indeed. That Atwood publishes a book of poems after *Interlunar,* quelling suspicions that she abandoned poetry during the eleven-year breach, may suggest her own renewed belief in the future of the poem.

4
· · · ·

(Dis)unified Field Theories:
The Clarendon Lectures Seen through (a)
Cat's Eye

MARY K. KIRTZ

> I thought about *Cat's Eye* for twenty-five years before starting it.
>   Margaret Atwood, *Two Solicitudes* (98)

In her introduction to the published version of the lectures she gave on
Canadian literature at Oxford University in 1991, Margaret Atwood
points out a rationale for choosing this particular subject for such an
audience: She can count on the "material being almost completely *terra
incognita*" (*Strange Things*, 2) to those listening. Indeed, she worries
that this very fact might make them bored, since, in the hierarchy of
former colonies, "Canada—lacking the exoticism of Africa, the strange
fauna of Australia, or the romance of India—still tends to occupy the
bottom rung on the status ladder of ex-British colonies" (*ST*, 2). Even
worse, she notes, is the view of Canada's literature "in the English literary mind . . . [as] an unexplored and uninteresting wasteland, punctuated by a few rocks, bogs, and stumps"(*ST*, 2). Although these
remarks exhibit Atwood's characteristic humor, the intent beneath the
wit is a serious one: to explain to people outside Canada at least some
aspects of its literature that can be recognized as distinctly Canadian.

More than twenty years earlier, her reasons for writing *Survival* for
people *inside* Canada were presented in similar terms. In 1995, speaking to Victor-Lévy Beaulieu, she pointed out that she had written that

guide "to establish, one, that Canadian literature existed, and two, that it was different from English and American literature . . . it is logical to assume that, if a country is different, its literature will be too" (*Two Solicitudes,* 100). By the time she gave the Clarendon lectures, Atwood no longer needed to prove the existence of Canadian literature; its development as a valid field had taken hold through the intervening years, spurred on by a growing nationalism and considerable government support. Nevertheless, as the quotes above suggest, she still feels the need to prove that its terrain, like that of ex-colonies displaying a more obvious sense of "otherness," was worth exploring by those outside Canada's territory.

Establishing that otherness remains particularly problematic for writers and scholars of Anglophone Canadian literature. (Québecois works have been successfully turned into a distinct literature of their own not only because of the language difference and the separatist movement in that province, but also because academic scholars began making clear distinctions between the two literatures in their own published works.) The federal government's official efforts to establish Canada's national difference through the Multiculturalism Act, declaring Canada to be a "multicultural nation within a bilingual framework," have indeed brought greater awareness of Canadians as something "other" than descendents of people from France, England, and the United States. By adding the work of the First Nations, visible minorities, and more recent immigrants to the literary mix comprising Francophone and Anglophone writers, the federal government has emphasized Canada's simultaneous status as both a conquering and a conquered nation. This duality continues to blur the clarity of federal Canada's current "othered" image and contributes to the ongoing difficulty of Canadian efforts to establish some sort of monolithic national identity, particularly for its own people (it is not clear to what extent the rest of the world worries about this). In the lectures, Atwood likens the search for this elusive concept to a paradigm of canine frustration:

> But surely the search for the fabled Canadian identity is like a dog chasing its own tail. Round about and round about it goes, with the tail whisking out of sight; whereupon it proclaims the tail elusive, fragile, threatened, or absent. And yet, as everyone can plainly see, there is the tail, as firmly attached to the dog as ever. (*ST,* 8)

It is one of the paradoxes of contemporary Canadian existence that the period during which Canadian nationalism asserted itself most vigorously—the 1960s and 1970s—coincided both with the rise of Québec's desire to redraw Canada's boundaries and with the kind of transnational globalism that appears to be erasing national boundaries everywhere. The simultaneous existence of the centripetal desire to declare a specific identity for Canada and the centrifugal insistence on its irrelevance is aptly served by Atwood's simile of the disappearing tail that, seen or unseen, continues to wag the dog. In Atwood's own novels, starting with *Surfacing,* she has explored—sometimes satirical-ly, sometimes elegiacally—both the tail and the reasons for its contin-uous disappearing act.

That she herself believes in the existence of both the dog and its tail is never in doubt. In the Clarendon lectures, Atwood postulates that whatever we may say about their actuality, national identities do exist and they inevitably possess certain characteristics. According to her analysis, a nation's cultural identity is composed of "cliché-images . . . based on fact or historical reality of some sort [and are then used by artists and writers who can] make variations on them, explore them more deeply. . . . What art can't do is ignore them altogether" (8). In addition to

> such images, every culture has stories that are told and retold, and such recurring stories bear examining . . . [because] story-tellers come back to them time and time again, approaching them from various angles and discovering new and different meanings each time the story, or a part of it, is given a fresh incarnation. (11)

For the lectures, Atwood concentrates on images and stories of Cana-da's "malevolent North" as it is represented in four different areas: in literary approaches to the story of the disastrous search for the North-west Passage by Sir John Franklin; in the efforts of white men to "go native"; in the folkloric figure of the Wendigo; and, finally, in women's responses to the wilderness experience. These stories and images, focused as they are on the primeval landscape, on the native peoples, or on women, emphasize, in Atwood's view, the "otherness" of the Canadian experience (and, by extension, its identity). All of these images and stories in fact are ones that, along with her thinking about *Cat's Eye,* have occupied Atwood's own approach to her literary out-put for over twenty-five years and appear in her own work, as she her-self mentions in her final lecture. She cites the texts more obviously connected with the content of the lectures: *Surfacing, The Journals of Susanna Moodie,* and some stories in *Wilderness Tips.* Less obviously, they can be found in a more deracinated, denatured, or disguised form in some of her other works as well, particularly in *Cat's Eye,* published in 1988. In this novel, they have become pale urban versions (or "subversions," if you will) of the powerful originals, taking on an ambiguity that marks Canada's own lack of definition. I will argue that their transformation parallels Atwood's increasing concern about the stability of Canada as a distinct national entity. In that sense, these stories and images become allegorical representations of Canada's shifting sense of nationhood.

Atwood's first major use of the characteristics she outlines in the lectures occurred in *Surfacing,* a text that has been elucidated extensively by critics since its publication, most often in feminist terms. Having been published almost simultaneously with *Survival,* the novel has also frequently been interpreted in terms of the stages of victimhood outlined in that text, and, not surprisingly, given Atwood's desire to "prove" the existence of Canadian literature at this time, she incorporates all of the characteristics of the "malevolent North" into this early novel: The wilderness described is that of northern Québec, the Wendigo becomes a mysterious apparition, the protagonist "goes native" and also treats her cottage as a "linoleum cave"—the metaphor Atwood uses in the Clarendon lectures for the female response to the wild.[1] Unlike the malevolence exhibited by these characteristics in many of the texts Atwood mentions in the 1991 lectures, in her own novel they benevolently lead the protagonist to a resolution, however tentative it may be, of her angst. Atwood transforms the usually murderous Wendigo into a powerful healing figure whose appearance is the culmination of the protagonist's journey toward self-forgiveness and self-acceptance after having had an abortion.[2] The spiritual journey itself is enacted through a version of "going native," when the protagonist throws off all trappings of civilization in her quest and turns her parents' cottage into a kind of cave; at the end, she restores order before leaving for the city.

These two aspects of the north are seen in a positive light, but the wilderness and Canadians' relationship to it are presented in more ambivalent terms. Although the protagonist has been able to make peace with herself and her parents as a result of her stay in the bush, suggesting the importance of the wilderness as a sacred space that should be left undeveloped, the Québec government is about to flood the area in the name of technological progress, and American speculators are ready to transform the rest into cozy camping and fishing grounds. Once again, the Canadian landscape is threatened by Québecois insistence on its prerogatives and American desire for economic conquest. Perhaps the starkest betrayal comes from those who might have been thought to value it most, ordinary Anglophone Canadian citizens. Seeing a canoe full of fisherman whom she assumes to be Americans, the protagonist discovers that they are in fact Canadian; in a classic Atwoodian ironic turn, the fishermen have made the same assumption about the protagonist and her friends: "'We thought you were Yanks, with the hair and all'" (151), they declare. She is furious with them for having "disguised" themselves (their boat sports a "Go Mets" sticker) and meditates on the logical conclusion to this case of mistaken identity. If Canadians do not value homegrown culture, then Americanism is

> what's in store for us, it's what we're turning into. . . . Like the Late Show sci-fi movies, creatures from outer space, body snatchers injecting themselves into you, dispossessing your brain, their eyes blank eggshells behind the dark glasses. If you look like them and talk like them and think like them then you are them, I was saying, you speak their language, a language is everything you do. (151–52)

Atwood here delineates the ultimate Anglophone Canadian dilemma: By using the language they hold in common with Great Britain and the United States, such Canadians have great difficulty not only in distinguishing themselves from citizens of these other countries, but also in creating their own cultural artifacts. Again, we see Atwood's irony at work as she describes the problem in the very terms created by it, by using an American popular film, *The Invasion of the Body Snatchers,* for her metaphorical presentation of the dilemma.[3]

Atwood's concern for Anglophone Canadians' inability to distinguish themselves from Americans is elucidated even more succinctly in her next novel, *Lady Oracle,* published in 1976. In this work, Atwood begins transforming the characteristics of the "malevolent North" by bringing them to bear upon a southern urban Anglophone Canada. Following the tendency of storytellers that she had noted in the Clarendon lectures, Atwood approaches these characteristics "from various angles and discover[s] new and different meanings each time the story, or a part of it, is given a fresh incarnation" (11).

Their use here, as in *Surfacing,* emphasizes the still tenuous status of Canadian identity. Atwood uses the life journey of Joan in *Lady Oracle* to suggest that Anglophone Canadian culture, given its proximity to the United States and its continuing, if sometimes tepid, fealty toward Great Britain, can never be anything but derivative.[4]

Joan, named after American movie star Joan Crawford, learns about life by watching non-Canadian movies like *The Red Shoes* (a British-made movie about a doomed English ballerina whose career takes her to Paris, thus evoking here both of Canada's imperial parents). In addition, she reads trashy romance novels and then learns how to write them while living in London. Paul, the Polish count who introduces Joan to this line of work, cannot distinguish between Americans and Canadians:

> [H]e would only smile his twisted little smile and say, "You Americans are so naive, you have no history." I'd given up trying to tell him I was not an American. "It's all the same thing, isn't it?" he would say. "The lack of one kind of history is the same as the lack of another." (159)

Another of Joan's lovers, an artist who calls himself "The Royal Porcupine," suggests the continuing adherence of Anglophone Canadians to England. When Joan asks him about this name, he proclaims himself a "Royalist . . . I really dig the Queen. I felt I should have a name that would reflect that. It's like the Royal Mail or the Royal Canadian Mounted Police" (241–42). Note here the complete lack of differentiation between the British postal system and the Canadian peacekeepers. He chooses "Porcupine" because he thinks it's a better national symbol for Canada than the beaver:

> I've always figured the beaver was wrong, as a national symbol. . . . I mean, the beaver. A dull animal and too nineteenth century; all that industry. And you know what they used to be hunted for? The skin was for hats, and then they cut the nuts off for perfume. I mean, what a fate. The porcupine, though, it does what it likes, it's covered with prickles so nobody messes with it. (242)

As represented by Joan and the Royal Porcupine, then, it appears that the Canadian cultural identity in the 1970s remains a pastiche of British and American influences, distinguishable from neither.

Atwood also satirizes Anglophone Canadian radical groups who, busy protesting a war being fought by those south of the border, remain blissfully ignorant of the incipient one beginning just east of Ontario. Even worse is the oxymoronic status of being a radical in Ontario (as opposed to being a member of the *Front de Libération de Québec*). Joan tells the anticommunist Polish count, "[I]t doesn't mean anything here, it's respectable, sort of. They don't *do* anything; they just have meetings and talk a lot, sort of like the Theosophists" (282). Their efforts to support a strike fail because "the workers are Portuguese, and . . . Canadian nationalism means bugger all to them. . . . Not that we can get it across to them, we're still looking for an interpreter" (262).

As this mention of the Portuguese suggests, there are brief infusions of "otherness" within the story, exemplified primarily by recent immigrants residing in Toronto. In the person of John/Zerdo, Atwood succinctly renders the immigrant experience before and after the enactment of the government's multicultural policy. As "John" in the 1950s, the restaurant owner works hard to assimilate into the larger Anglophone culture; as "Zerdo" in the 1970s, he flaunts his ethnicity. Like his name, his restaurant has been transformed from the generically North American diner named "Bite-a-Bit" to a grapevine-festooned Greek cantina. Nevertheless, such groups remain peripheral; Atwood's main concern is to elucidate the overwhelming hold Anglophone Canada's two imperial masters, the British and the Americans, have on the country's cultural imagination.

Indeed, the easily recognizable "cliché-images" and stories of the "malevolent North" in *Surfacing* have undergone a considerable transformation in their migration south to Toronto, but their presence can still be discerned within the text. The ravines of Toronto snaking their way beneath the civilized surface of the city prove themselves to be a dangerous terrain for young Joan to traverse; they appear in still a different form as the dangerous maze in the adult Joan's costume gothic. The cannibalistic Wendigo is reincarnated as Joan's alcoholic mother's ghost, and Joan's efforts to morph herself into the kind of woman idealized by Western culture is a satirical, if poignant, inversion of "going native." Inverting this particular concept does not eliminate it; whether one is "going" or "returning" to native, it remains a point of reference for Canadian identity. Like the dilemma of deciding who are the conquerors and who are the conquered, the question of which is the "native" side has shifting answers. While the British Archie Belaney passed himself off as the Indian Grey Owl, Joan Foster is the "uncivilized" native who tries to pass herself off as a socially acceptable Stepford wife. Just as Belaney's real identity was discovered only after his death, so Joan, after her (fake) death, is finally revealed as the person behind both Lady Oracle, the "poetess," and Louisa K. Delacourt, the romance writer. But are these identities any more authentic (that is, more "native") than her identification as Arthur's wife? As the women at the center of the maze point out, they are all Lady Redmond; the thing signified may never be found beneath all these signifiers.

Lady Oracle also presents Joan with many "linoleum caves" to inhabit, perhaps the most dangerous being her mother's kitchen, in which her mother, prefiguring her ghostly role as Wendigo, stabs her daughter with a paring knife. As a woman negotiating the tangled maze of her life, Joan, like the protagonist of *Surfacing*, has a vision before finally arriving at an accommodation with the fate she's been handed and reconciling the many contradictions within her several selves. The apparition of her mother, crying soundlessly through her lipstick-doubled mouth and stretching out her arms toward Joan, tries to lure her to her death. Together, Joan thinks, they "would go down the corridor into the darkness" (330). Waking from this trance when she is unable to open the door, Joan realizes that she must become her own person. Just as the protagonist in the earlier novel sets pathways and boundaries for herself as she travels to the depths of her psyche, so too does Joan send herself onto the path of her fictional maze in order to discover who she really is. Both novels end in ambiguity, with each protagonist's newly formed sense of self-identity presented as tentative at best, even as each prepares to return "home," a classic metaphor for the center. Twelve years later, many of these themes and images reach their full expression in *Cat's Eye*.

Frank Davey, in his analysis of the novel, suggests that *Cat's Eye* veers between two points of political ideology, the local and the universal. "The national," he asserts, "is present as a kind of freedom from the power of transnational 'fashion,' and as a composite of particular, local images" (*Post-National Arguments*, 238). Furthermore, the local images themselves, as a composite of a "human Canada . . . are narrowly individual and almost totally lacking in social codes and discourses" (238). In other words, Davey detects no clusters within the text of a society's "cliché-images" or stories that help to create an identifiable national literature. A close reading of the text, however, suggests both the presence and a critique of the constituent components identified by Atwood in her Clarendon lectures.

Atwood's depiction of Elaine's childhood, particularly its focus on the nasty games young girls play, has been analyzed extensively, with people lining up on one side or the other of the claim that Atwood's description is a disservice to the feminist cause. The use of this material as an allegorical representation of Canada's national zeitgeist during World War II and the decades following, however, has received far less attention.[5] Atwood is not merely recreating what being a girl in the

1940s and '50s was like; she is also depicting what English Canada, specifically southern Ontario—as a bastion of Anglophiles being transformed by immigrants from less loved regions—was like. Davey calls Elaine's experiences a division between the local and the global. Between these two polarities, however, one can also see her experience as an exemplar of the sense of nationhood experienced by all urban Anglophone Canadians of this period, strung as they were within two hundred miles of the porous American border and still being inculcated with a belief in the virtue of having Great Britain as an imperial parent. Atwood once again uses the "cliché-images" she most closely identifies with Canada's sense of "otherness" to focus on this problem. In the urban context of the novel, she has revisioned them into images more readily grasped by a typical urban Anglophone Canadian. Although they remain recognizable as indicators of Canada's sense of itself, this transformation also suggests their adaptability. More pessimistically, it may also suggest their instability as purveyors of a distinct national identity.

As Elaine returns to Toronto, she notes the malevolence lurking beneath the "*world-class city*. . . . Underneath the flourish and ostentation is the old city, street after street of thick red brick houses, with their front porch pillars like the off-white stems of toadstools and their watchful, calculating windows. Malicious, grudging, vindictive, implacable"(*CE*, 14). In this frightening landscape, she feels lost. Even more, she feels that she is in disguise. In a reversal of the male trend outlined by Atwood in the Clarendon lectures, rather than "going native," Elaine, like Joan before her, is a native "going civilized." Like the protagonist in *Surfacing*, she spends her earliest years as a nomad in the bush, along with her parents and brother, Stephen. Once they move to the city, Elaine realizes that her family is different somehow; the Anglican Carol Campbell, living in a house decorated in chintz, describes Elaine's family to her other friends "as if she's reporting on the antics of some primitive tribe: true, but incredible" (52). This Anglophiliac friend sees the workplace of Elaine's father as equally strange and exotic, even repellent, as she examines the native fauna he has preserved. Elaine quickly learns to hide her true responses and turns herself into "an imitation of a girl" (55), never feeling that she's the real thing. In fact, she identifies with her father's graduate student from India, Mr. Banerji, and dreams at one point that he and her Jewish neighbor, Mrs. Finestein, are her parents. In the dream, her house has been destroyed and her real parents are dead, "sinking down through the earth, which is hard but transparent, like ice" (179), recalling in this image the doomed Franklin expedition. The Indian and the Jew, then, provide a greater sense of "otherness" than do her parents. The latter's having roughed it in the bush is apparently not enough to save them from the Franklin team's fate. Elaine divides the people she knows into two groups, the wild and the tame:

> Wild things are smarter than tame ones, that much is clear. Wild things are elusive and wily and look out for themselves. I divide the people I know into tame and wild. My mother, wild. My father and brother, also wild; Mr. Banerji, wild also, but in a more skittish way. Carol, tame. Grace, tame as well, though with sneaky vestiges of wild. Cordelia, wild, pure and simple. (139)

As this categorization shows, there is no simple correspondence between being "wild" and being "native" or between being "tame" and "civilized."

Atwood's intricate play in this text with the concept of "going native" is an accurate reflection of the complexity governing what it means to be "native" in Canada. In a country with several waves of settlers, who exactly are the natives, especially after the federal multi-cultural policy has embraced everyone within its mosaical grasp? Although Elaine and her family have spent years in the bush, they remain, however uneasily, part of the Anglophones, while the First Nations themselves are virtually invisible. As the Risleys drive north for another summer in the bush, Elaine sees three Indians standing beside the road

> as if they've been doing it for a long time. They're familiar to me but only as scenery. Do they see me as I stare at them out of the car window? Probably not. I'm a blur to them, one more face in a car that doesn't stop. I have no claim on them, or on any of this. (152)

The Risley family's difference is based on their different experience of the Canadian landscape rather than on their race, making them culturally rather than physically native in the eyes of the urbanites.

Mr. Banerji and Mrs. Finestein, on the other hand, represent a physical "otherness" that is not "native" to Canada, but imported and therefore even more exotic and strange. Indeed, Elaine discovers that the inhabitants of this civilized wilderness view their strangeness with suspicion and prejudice. Mr. Banerji finally gives up and returns to India because, Elaine's father explains, "'They wouldn't promote

him,'. . . There's a lot behind *they* (not *we*), and *wouldn't* (not *didn't*)"
(307). When Elaine becomes young Brian Finestein's babysitter, she
enters an even harsher arena of hostility. Carol and Grace refer to Jews,
including the Finesteins, as kikes and Christ killers, and little Brian as
"an old Jew baby" (144). Already tormented by these friends, Elaine
believes that she is too weak to protect the baby from them, imagining
him "hurtling in his carriage down the icy hill by the side of the bridge,
straight toward the creek full of dead people" (144). This image
evokes those of Jews murdered by the Nazis, connecting the cruel
behavior of her "civilized" friends to these perpetrators of unspeakable
evil.

Two of Elaine's teachers, Miss Lumley and Miss Stuart, exemplify
the confusion that begins to develop at this time over the constitutive
components of nationhood. Miss Lumley upholds the British image of
an empire that has civilized the world and, in Canada specifically, conquered another imperial power, the French, and saved the First Nations
from their heathen ways. A firm hierarchy is established among these
groups. The students sing "God Save the King" and "Rule Britannia"
in class, but Elaine notes, "we aren't real Britons, because we are also
Canadians. This isn't quite as good, although it has its own song" (84).
Miss Lumley castigates the Canadian students for not having suffered
as did the children of Europe, the mother continent. The Scottish perspective presented in Miss Stuart's class, in which the English are seen
as the ruin of Bonnie Prince Charlie, only confuses the issue further,
since in Canada the Scots are very much a part of the colonizing Brits,
who remain the pinnacle of culture and civilization among these
"natives." Like the question of who are the natives, here we ask which
is the empire, which is the colony? Burnham High School is awash in
Scots memorabilia, and the students sing "'The Skye Boat Song,' about
Bonnie Prince Charlie escaping the genocidal English" (220). Elaine
thinks, "all this Scottishness is normal for high schools, never having
gone to one before; and even the several Armenians, Greeks, and Chinese in our school lose the edges of their differences, immersed as we
all are in a mist of plaid" (220–21).

The Brits remain in the ascendancy during this immediate postwar
period. Miss Stuart's Scottish brogue is far more acceptable than is Mr.
Hrbik's pronunciation of "body" as "bowdy" and "woman" as
"voman." Indeed, his students call him "a D.P., which means *displaced
person,* an old insult I remember from high school. It was what you
called refugees from Europe, and those who were stupid and uncouth
and did not fit in" (299). In the late '80s, as the adult Elaine glances

through a telephone directory, she sees that "[t]here are more Campbells than you can shake a stick at. . . . No Josef Hrbik, though there are Hrbeks, Hrens, Hrastnicks, Hriczus" (189), indicating, perhaps, that the later immigrant groups are gaining on conquering settlers and aspiring to "native" status themselves. The addition of refugees and displaced persons, represented by her art professor, Josef Hrbik, who has come "'from a country that no longer exists . . . [to] a country that does not yet exist'" (324), also emphasizes the instability of nationhood and identity in an era of increasing globalization. Canada seems doomed to remain a work in progress rather than ever to become a finished entity. Each new layer of immigration extends the definition of "native" to those coming immediately before the most recent crop of immigrants, blurring all divisions and definitions of nationhood. "Homelessness," Elaine thinks, "is a nationality now" (334), implying that the average person's state is governed by rootlessness rather than roots.

The depiction of Elaine's brother, Stephen, exemplifies this status, giving us yet another version of both the immigrant experience of displacement and its connection to the notion of "going native." Stephen, unlike his sister, seems to adapt rather easily to the urban environment and eventually moves to the United States to study astrophysics. While he himself seems to feel at ease moving among these different people, he appears as strange to the Americans as Josef Hrbik and his kind are to Anglophile Canadians in southern Ontario. When Stephen accidentally trespasses onto a restricted military zone, he's arrested as a spy. It is his casual approach to national differences that puts him into such dangerous situations. His area of study, the nature of the universe, makes him ignore such mundane things as national boundaries and identities, and it is this very attitude that leads to his death: He is simply another kind of "native" unable to "go civilized." Elaine recognizes this, worrying that "he should be more careful. What I have always assumed in him to be bravery may be merely an ignorance of consequences. He thinks he is safe, because he is what he says he is. But he's out in the open, and surrounded by strangers" (310).

Being so true to his "native" self, he cannot adapt to, adopt disguises for, "go civilized" in the various environments in which he finds himself. Stephen becomes a world traveler, lighting momentarily here or there. When Elaine next sees him, he looks "like a creature from an alien planet disguised in human clothing" (351) and speaks "'the one truly universal language: mathematics'" (353). Stephen's refusal to acknowledge boundaries ironically collides with the increasingly global approach to asserting national rights by various groups. The Second

World War, so clear in both its missions and its boundaries, has mutated into a global affair that "gets in everywhere, you can't shut it out. Killing is endless now, it's an industry, there's money in it, and the good side and the bad side are pretty hard to tell apart. . . . This is the war that killed Stephen" (334). The mission of the terrorists who kill her brother is unclear. In their pillowcase disguises, they look like yet another version of the Wendigo figure, "caught halfway through their transformation: ordinary bodies but with powerful, supernatural heads, deformed in the direction of heroism, or villainy" (412). As the man chooses Stephen for death, "his oversized head moves ponderously left, like the head of some shortsighted, dull-witted monster" (413). The ambiguity of their cause only heightens the futility of Stephen's demise.

Not just the status of the various groups, but also the urban wilderness through which they traverse is confusing to those unfamiliar with its terrain. Carol first introduces Elaine to the most frightening aspect of this particular wilderness, the ravine, as they walk home from school. It becomes the site for the confluence of all four of the "cliché-images": the frozen north, "going native," the Wendigo, and linoleum caves.

As punishment for once again having transgressed the unfathomable rules of preteen girlhood, Elaine must go down into the ravine, "where the bad men are, where we're never supposed to go" (200) and retrieve her hat, thrown down onto the ice-covered creek by the malevolent Cordelia. As she steps onto the ice, it breaks and Elaine falls through. The water, Elaine realizes, "comes straight from the cemetery, from the graves and their bones. It's water made from the dead people, dissolved and clear" (201), and if she doesn't get out, she will be one of them, like the men in the Franklin expedition. Climbing out of the creek, waterlogged and reeling with pain from the cold, Elaine lies down in the snow, only to be brought out of her cold-induced lethargy by a vision of a woman with "her heart, on the outside of her body, glowing like neon, like a coal" (203). Elaine identifies her as the Virgin Mary, but given Atwood's penchant for ironic reversals, she might also be seen as a benevolent version of the Wendigo, with her dark dress and glowing heart replacing the icy body and heart of the monster. This episode sets Elaine free from her entanglement with her so-called friends, the "native" in her finally seeing through the subterfuge of their "civilized" behavior. The threat developed out of a kitchen metaphor and used by the girls to intimidate her, "ten stacks of plates" symbolically brought crashing down on Elaine's head, no longer frightens her as she walks away from them.

The Wendigo is presented in various manifestations in this text, exemplifying Atwood's own complex view of this figure. Its most obvious incarnation is in the figure of Mrs. Smeath. Mrs. Smeath has a bad heart, according to her daughter Grace. Elaine remembers her lying on her couch, "her scrubbed face, without her glasses, white and strangely luminous in the dim space, like a phosphorescent mushroom" (62), evoking the glowing eyes of the Wendigo. In the fundamentalist Smeath family's eyes, Elaine is a heathen—yet another kind of "native"—who might be saved. Elaine has been working to overcome her heathen ways, going to Sunday school with Grace, memorizing psalms, writing pious essays, and singing hymns. Coming upon Mrs. Smeath talking with her sister in the kitchen, their "linoleum cave," Elaine discovers that the woman has known all along about the girls' cruelty toward her, justifying it as "God's punishment," indeed, declaring that "[i]t serves her right" (193). When Mrs. Smeath realizes that Elaine has been eavesdropping on this conversation, she smiles smugly and her "bad heart floats in her body like an eye, an evil eye, it sees me" (194). Shortly thereafter, Elaine finds on the sidewalk a picture of the Virgin Mary, with her heart shown outside her chest, "large, red and tidy, like a satin heart pincushion, or a valentine. Under the picture is printed: *The Seven Sorrows*" (195). The non-Catholic students have dubbed the local Catholic school, where holy pictures like this one are routinely given to students, "Our Lady of Perpetual Hell" (195). The actual name ends in "Help." This is of course the image that leads to her vision in the ravine. In both the case of Mrs. Smeath and the Virgin Mary, their benevolence/malevolence is held in ambiguous balance.

All the cliché-images and stories within the text are reinforced pictorially through the vehicle of Elaine's art. In her artwork, she has tried to create a unified field theory from her fragmented memories of a fractured childhood. When Elaine first starts painting Mrs. Smeath, her figure is "smiling her closed half-smile, smug and accusing. Whatever has happened to me is my own fault, the fault of what is wrong with me. . . . She multiplies on the walls like bacteria" (358). Although Elaine's memories of Mrs. Smeath have remained tinged with hatred, when she looks at her paintings of the woman in the present moment of the text, she realizes that Mrs. Smeath's self-righteous and smug eyes are also the eyes of someone "for whom God was a sadistic old man; the eyes of a small town threadbare decency. Mrs. Smeath was a transplant to the city, from somewhere a lot smaller. A displaced person; as I was" (427). Seeing herself through Mrs. Smeath's eyes, she realizes that taking Elaine in was an act of courage on the woman's part, and that Elaine has "not done it justice, or rather mercy. Instead I went for vengeance" (427). Elaine paints the Virgin Mary as a lioness because it seems more accurate "than the old bloodless milk-and-water Virgins of art history. My Virgin Mary is fierce, alert to danger, wild. She stares levely [sic] out at the viewer with her yellow lion's eyes. A gnawed bone lies at her feet" (365). Since being wild is associated in the young Elaine's mind with Cordelia as well as with her parents, its nature as an attribute of the Virgin Mary is not clearly marked as good or bad, particularly with the gnawed bone lying at her feet. Does the gnawed bone suggest the nurturing mother getting food for her young, or is it an expression of the Wendigo's cannibalistic tendencies?

The trajectory taken by the relationship between Cordelia and Elaine is also revealed in Elaine's art. She commemorates Cordelia in a painting titled *Half a Face* after a story the two read in a horror comic book. Cordelia stares out of the foreground of the picture, and hanging on the wall behind her is "another face, covered with a white cloth" (243). Cordelia appears afraid of Elaine in this picture, and Elaine acknowledges her own fear of Cordelia, not "of seeing Cordelia. I'm afraid of being Cordelia. Because in some way we changed places, and I've forgotten when" (243). Until the incident in the ravine, Cordelia's power over Elaine is both immense and mysterious. When they once again become friends in high school, they begin to trade places. On the day that the teenage Elaine, long after the ravine incident, frightens Cordelia by jokingly declaring herself a vampire who's "been dead for years" (249), Elaine realizes that she has a "malevolent little triumph to finger: energy has passed between us, and I am stronger" (250). This "cross-over" keeps the image of the Wendigo, particularly as it is manifested in the relationship between Elaine and Cordelia, in constant flux within this text. Cordelia, who is purely and simply "wild" in spite of her "civilized" veneer, had claimed that dead people populated the ravine into which she had forced Elaine to go.

Elaine's claim here to be one of the dead people reverses their roles from those they held vis-à-vis one another in childhood. In their childhood, Cordelia is relentless in her pursuit of Elaine until the latter is tearing the flesh off her feet, biting the skin off her lips, throwing up, fainting, and missing school. Her response to Cordelia's cruel badgering is similar to being under a Wendigo's spell: "I begin to spend time outside my body without falling over. . . . My eyes are open but I'm not there. I'm off to the side" (183). Elaine begins to pray to the Virgin Mary, a false idol to the Smeaths, a saint to the Catholics they despise. The vision of this figure rescues Elaine from the hell of her friendship with Cordelia who, along with Grace and Carol, grows "paler and paler every day, less and less substantial" (208), as if they themselves had embodied the evil curse of a Wendigo whose spell is now broken. Elaine's self-portrait, titled *Cat's Eye*, is the companion piece to her portrait of Cordelia. In this portrait, Elaine portrays only the top half of her face, while in a pier glass behind her, part of the back of her head, "different, younger," is showing, and in the distance "are three small figures, dressed in the winter clothing of the girls of forty years ago. They walk forward, their faces shadowed, against a field of snow" (430).

In high school, friends once more, Cordelia and Elaine read a horror comic about a woman with a burned face who enters the unblemished body of her twin sister when the latter looks in the mirror. That night, Elaine is afraid she'll "find out that there's someone else trapped inside my body; I'll look into the bathroom mirror and see the face of another girl, someone who looks like me but has half of her face darkened, the skin burned away" (227). Cordelia becomes this "other half" as she begins to take on Elaine's earlier role of "native." Cordelia's behavior with boys is no more than an "imitation" of such social behavior, as if she's "mimicking something, something in her head, some role or image that only she can see" (262). She fails where Elaine succeeds—in school, with boys, with life in general. When they meet again, Cordelia, temporarily all right, is like the badly burned twin, and Elaine, involved in an emotionally draining affair, sees herself reflected in Cordelia's sunglasses, "in her mirror eyes, in duplicate and monochrome, and a great deal smaller than life-size" (322). This brief re-reversal of their roles evaporates quickly, however. In their next meeting, when Cordelia asks Elaine to rescue her from the private asylum in which she's incarcerated, Elaine imagines Cordelia hiding out in her apartment "sleeping on an improvised bed like the draft dodgers, a refugee, a displaced person" (380), and doesn't feel up to such a rescue. After Cordelia disappears from the asylum, Elaine dreams of a mannequin statue that's "wearing nothing but a gauze costume covered with spangles. It ends at the neck. Underneath its arm, wrapped in a white cloth, is Cordelia's head" (382). The failure of Cordelia's efforts to act her way back to sanity at the Stratford Shakespearean Festival is emphasized by this image tying together her roles in both *The Tempest* and *Macbeth*. In the latter, she embarrassed herself, and in the former, she could barely be seen.

As the adult Elaine returns to the ravine, acknowledging that the Virgin Mary had not appeared to her the day of her fall into the creek, a different vision, that of Cordelia at the age of nine, takes hold. Because this apparition allows Elaine to engage in a kind of healing ceremony, Cordelia here becomes the form of Wendigo that serves as a catalyst for healing. The scene is similar to the encounters that occur in *Surfacing* between the protagonist and the Wendigo-like figure and in *Lady Oracle* between Joan and her mother before their own healing can move forward. Realizing that the fearful emotions she felt as a child were Cordelia's as well her own, Elaine is finally able to forgive both Cordelia and herself for the monstrous behaviors that were, in many ways, all too human.

> "I am the older one now, I'm the stronger. If she stays here any longer she will freeze to death; she will be left behind, in the wrong time. It's almost too late.
>
> I reach out my arms to her, bend down, hands open to show I have no weapon. *It's all right,* I say to her. *You can go home now.* The snow in my eyes withdraws like smoke.
>
> When I turn finally, Cordelia is no longer there. (443)

Elaine's urging Cordelia to "go home" underscores the identification of Elaine, Mrs. Smeath, and Cordelia as "displaced persons" and broadens this category beyond the narrow one she had constructed earlier around the figure of Josef Hrbik. Anyone caught between having to be "civilized" or "going native" is dispossessed, rootless, displaced. In a country like Canada, with its sense of nationhood constantly challenged and in flux, such feelings are the prevailing ones.

The second painting in Elaine's retrospective, called *Three Muses,* portrays Mrs. Finestein, Mr. Banerji, and Miss Stuart, each holding, respectively, an orange the size of a beach ball, a flat disc with spruce budworm eggs displayed, and a globe of the world. As opposed to the three little witches of her childhood, these are the three people who have graced her with kindness. They are also, each in a different way, displaced persons, here brought from the margins to the very center, standing in for one of the great cliché-images of Western art, the classical Graces. They offer their gifts of kindness in circular forms, suggesting images of wholeness, like the space-time continuum bent in on itself, with no beginning and no end.

The last painting in Elaine's retrospective bears the name *Unified Field Theory* and is a portrait of the Virgin of Lost Things. It is the final transformation of her memory of the ravine incident, holding within it all the terror and the magic of childhood. Instead of a visible heart, however, the virgin "holds a glass object: an oversized cat's eye marble, with a blue center" (430). Like the circular objects in the portrait of the muses, the globe suggests wholeness, and since *Cat's Eye* is the name of Elaine's self-portrait, it also suggests that Elaine herself has come full circle, become whole. Similarly, Atwood's effort to re-create the "lost things" of childhood can be seen as an effort to create a unified field theory of Canada's recent past, transforming its most visibly "different" cliché-images and stories, those connected with the "malevolent North," to the predominately urban environment of post–World War II southern Ontario. But the final pages of the novel resist closure. Elaine has forgiven Cordelia and accepted the events of the past, but she continues to regret their impact on the future, a future in which Cordelia, and the friendship they might have had, is forever lost. In a shifting landscape, even the most durable cliché-images can be irretrievably buried by layers of new images heaped upon them. In her conversation with Victor-Lévy Beaulieu, Atwood notes that she ended *Survival* with the question *Have we survived?*

> That question is still very current. I wrote the book almost twenty-five years ago, and since then our economic domination by the United States is even greater. The Canadian government is dismantling all its structures for supporting the arts, social programs, the health-care system, care of the elderly, and so on. The question of Québec's separation also has a potential impact on this. Canada will be transformed into several little countries, including the country of Ontario. (*Two Solicitudes*, 103)

For over twenty-five years, Atwood has worked to identify and disseminate the cliché-images and stories of Canadian literature for the rest of the world. The Clarendon lectures exemplify this mission. In her own work, such images are clearly evident, albeit transformed, seen, as Elaine sees time, "like a series of liquid transparencies" (*CE*, 3) taking on the shape and form of the stories in which they appear. But if the country that they are intended to represent is itself fractured and divided into unrecognizable shapes, can they carry the burden of national identity forward into these new territories? Or, as Stephen says of Cordelia, suggesting the elusive and ephemeral nature of such iconic figures, do they have only a tendency to exist? Will they, like this pathetic creature, simply disappear into the light and be mourned by a world that never recognizes their value? Atwood has worked diligently to reconstruct the past into a form of identity for Anglophone Canada; whether a future will be built upon that past remains unknown.

NOTES

1. Atwood borrowed this metaphor from Alice Munro, noting that it "comes from a sentence in Alice Munro's 1971 novel *The Lives of Girls & Women* (253): 'People's lives in Jubilee, as elsewhere, were dull, simple, amazing and unfathomable—deep caves paved with kitchen linoleum.' What struck me about that last phrase was the juxtaposition of 'caves' and 'linoleum'—the idea of domesticity as simply a thin overlay covering a natural, and wild, abyss. Or, conversely, the suggestion that you can pave the wilderness over, making it into a kitchen, however thin the linoleum veneer" (*Strange Things*, 88).

2. Atwood notes in the Clarendon lectures that however variable are the folkloric versions of the Wendigo, "all agree that the Wendigo is—among other things— a giant spirit-creature with a heart and sometimes an entire body of ice, and prodigious strength; . . . its prevailing characteristic seems to be its ravenous hunger for human flesh" (66). In more figurative terms, the Wendigo "has been seen as the personification of winter, or hunger, or spiritual selfishness, and indeed the three are connected: winter is a time of scarcity, which gives rise to hunger, which gives rise to selfishness" (67). Even more pertinent for the texts under discussion, in which the boundaries between the Wendigo and various human characters are blurred, Atwood suggests that in the hands of "non-Native" writers, the image of the Wendigo is often transposed upon the human beings in the story: "It's not that monsters are human, but that humans themselves are potential monsters. The Wendigo is what you might turn into if you don't watch out" (69). The apparition in *Surfacing* follows the more traditional form of the Wendigo, while Joan's mother in *Lady Oracle* and Mrs. Smeath and Cordelia in *Cat's Eye* exemplify the more cautionary, non-Native version of this cliché-image: All three seem to turn into potential monsters. The Virgin Mary in *Cat's Eye* is the most enigmatic of these Wendigo-like figures. With her heart burning like coal instead of ice, she suggests what such a monster might turn into if it were kind rather than cruel, making the "monster" potentially human, or at least humane. Looked at from this perspective, the Virgin Mary may be seen as what the monster might turn into if it were to lose its evil tendencies. In this ironic reversal of Atwood's point, the apparition here, emphasizing the Virgin Mary's connection with "Help" rather than with "Hell," saves Elaine from a death within an ice-covered habitat that resembles the traditional Wendigo's frozen body. In all the cases mentioned above, however, the boundaries between human and monster, good and evil, heroism and villainy are blurred and often difficult to define.

3. This submersion of Canadian identity into an American one works in equally subversive ways in real life: I first read *Surfacing* as a graduate student in the United States during the middle 1970s in a seminar titled "The Contemporary American Novel"; the novel's—or even the author's—Canadian identity was never discussed. The protagonist was seen primarily in terms of the issues being raised by the American women's movement of the time. The anti-Americanism was explained away as a reflection of the divisiveness caused in the United States by the Vietnam War. Not wishing to draw attention to her own otherness as a Canadian and easily able to "pass" as one of "them," the young self I was then sat quietly and merely listened.

4. I develop this discussion of *Lady Oracle* more fully and from a somewhat different perspective in my article "Canadian Literary Cultures Observed: Carol Shields' *Small Ceremonies* and Margaret Atwood's *Lady Oracle*."

5. The most extensive treatment of this topic can be found in *Post-National Arguments: The Politics of the Anglophone-Canadian Novel since 1967,* by Frank Davey. His view—that Atwood deals only with the local and the global rather than the national—differs considerably from my own. Arnold Davidson also considers postcolonial aspects of *Cat's Eye* in one section of his critical volume on the novel, *Seeing in the Dark: Margaret Atwood's* Cat's Eye. Works that view the novel primarily in feminist terms include the following: "Images of Women's Power in Contemporary Canadian Fiction by Women," by Carol Beran; *Brutal Choreographies: Oppositional Strategies and Narrative Design in the Novels of Margaret Atwood,* by J. Brooks Bouson; *Margaret Atwood's Power: Mirrors, Reflections and Images in Select Fiction and Poetry,* by Shannon Hengen; "Contrary Re-memberings: The Creating Self and Feminism in *Cat's Eye*," by Judith McCombs; "Margaret Atwood and Julia Kristeva: Space-Time, the Dissident Woman Artist, and the Pursuit of Female Solidarity in *Cat's Eye*," by Martha Sharpe; and *Margaret Atwood's Fairy-Tale Sexual Politics,* by Sharon Rose Wilson.

5

. . . .

Strangers within the Gates:
Margaret Atwood's *Wilderness Tips*

CAROL L. BERAN

I am convinced that I cannot exaggerate enough even to lay the foundation of a true expression.
  Henry David Thoreau

In each of the ten stories in Margaret Atwood's *Wilderness Tips*, readers encounter a stranger in an enclosed world. The invaders in these stories—unlikely doubles, members of the opposite sex, immigrants, aliens—bring the unknown, the foreign, the bizarre into everyday life in flat, dull Canada. However, strangers in these stories do more than enliven cabin-fevered Canadian characters. Critical assessments of Margaret Atwood's writings, in the detached academic mode, generally fail to voice the intensity of Atwood's commitment to teach and to delight. The stories in *Wilderness Tips* illustrate how Atwood demands of her readers a strong engagement that goes beyond the stance that David Staines considers typical of Canadians and Canadian literature: the "dispassionate witness" (*Beyond the Provinces*, 60). These stories challenge readers to acknowledge the human predicament in the latter half of the twentieth century, consider possible responses, and finally transform themselves into "creative non-victims."[1] Reading *Wilderness Tips* as variations on the theme of the stranger clarifies Atwood's critique of contemporary society, reveals her metacriticism of those who write literary criticism about her works, and underscores the intensity with which she attempts to arouse her audience to respond to typical Canadian situations with *un*-Canadian impoliteness and intensity.

An initial look at strangers in *Wilderness Tips* suggests that Atwood has set up groups of stories that tempt readers to analysis by particular currently fashionable literary theories. Critics have frequently found Atwood creating characters who are doubles of one another. For these critics, Atwood provides strangers who are also doppelgangers. Functioning as a self outside of the self, a stranger whose invasion of personal space sparks introspection and epiphany, is a key role of Ronette in "True Trash," Molly in "Weight," and Marcia in "Hack Wednesday." The difference between two women—a relatively small degree of strangeness—becomes space in which to work out the question of identity. Joanne, her double name suggesting the split in her identity, follows from outside the less analytical, more lived life of her double, Ronette; in the end, Joanne cannot know for sure what has happened to her other, nor become like her, nor enter into the true story of her life: "The melodrama tempts her, the idea of a revelation, a sensation, a neat ending" (*WT*, 30). The terms Atwood uses here suggest that Joanne resists creating a traditional, consciously shaped narrative out of Ronette's life ("melodrama," "revelation," "sensation," "neat ending"), preferring to see it as a "found" story: "an archaic story, a folktale, a mosaic artifact" (30). Joanne learns from Ronette's story that observing and analyzing put her at one remove from engaging in life: "What she wants is what Ronette has: the power to give herself up, without reservation and without commentary. . . . Everything Joanne herself does is surrounded by quotation marks" (18–19), marking her sensibility as postmodern. When she does try to engage, her borrowed dress becomes indelibly stained as she enters the world of a folktale.[2] In "Weight" the narrator, like Joanne, remains an outside observer of the aspects of life in which her friend Molly had been engaged: marriage, children, and a legal career representing people unable to pay her. Unlike Joanne, this narrator knows the end of the story of her doppelganger: Hacked up by her husband, Molly's body has been scattered across Ontario. The narrator's power over the men that she cajoles, seduces, and blackmails into donating to the battered women's shelter may avenge the murderous power of Molly's husband. However, when it occurs to the narrator that she doesn't have to go to dinner or have an affair with the latest contributor, the options of being like Molly (a victim) or being the opposite of Molly (a victimizer) give way to a third possibility: being a creative non-victim, someone who moves out of victim patterns, transcends traditional roles, and learns to tell her own story (*Survival*, 38–39). Marcia in "Hack Wednesday" is her own double. She is a stranger to herself as past and present selves seem to exist simultaneously. For her, "Time is going faster and faster" (207). She must cope with changes within her body (aging) and outside it (her partner aging, her children growing up, computers in the workplace, "Rex Morgan, M.D." disappearing from the newspaper). Her psyche is also double: She is both immersed in and ironically detached from quintessential Canadian attitudes—the stories Canadians tell themselves about themselves: "the supposed Anglo-Canadian prudery, inhibition, and obsession with public opinion" (208), the "moral obligation to deal with winter instead of merely avoiding it" (213), and the anti-Americanism of her husband's refusal to eat Cheerios "because they're American" (209). Exploring the theme of the double in these stories could expand beyond traditional thematic criticism into psychological or feminist interpretations of the other self, with emphasis on how Atwood's ideal of the creative non-victim emerges or fails to emerge in each case, or into postcolonial analyses of the stories, showing how Joanne, the narrator of "Weight," and Marcia each have a hybridity of perspective that reflects Canada's colonial status (with respect to both Britain and the United States) and marks the characters' position in a postmodern world.

Critics who explore gender differences and the power politics between men and women are likely to be interested in the interactions of Percy Marrow and Susanna in "Uncles" and Selena and Richard in "Isis in Darkness." In "Uncles" Atwood observes the interrelationship between the genders as Percy creates and destroys Susanna professionally, causing her to perceive an uncomfortable revisionist history of her life that makes him a stranger to her and her a stranger to herself: "'Maybe I've remembered my whole life wrong'" (143). The differences she perceives between males and females—that boys were told "Don't be a smart aleck" (124), whereas she "could do whatever she liked and still be cute as a button" (125)—prove inaccurate or at least inadequate; the lack of deference between males and females in spite of seeming mutual politeness comes as a shock, making all men as much strangers to Susanna as Percy makes himself by writing the exposé. Susanna assumes that the version of her story that men tell is accurate, letting men make her a stranger to herself. In contrast, the poet Selena in "Isis in Darkness" writes her own story that eludes man's synthetic power. As Richard tries unsuccessfully to analyze the elusive and changeable Selena, Atwood leads the reader into an inquiry about the feminist concern with difference. Richard's scholarly note cards become mosaic pieces from which he tries to reconstruct Selena with deference bordering on reverence: "He is the one who will sift through the rubble, groping for the shape of the past. He is the one who will say it has meaning" (74). Nevertheless, trying to reassemble her makes his "eyes hurt" (74). Here, the man seems to have the power to create meaning; yet the woman, through her complexity, cannot be adequately reduced to the note cards that seem to contain her, nor synthesized from them. In Atwood's theory of victimization, Susanna allows herself to be a victim of what she perceives as a male-dominated world (Victim Position Two [*Survival*, 37]), whereas Selena makes herself a creative non-victim (Victim Position Four [*Survival*, 38–39]). Reading the two stories together clarifies that what apparently reflects a difference in power between males and females can be transformed by a difference in how and by whom their stories are told. In these stories Atwood challenges simplistic views that men have all the power and use it to victimize women. Susanna makes herself a victim of male power by letting men create her identity, whereas Selena creates her own identity and is unaffected by whatever identities Richard may create for her. For feminist critics interested in the ways that men have power to control what is seen as real and to discriminate against whatever lies outside their reality paradigm, these stories offer abundant material.

Lucy in "Death by Landscape" comes from the United States, and George in "Wilderness Tips" comes from Hungary, inviting cultural critics to discuss clashes of customs and beliefs as these characters interact with Canadian characters. As Atwood explores characters who are strangers to each other due to cultural differences, she creates political allegories about Canadian multiculturalism. Canadian writers frequently attempt to define the ever-elusive national identity by contrasting Canadians with people from the United States and by including distinctly different people from various ethnic groups within the Canadian mosaic. American Lucy influences the entire life of Canadian Lois, although Lucy disappears when the girls are teenagers. Lois stares at Canadian paintings on her wall, looking for Lucy the way other Canadians might stare at American programs on the television screen, and she seems to deny her own life because of her feelings about Lucy: "She can hardly remember, now, having her two boys in the hospital, nursing them as babies; she can hardly remember getting married, or what Rob looked like" (117). American culture as center marginalizes Canadian culture.[3] George similarly invades the life stories of Canadians. The three sisters of the story represent types of Canadian women: Prue is a sexual adventurer; Pamela, a reserved academic; and Portia, a loving but betrayed wife. Hungarian George—not a

British Saint George—seduces them all. Portia's vision at the end of the story, evoked by her realization of what George with his different code of behavior has done to them all, shows Canada as the sinking *Titanic* with its passengers "still not aware of the disaster that has already overcome them" (204). However, envisioning herself as Cassandra, "running naked through the ballroom" predicting catastrophe, reminds her that "nothing has happened, really, that hasn't happened before" (204). These two stories offer more than an entertaining read. By critiquing stories Canadians tell about themselves, they demand that we see the potentially destructive aspects of Canada's ways of defining itself, whether by its attraction/repulsion response to the United States or its mosaic response toward immigrants, naively valuing them without understanding the cultural differences that make them truly strangers.

The tumor in "Hairball," the preserved 2,000-year-old body in "The Bog Man," and the 150-year-old frozen body of John Torrington in "The Age of Lead" are the most alien of the strangers in *Wilderness Tips*. For Freudian critics who want to discover what is inside a character, "Hairball" presents a hidden self brought to light. For new historical critics, the exhumed bodies of the bog man and John Torrington shed light on the past, present, and future. For critics interested in the myths and symbols that define Canada today, these stories present a plethora of material that challenges and deconstructs key cultural myths. Hairball, who is benign only in the doctor's diagnosis, invades Kat's body and the party held by Ger's wife. The potentially slapstick comedy of the untold opening of the truffle box containing the tumor is funny because of its incongruity. But Kat's behavior—which readers sympathetic to Kat's predicament applaud—is not polite; it not only joyously transgresses the Canadian code of good manners, but also violates the biblical injunction, "Be not forgetful to entertain strangers: for thereby some have entertained angels unawares" (Hebrews 13:2, King James Version),[4] satirizing two cultural beliefs.

In "The Bog Man" the well-preserved human body may be an object of wonder, yet the bog man represents a past that Julie repudiates when she envisions her lover changing into a bog man. Julie goes into a telephone booth and ultimately transforms herself; Connor's failure to get inside the booth to metamorphose into Superman nullifies cultural myths concerning male power. Years later Julie wonders, "how can she explain him, him and his once golden aura? She no longer tries" (94). Bereft of his saintly halo, Connor, like the bog man, is ultimately a total stranger. Julie prefers a story that "is now like an artifact from a vanished civilization, the customs of which have become obscure" (95). This allows her to be a dispassionate witness to the stranger she once confronted. But as readers who watch her story-making, can we be as dispassionate? Are we to feel no outrage at the professor for beginning an affair with his student without mentioning that he is married? Do we feel it is appropriate that Julie takes revenge on him as he declares his love for her while he pounds on the door of the phone booth? Because she "is truly frightened of him" (93), she is caught between her fear and the social code of good manners and kindness that says she should listen with sympathy, especially since she is a woman. Is the story she constantly revises and retells for thirty years adequate? Is she a creative non-victim or a victimizer? We are told that "She knows the damage was done, was severe, at least at the time; but how can it be acknowledged without sounding like a form of gloating?" (94–95). Neither Julie's nor Connor's actions are charming or polite. The brutal, transgressive worlds of Connor and the bog man have great power and energy, now lost. We should grieve for the diminution: "By this time he is almost an anecdote" (95). Julie may feel that way because the story is from her distant past; for us, however, the story is present. We should feel strongly because we know that this is no anecdote, but an indictment of viewpoints characteristic of our time.

In "The Age of Lead" John Torrington and his companions on the Franklin Expedition, we are told, died because of the new technology that was intended to save their lives, just as Vincent, dying of "a mutated virus that didn't even have a name yet" (160), may be the victim of a modern malaise, symbolized by the clutter of "plastic drinking cups, crumpled soft-drink cans, used take-out plates . . . like a trail left by an army on the march or by the fleeing residents of a city under bombardment" (162), an image that magnifies a kind of environmental pollution that some might consider trivial by linking it with the devastation of war. Neither Jane's sympathy (Atwood's choice of Lady Franklin's first name for her modern character suggests the story is a retelling of Jane Griffin Franklin's efforts to rescue her lost husband), nor technology's latest advances, nor the health care system in which Canadians take such pride are effective in this situation. But are we just dispassionate observers of the destruction by technology that this story recounts? By the end of the story, Atwood overthrows any sense of superiority we may have felt as we began to read about John Torrington. Atwood presents us with our world. We should be upset. Because the mysterious disease killing Vincent is specifically not AIDS, we become aware that AIDS may only be a precursor to dreadful diseases yet to come; even as knowing and being able to prevent the mysterious disease that killed John Torrington does not end human suffering, solving the puzzle of AIDS or cancer will change rather than end the story of sickness and death. "The most troubling warning," embodied in both John Torrington and Vincent, "is that there are some secrets, mysteries, truths that will always escape our desire to possess, label, control" (Grace, "Franklin Lives," 162). In these three stories, by means of the outrageous character of the stranger, Atwood not only satirizes both the myth of the polite Canadian and the myth of technology's ability to improve human life, but also pokes fun at those critics who espouse artistic detachment, who see reading as a dispassionate way of gazing on the problems of other people, problems that they themselves expect never to encounter, rather than as a way of engaging in a transformative process set up by a writer who bears witness to the problems confronting humanity now. "Witness is what you must bear," Atwood writes in "Notes towards a Poem That Can Never Be Written" (*Selected Poems II,* 73).

Of course, Atwood's stories also tempt subtle or devious readings. Doubles may be more obviously present in "True Trash," "Weight," and "Hack Wednesday" than in the other stories, but surely George is the evil twin of the women's ineffectual brother, Roland, and Lucy is the lost half of Lois. Hairball, the bog man, and John Torrington might be discussed as doubles that manifest inner worlds of Kat, Connor, and Vincent. Using Sharon Wilson's notion that doppelgangers can be opposite sexes (270), Susanna and Percy or Richard and Selena might be seen as doubles in opposition, with one in each pair representing fantasy and the other reality. Stories other than "Uncles" and "Isis in Darkness" explore gender differences. In "True Trash," Joanne and Ronette become tainted by experiences that seem not to affect the male characters in the same way. In "Wilderness Tips," the battle of the sexes and the double standard provide both the tragedy and the humor as the patriarch watches from the washroom wall. Although the sisters in "Wilderness Tips" have become very different people, all can be hoodwinked by same male and all fail to support each other in the sisterhood of women. Marcia and Eric reveal differing aging patterns in women and men. Lois's childhood experiences at camp reveal part of the process of gender role acquisition for women. Kat, Julie, and Jane all fight for the man they think they love, engaging unsuccessfully in the battle of the sexes. And although Hairball, the bog man, and John Torrington may be the strangest of the strangers in these stories, all the stories do contain strangers whose presence reveals inadequacies in the perceptions of the other characters.

In providing obvious fodder for certain types of critics and more subtle gleanings for more ingenious critics, is Atwood mocking the literary critical establishment? Are we ridiculous to be tracking down one more example of the doppelganger, one more battle of the sexes, one more appropriation of voice, one more example of the workings of the multicultural mosaic, one more wild conceit in Atwood's writings? Is there folly in not simply enjoying these stories as a good read? As readers, should we be Ronettes rather than Joannes? If Atwood reuses her best known motifs, we critics cry, "nothing new here." Sherrill E. Grace, for example, calls the stories in *Wilderness Tips* "too familiar, even boring," comparing them to "pictures at a retrospective exhibition" that "seem to have been chosen deliberately to evoke, echo and recall" ("Surviving," 31). Yet if Atwood does not reuse her most familiar motifs, her signature is missing—she loses her way of saying, "Margaret Atwood is present in this story as its maker; listen for her distinctive voice." Furthermore, if as critics we read the story for other readers, are we appropriating their voices with patriarchal (or matriarchal) voices, preempting their individual analyses, their right to tell their own story from the story Atwood provides?

The three stories of very strange strangers offer a key to reading this book: rage. The words "rage," "outraged," "anger," and "angry" recur throughout *Wilderness Tips*. In "Hairball" Kat wants to name a magazine "All the Rage," but "the board was put off by the vibrations of anger in the word 'rage'" (41); she later writes of Hairball disguised as a truffle, "This is all the rage" (47). In "Hack Wednesday," Marcia remembers "when airlessness was all the rage" (214). The waitresses in "True Trash" are "outraged" at a story (8). Donny in "True Trash," Richard in "Isis in Darkness," and Lois in "Death by Landscape" are described as "angry" (27, 56, 115). Susanna feels "anger" in "Uncles" (125). In the stories in *Wilderness Tips,* Atwood's strangers are not nice polite Canadians who, with infinite tact, help needy and grateful friends to graceful epiphanies, but foreigners, trespassers, meddlers, non-natives who jab alien elements into the peaceful, orderly, well-governed lives of Canadians. Hugh MacLennan writes that he was told by a movie mogul, "Boy meets girl in Winnipeg and who cares?" ("On Being," 23). But in *Wilderness Tips* Atwood demands that we care: The exaggeration of the interloper clashes with the diminution of the Canadian to produce a kind of humor that, in spite of its understated tone, should make the reader angry about the way things are. Readers who find the "consistently muted palette" of the stories in *Wilderness Tips* "too much of the same thing" (Grace, "Surviving," 31) have missed the demanding role that Atwood assigns to readers of this volume: responding with rage and then transcending it.

Atwood is defining Canada and trying to improve it, just as she has frequently done throughout her career. In a 1999 reassessment of *Survival*, Atwood asserts that "its central concerns remain with us, and must still be confronted. Are we really that different from anybody else? If so, how? And is that how something worth preserving?" ("Survival Then and Now," 58).[5] Taken together, the stories in *Wilderness Tips* explore ways that outsiders affect Canadians and Canadian society. However, this exploration is not dispassionate, because Atwood calls on readers to react with the passion sometimes lacking in the reactions of the characters.

For Atwood, the detached, dispassionate gaze is insufficient (Victim Position One [*Survival*, 36]). So is assent to victimization (Victim Position Two [*Survival*, 37]). So is activism against victimization (Victim Position Three [*Survival*, 37–38]). Only transformation into creative non-victims (Victim Position Four [*Survival*, 38–39]) proves adequate to the demands of the human predicament. In *Wilderness Tips* Atwood offers that next moment, the moment beyond the ends of stories, as the transforming moment, the moment in which each reader begins or continues the journey toward being a creative non-victim by his or her responses to the story. Readers' roles can go beyond Staines's concept of the "dispassionate witness" ("Beyond the Provinces," 60). By the end of her story as told by Atwood, Joanne is no longer threatened by the kinds of victimization experienced by Samuel Richardson's Pamela or her descendant in "True Trash," Ronette. Joanne puts together stories, understanding that they may not take standard shapes or have traditional endings. But she has missed the fact that the owner of the camp, Mr. B., has the same name as the man who attempts to seduce but later marries Pamela; Ronette's life may not be a story of a woman's generous act toward a boy (following the archetype of the experienced older woman who initiates the inexperienced male into the mysteries of sex, satirized in Atwood's version by the extreme youth of the boy and the resulting pregnancy for the theoretically knowledgeable woman), but the age-old story of a powerful man victimizing a defenseless woman. The story of the Canadian charm and politeness with which Ronette gives herself to Donny omits the alternative story that Mr. B.'s name suggests, leaving us to feel an outrage that the characters don't feel. Ronette's politeness and feminine nurturing are not affirmed by the outcome—pregnancy with no possibility of marriage in an era when that would have seriously stigmatized a woman. Joanne is a creative non-victim in that she is composing a story rather than simply experiencing it; yet the story that she constructs is too incomplete to make adequate sense of the world. Atwood constructs a larger story; readers who construct a story that includes Joanne's version of Ronette's story and Atwood's version of Joanne's story have learned what Atwood is teaching, which is less about women still being victimized sexually by men than about old patterns that repeat, stories that define a culture, and a vision that might move a society beyond its no longer productive archetypes and myths.

Readers of "Weight" experience outrage at the way that the narrator uses her sexuality to gain power over men. Yet, as we watch this exaggerated scenario, we begin to recognize that this is exactly what some women have always done. Hasn't sexuality been a major source of power for women? At the end, the narrator revises her vision when she realizes that she does not have to have sex with this man in order to have power over him. However, she has not yet found a way out of the age-old battle of the sexes—the same battle that killed her double. If readers can experience anger at the narrator's initial vision, applaud her revised vision, and then move on ultimately to see more than she does, Atwood's story will not only have brought delight, but will also have initiated a learning process.

For some readers, the elegiac tone of "Hack Wednesday," sweetly sentimental about aging to begin with, becomes cloying by the end of the story. Yet, as in the story of John and Mary that Atwood satirizes in "Happy Endings" in *Murder in the Dark*, the "only authentic ending" is "*John and Mary die. John and Mary die. John and Mary die*" (40); fact, not nostalgia. Alzheimer's disease may one day obliterate bittersweet memories and make Marcia a real stranger to herself. Her partner's futile crusades may devolve into more meaningless symptoms of old age. Amid the sentimentality, we can recall Dylan Thomas's plea: "Do not go gentle into that good night. / Rage, rage against the dying of the light" (128). From there we can move beyond rage into being creative non-victims, people who can accept their own experience "for what it is, rather than having to distort it to make it correspond with others' versions of it" (Atwood, *Survival*, 39), which may be precisely what Marcia does.

When Selena and Susanna allow strangers to tell their stories, and thereby make them strangers to themselves, we should be incensed that the characters let what the males say be given the status of single truth;

we should then move on to tell their stories as our own vision dictates. Because Richard is a literary critic and obviously cannot tell Selena's whole story, reviewing this story reminds us not to let literary critics or our adherence to various schools of literary criticism tell the story for us. Because Percy's subjectivity colors his vision of Susanna, "Uncles" serves as a call to assert one's own view in the face of conflicting alternative stories, thereby allowing the process of reading to become transformative.

Outsiders Lucy and George have taken over the stories of the Canadian characters. Why aren't we outraged at this? Can Lucy's and George's stories coexist with rather than co-opt other stories? These stories ask questions regarding the multiple stories current in the Canadian mosaic. In "Survival, Then and Now" Atwood writes, "Canada's well-known failure to embrace a single 'identity' of the yodelling or Beefeater variety has come to seem less like a failure than a deliberate and rather brave refusal" (57). Yet these stories raise the question of whether all of the multiple identities available to Canadians are equally conducive to the well-being of the community as a whole and its members individually; Atwood challenges the stories her nation tells itself about the destructive power of the United States and the value of generously embracing refugees.

Moreover, the stories in *Wilderness Tips* appear to contradict each other. What seems clear in one story gets muddied by another. Is Lucy a good summer visitor while George is a bad immigrant? Lucy seemingly fails to cope with the Canadian wilderness and apparently does not survive; yet in another sense her disappearance makes her potent and pernicious. George has learned to survive in the Canadian wilderness, yet he hardly seems a role model for survival. Perhaps survival is not the only goal for Canadians, and "Wilderness Tips" contains a revision of Atwood's former thesis. Naming George's wife Portia suggests that she represents the Christian virtue of her predecessor in Shakespeare's *The Merchant of Venice* who asserts, "The quality of mercy is not strained" (606). Does Atwood's Portia look foolish to us as she acts out this ideal? Or does mercy truly bless "him that gives and him that takes" (Shakespeare, 606)? Would we want to live in a world in which Atwood's story is the final revision of Portia's story? John Torrington seems to symbolize how we retell and revise the past but forget to learn from it. In contrast, Julie begins to learn how to tell her own story from her experiences with the bog man. But is she an acceptable storyteller when her retelling loses so much of the energy of the past? Is the powerfully assertive narrator of "Weight" a better role model for women than Marcia, who seems adrift in passing time, yet perhaps lives her daily life more richly than Molly's friend? Do the fates of Ronette and Molly warn against actively engaging in life? Yet detachment in Joanne and in Molly's friend seems lacking if slightly less dangerous than engagement. Is Kat's revenge on Ger and his wife more acceptable than the revenge that Molly's friend takes on males? Should we prefer Joanne or Julie to Richard as a collector of stories? Is Atwood suggesting that men and women are equally unfit to tell the stories of others? Should we blame Percy for destroying Susanna or Richard for not rescuing Selena?[6] Should we be angry with Atwood for this muddle of contradictions? Is she playing games with thematic critics and critics who look for consistency? Atwood as postmodern trickster invites us to listen to a narrator or see with a focalizer whose vision seems plausible and pleasing to accept, but then Atwood reveals how foolish we have been in not thinking for ourselves. The shifts of vision and the independent thought required of the reader make these stories unsettling, yet the discomfort is part of the process of transformation that these stories set in motion.

Often literary critics want a writer such as Atwood to be politically correct, by their definition of correctness, desiring her stories to fit into their categories of belief. Looking at all ten stories in *Wilderness Tips* demonstrates how Atwood satirizes these critics with stories that seem to contradict one another or create ambiguity rather than eliminate it. Atwood's role as a satirist requires no consistency except the consistency of ridiculing folly wherever it may be found. Literature's function to teach does not mean to Atwood that stories should offer clearly stated rules to live by; there is no "moral of the story" in the traditional sense. Rather, the stories in *Wilderness Tips* open up subjects for discussion, leading into a process of thinking and rethinking. Atwood delights us by her outrageousness even as she evokes passionate responses that move us away from being mere dispassionate observers of absurdity and injustice. By tempting readers to various kinds of rational analyses, Atwood makes them complicit in their own victimization, because they think that they are not victims at all (Victim Position One); failing to acknowledge their own victimization, they victimize others by constructing the story of the story for other readers out of theories about literature rather than letting other readers speak in their own voices. Yet if we do react to the stories in our own ways rather than in any prescribed way; if, remembering that "Art is anger" (Van Herk, 330), we let rage take us into our own reading of each text, we can move toward becoming creative non-victims, able to tell our own stories. For Atwood, the value of reading and writing fiction is that we broaden our vision by identifying ourselves with strangers: "If writing novels—and reading them—have any redeeming social value, it's probably that they force you to imagine what it's like to be some-body else" (*Second Words,* 430). As we read these stories, Atwood makes us entertain strangers—and it may be that in her wily art she is making us entertain "angels unawares," characters who change us as we encounter and react to them and their interactions with other char-acters, pushing us along one more step in our own journeys toward becoming creative non-victims able to move beyond the myths and archetypes that have defined us in the past, able to retell our own sto-ries in new ways in a world where a tiny piece of the Berlin Wall may be the largest possible symbol of hope for peace and freedom.

NOTES

1. Atwood uses the term "creative non-victim" in *Survival: A Thematic Guide to Canadian Literature* to describe people who are free to be creative because they do not divert their energy into suppressing, displacing, or protesting victimization (38–39). Atwood's discussion of Victim Positions in *Survival* is sometimes dismissed as trivial, derived from popular psychology (see, for example, James Steele's "The Lit-erary Criticism of Margaret Atwood," p. 77). However, I disagree. The Victim Posi-tions seem to me a reworking of the highly respected psychological stages outlined by Elisabeth Kubler-Ross in *On Death and Dying* (Denial, Anger, Bargaining, Depres-sion, Acceptance, Hope). The positions Atwood defines, taken in order, not only mark a progression often seen in the thinking of the characters in Atwood's stories, from the earliest to the most recent, but also explain (as I show in this essay) the process that readers of Atwood's stories undergo.

2. Bruno Bettelheim sees the staining associated with the young woman in the folktale "Bluebeard's Egg" as indicating that her curiosity has caused her to lose her innocence/virginity (300–2). In *Margaret Atwood's Fairy-Tale Sexual Politics,* Sharon Rose Wilson traces the "Bluebeard's Egg" motif in many of Atwood's works.

3. See, for example, Staines's comment on L. M. Montgomery's *Chronicles of Avonlea:* "For Avonlea residents, the United States is the foreign, the exotic, the cen-tre that makes them seem on the periphery" (11).

4. Atwood paraphrases this verse and connects it with the Canadian virtue of good manners when she writes about the Canadians whom George takes advantage of in "Wilderness Tips": "These people were lax and trusting, and easily embarrassed by a hint of their own intolerance or lack of hospitality to strangers. They weren't ready for him" (190).

5. Coral Ann Howells notes that *Wilderness Tips* gives "a bleaker vision of sur-vival on a globalized scale" (59) than Atwood's previous works, and after discussing Atwood's critiques in various stories, concludes that "Atwood's conception of futures already being shaped by the present and foreshadowed by the past makes for dire warnings, yet she continues to write, diagnosing the symptoms of a general malaise

as they appear in her specifically Canadian context" (68). Howells believes that "it is through the very power of myth to transform perceptions that hopes for regeneration and survival may lie" (68).

6. See Arnold E. Davidson's "Negotiating *Wilderness Tips*," pp. 184–86, for a discussion of additional ways in which "the obvious interconnections between the stories modifies their meanings, individually and collectively" (186).

6

. . . .

The Robber Bride; or, Who Is a True Canadian?

CAROL ANN HOWELLS

Even the real thing looks constructed. When Roz saw her first Alp, she thought, Bring out the chorus line in bodices and dirndls, and let's all yodel. Maybe that's what people mean by a national identity. The hired help in outfits. The backdrops. The props. (*Robber Bride,* 88)

This parodic representation of national identity as staged performance resonates against Margaret Atwood's more serious remarks in *Macleans* ("Survival," 57): "Canada's well-known failure to embrace a single 'identity' of the yodelling or Beefeater variety has come to seem less like a failure than a deliberate and rather brave refusal. . . . The former Canadian-identity question, 'Where is here?' has been replaced by 'Who are we?'." It is within these parameters that I want to consider *The Robber Bride* as part of Atwood's ongoing inquiry into what "being Canadian" means.

Atwood has always been an astute and sensitive cultural critic, charting shifts in Canada's social attitudes and nationalist ideology, speaking from her own position as a white Anglophone Canadian woman, born in Ontario and living in Toronto. The narrative voices in her novels may speak out of that specific location of culture, gender, and race; but her fictional territory extends beyond that to include other and "othered" ethnic and racial identities in Canadian society, their presence sharpened by Atwood's critique of widespread English Canadian prejudice and what nonwhite writers refer to as the systemic violence of racism in Canada (Bannerji, 11). Though signaling the presence of those "others," Atwood does not attempt to negotiate racial politics; instead, she engages with issues of white immigrancy and ethnicity in *The Robber Bride* (as she had earlier in *Life before Man* and as she does in *Alias Grace*), in answer to her question, "Who are we?" The novel primarily addresses English Canadian anxieties about changing representations of national identity, focused at a precise point in time and place: Toronto in 1990–1991, while that city is itself situated in the international context, with events in Eastern Europe and the Gulf War whirling around. Atwood's concerns with late-twentieth-century Canada's malaise have shifted from anxieties about the country's political survival expressed in *Wilderness Tips* (1991), where the title story registers a "slippage in the bedrock" of traditional English Canadian myths of nationhood under pressures of Quebec separatism and the cultural and political resurgence of First Nations People (Howells, *Margaret Atwood*, 33–37). In *The Robber Bride* she is asking, "Are we really that different from anybody else? And if so, how?" ("Survival," 58) What do distinctively Canadian identities—personal and collective—look like in the nineties? And is Canadian identity always in the plural, to take account of cultural differences in revised narratives of Canada's national heritage?

In seeking answers to these questions in *The Robber Bride*, Atwood appeals to the present "nation-space" as it is represented by Toronto, one of the three most ethnically and racially diverse cities in Canada.[1] She also, characteristically, looks back to history, for "nothing has happened, really, that hasn't happened before" (WT, 221). However, the answers vary from one historical period to another, for political choices change as power relations within a country shift in response to constantly changing relations between dominant and formerly marginal groups. The social space of postwar Toronto in *The Robber Bride* (from the 1940s to the early 1990s) might be interpreted through Homi Bhabha's "discourse of nation," for whatever else Atwood may be doing here, she is also narrating the nation. Any discourse of nation

> investigates the nation-space in the *process* of the articulation of elements: where meanings may be partial because they are *in medias res*; and history may be half-made because it is in the process of being made; and the image of cultural authority may be ambivalent because it is caught, uncertainly, in the act of "composing" its powerful image. (Bhabha, *Nation and Narration*, 3)

It is within that context of what Bhabha calls "the problematic unity of the nation" and "the articulation of cultural difference" (*Nation and*

Narration, 5) that we can most clearly situate *The Robber Bride* as a postcolonial Canadian novel that displays the "cultural temporality of the nation" and its "always transitional social reality" (*Nation and Narration,* 1).

It is true that as a result of its changing immigration policies and demography since the end of World War II, Canada has shifted its ideological discourse of nation beyond the traditional Anglophone/francophone pattern that reflects its founding history so as to take account of widespread cultural and racial differences. This revised discourse of nation is codified in the 1988 Multiculturalism Act, which recognizes that ethnic, racial, religious, and cultural diversity are a "fundamental characteristic of the Canadian heritage and identity." Such recognition of the heterogeneous histories of its citizens fundamentally revises traditional colonial concepts of a dominantly British Canada, opening up the nation-space and necessitating a redefinition of the terms in which it is possible to think about Canadian nationhood and identity in a postcolonial context.

The most appropriate terms for this redefinition of Canadianness would seem to be those offered by postcolonial theory and criticism, with its emphasis on immigrancy and nomadism, hybridity and diaspora, and its analysis of split selves and socially constructed "others." The pervasive emphasis is on displacement and shifting subject positions where reinventions and transformations of the self become mechanisms of survival. (My frames of reference are Bannerji, 70–74; Bhabha 1994, 1–18; Brydon, 193–97; Hall, 392–403; and Mukherjee, 24–40.) If we look at *The Robber Bride* from these postcolonial perspectives, we begin to notice that Atwood is peering beneath the surface of English Canadian narratives of identity as she looks into the life stories of three white Canadian women born during World War II, growing up and still living in Toronto in the 1990s. And what does she see? She sees hidden histories of immigrancy and cultural displacement, split subjects, dislocated identities, reinventions and renamings, a pervasive sense of otherness and not belonging. To read *The Robber Bride* in postcolonial terms reveals how the white subject fractures under this analysis too. This is in no way meant to trivialize or minimize the experience of nonwhite subjects in Canada, nor the painful experiences of "negative othering," but rather to highlight how Atwood's fictional representations of subjectivity reveal the nonfixity of identity, and how her narrative strategies uncover secrets hidden in the past as she deconstructs myths of white English Canadian authenticity, showing how difference is a crucial factor in any identity construction.

Of course the catalyst in the novel is the Robber Bride, for Tony, Roz, and Charis are all threatened by Zenia, the European postwar immigrant, the Other Woman. Yet those three protagonists survive, and it is Zenia whose death is recorded (twice, as it happens). They are all there for both of her memorial services and the scattering of her ashes, and the novel ends with the three of them together, ready to tell more stories about their experiences with Zenia. So what exactly is Zenia's role, and why is she the focus of the plot? Her role as the Other Woman has usually been interpreted in feminist terms focusing on issues of sexuality and gender in the novel, and I have seen only two essays that go beyond a feminist heading into "postimperial or nationalist interpretations (Hengen 1995, 271–86; Potts, 230–38). Thinking in postcolonial terms, would it not be possible to see a second frame of "othering" here, with the focus on Zenia as immigrant, in Atwood's discourse of Canadianness?[2] It is Zenia's otherness that forces these women to confront dimensions of otherness within themselves, a fact obscurely recognized at the beginning by Tony, who like her creator is given to deconstructing the myths of history:

> *Pick any strand and snip, and history comes unravelled. . . .*
> But Zenia is also a puzzle, a knot: if Tony could just find a loose end and pull, a great deal would come free, for everyone involved, and for herself as well. Or this is her hope. She has a historian's belief in the salutary power of explanations. (*RB*, 3)

Life histories do unravel in the course of the novel—not Zenia's, but those of Tony, Roz, and Charis—and a great deal does come free. Storytelling becomes the agent of exorcism and opens the way for regeneration and new figurings of identity. Zenia herself remains an enigma to the end, and her multiple life stories seem like a series of magic mirrors held up to the Canadian women, magnifying and distorting their own deepest fears and desires: "She did it with mirrors. The mirror was whoever was watching" (*RB*, 461). As Hengen pertinently remarks, "Zenia's foreignness, her difference, is precisely what each of the other three main characters must come to understand, and that difference is as powerful as any other force in their lives" (Hengen 1995, 278). Zenia is more than a threat; she is also a teacher, though her teaching methods are savagely painful. After all, as Atwood's first epigraph reminds us, "A rattlesnake that doesn't bite teaches you nothing." Zenia's lessons are about difference (which maybe should be spelled *differance* here), showing the three women how they might answer the questions that Atwood would pose six years later: "Are we really that different from anybody else? And if so, how?" ("Survival," 58)

In this reading of Canadian female postcolonial subjectivities, my emphasis is less on Zenia and more on the three protagonists. Zenia herself is Rosi Braidotti's Nomadic Subject par excellence, "Nomadism is . . . an acute awareness of the nonfixity of boundaries. It is the intense desire to go on trespassing, transgressing" (*Nomadic Subjects,* 36). Zenia is always outside and on the loose, an exile and an invader. Incidentally these are the very terms that Atwood used to describe Canadians' immigrant heritage in *The Journals of Susanna Moodie* (1970). She crosses boundaries between nationalities as easily as she crosses between realism and fantasy, slipping in and out of these women's lives over three decades. Though Zenia is a world traveler and those women stay at home in Toronto, their life histories also demonstrate the "illusory stability of fixed identities" (Braidotti, 15) as well as those "unhomely moments" that Bhabha locates within narratives of postcolonial identity *(Location of Culture,* 11). The difference is that for Tony, Charis, and Roz, these fissures are entirely subjective and invisible to others, and it is only in Zenia's presence that what is repressed comes to light. Zenia disrupts the plots of their lives, forcing them to remember what they have forgotten and to redefine themselves in the crises that she precipitates.

Zenia may be a foreigner in Canada (a White Russian aristocrat on her mother's side and with any one of three possible fathers—Greek, Polish, English—in the version she tells Tony), but Tony herself has always felt like a foreigner in Canada. We see her as one of Atwood's *flaneuses* walking the streets of multicultural 1990s Toronto:

> She likes the mix on the street here, the mixed skins. Chinatown has taken over mostly, though there are still some Jewish delicatessens, and, further up and off to the side, the Portuguese and West Indian shops of the Kensington Market. Rome in the second century, Constantinople in the tenth, Vienna in the nineteenth. . . .
>
> . . . Among Chinese people she feels the right height, although she is not unaware of how she might be viewed by some of them. . . . Foreign, yes. Foreign here. (*RB,* 36)

From her perspective as a professional historian, Tony can compare Toronto with other earlier hybridized urban societies, just as in her war games the kitchen spices provide a more accurate representation of medieval populations not as "homogeneous blocks, but mixtures"

(111). Nevertheless, Tony feels a deep sense of personal inadequacy when her hairdresser tells her that she is "almost Chinese," which is rooted in her anxious early experience. As the child of an unhappy wartime marriage between a Canadian soldier and an English mother (who hated Canada and who later ran away to California), she grew up feeling not quite adequate to her parents' expectations, not being English and not being a boy: "Like a foreigner, she listens carefully, interpreting. Like a foreigner she keeps an eye out for sudden hostile gestures. Like a foreigner she makes mistakes" (145).

Tony has always been a split subject, aware of her mind and body as a site of contradictory impulses, with her left-handedness and her ability to read and write backward, indeed to speak and sing backward as well. This is more than a college party trick (when she sings "Clementine" backward in the junior common room) for it is also her own "archaic" language, her secret source of power and resistance:

> *Tomato,* she whispered to herself. *Otamot.* One of the Great Lakes. A stone war hammer used by an ancient tribe. If you said a word backwards, the meaning emptied out and then the word was vacant. Ready for a new meaning to flow in. (154)

Although Tony considers it absurd that people might think her speaking backward is Satan worship, there is a strong connection between spelling and spells here, as such language allows her to say what is otherwise forbidden. The voice of her other self speaks out of the anger and frustration that even as a child she has assiduously repressed, as in the startling example of the five-year-old Tony on a snowy slope with her mother. As her mother, utterly contemptuous of Tony's refusal to go on the toboggan, careers off on it by herself, Tony screams, "No! No!" However, "inside herself she could hear another voice, also hers, which was shouting, fearlessly and with ferocious delight: *On! On!*" (137). Such double voicing offers the spectacle of the self as site of estrangement, which has been a consistent motif in Atwood's writing from at least *Lady Oracle* through *Alias Grace*. Here we see Atwood's construction of a split female subjectivity, which finds its parallel with the construction of the nonwhite postcolonial subject or the immigrant subject (Bannerji, 24), where the conscious self is shadowed, indeed displaced, by its "unborn twin."

It is only in conversations with Zenia as a student in the 1960s that Tony manages to tell the story of her childhood with the pain of her mother's abandonment and her father's suicide shortly after she graduated. This telling is for Tony a kind of exorcism, while Zenia's response in its duplicitous way both convinces her that she is not alone and also reduces its significance. Zenia's story of her own wartime childhood experiences in Paris, though oddly parallel to Tony's, is much worse and far more exciting. By comparison, Tony's story looks "minor, grey, suburban . . . whereas Zenia's sparkles—no, it glares, in the lurid though uncertain light cast by large and portentous world events. (White Russians!)" (166). Zenia's foreignness represents for Tony her idealized other self, "herself as she would like to be: *Tnomerf Ynot*"(167). Indeed, it is this shadow self that Tony has normalized by becoming an expert in medieval military history. Tony's fascination with Zenia confronts us with what Hengen calls "the old oppressions of a Eurocentric view" (Hengen 1995, 272), highlighting Tony's Canadian sense of cultural inferiority, a phenomenon commonly referred to as the "Colonial Mentality. . . . It was part of a tendency to believe that the Great Good Place was, culturally speaking, elsewhere" ("Survival," 56). Potts traces a very similar pattern in the relationship between Tony and Zenia, arguing that Tony is "the perfect victim for Zenia" (Potts, 232). I would argue the balance shifts, however, for just as Tony's attitudes to Zenia change over thirty years, from admiration to deep distrust and finally to a more detached historicized perspective in the early 1990s, when Zenia is no longer seen as a threat, so does Tony revise to some extent her own Eurocentrism as she learns to live "at home" in Canada. When in the basement of her own house, where she lives with her beloved husband, West, Tony places the street map of Toronto on top of her sand-table map of medieval Europe; this is her decisive gesture of recognition that her own life's frame of reference is located in Toronto (Howells, *Margaret Atwood*, 163–64). The rest of the world is still out there and Zenia still lurks as a shadow on the periphery of Tony's mental landscape, but now she is History and the authority is in Tony's hands: She owes her only a "remembrance. She owes her an end" (464). Returning to the idea of Atwood's narrating the nation here, we might see Tony's story as a recapitulation of Bhabha's ambivalent national discourse, where the image of cultural authority is caught in the process of being composed; only here it is a process of shifting cultural affiliations.

For Roz, Zenia's disruptions highlight an altogether different set of dilemmas that speak to her personal history, and that are also representative in the Canadian context. These dilemmas cluster around the related issues of immigrancy, ethnicity, and social class. Living in a mansion in Rosedale as a wealthy company director with a smart office in a converted downtown brewery and cited in *Toronto Life* as one of "Toronto's Fifty Most Influential" citizens (88), Roz would seem to personify the immigrant New World success story—except that Roz is not an immigrant, although she feels like one. Born in Toronto to a working-class Irish Canadian mother and a Jewish refugee father from Winnipeg, it is Roz who is most keenly aware of the inauthenticity of either personal or national identity. What is the real thing when identities are continually being reinvented? "When you alter yourself, the alterations become the truth. Who knows that better than Roz?" (102) And how much does being Canadian depend on the passage of time rather than on a person's ethnic origins? Roz's thoughts on multicultural Canada reflect these dilemmas:

> [H]ow many immigrants can you fit in? How many of them can you handle, realistically, and who is *them*, and where do you draw the line? The mere fact that Roz is thinking this way shows the extent of the problem, because Roz knows very well what it's like to be *them*. By now, however, she is *us*. It makes a difference. (100)

The concept of an evolving ethnicity is certainly one favored by many historians and sociologists:

> New ethnic identities can emerge over time for identity is self-determined, whether Canadian, ethnic or recent newcomer. And the truth is that a majority of Canadians outside of Québec consider themselves ethnically Canadian and a majority of Francophone Québecois identify themselves as ethnically Québecois. (Buckner, 26)

Roz's life story reflects the "transitional social realities" that characterize Canada's postwar history. She herself has had several identities and changes of name, from Rosalind Greenwood to Roz Grunwald and later to Roz Andrews when she married Mitch. In those namings are encoded Roz's transformations and her upward mobility but also her insecurities, for every one of her identities is shadowed by the others. Brought up in Toronto during the war by her Roman Catholic mother who kept a rooming house, Roz was teased at her convent by speculations about her absent father: "Where's your father anyways? My Mum says he's a DP" (329). To be called a Displaced Person was a slur, and in Roz's memory of the daily harassment of European postwar refugees Atwood gives a sharp brief sketch of Canadian racial prejudice in the late 1940s: "DP! DP! Go back where you came from"

(324). In this context it is all the more traumatic when Roz's father does return a few years after the war and she discovers that he is a DP after all: "She can tell by the way he talks" (332).

With the arrival of her father and his two cronies, the "Uncles," Roz discovers that she is half Jewish. Her father becomes a rich Toronto property developer, though the original source of his wealth remains mysterious for a long time, and when her family moves north into an enormous house with a three-car garage near Upper Canada College, Rosalind is given a new identity to fit her family's new lifestyle. Her name is changed to Roz Grunwald, which was, she also discovers, her "real name all along" (343), but it was not safe to use it during the war because of Canadian anti-Semitic prejudice. (Indeed it had not been safe before the war, and was not entirely safe even in the late 1950s, it would appear, since Roz's father still received hate calls because of his last name, 308). Roz shifts from being Catholic and poor like her mother to being rich and Jewish like her father, though she still feels like an outsider, split in two by her dual cultural inheritance: "But whereas once Roz was not Catholic enough, now she isn't Jewish enough. She's an oddity, a hybrid, a strange half-person" (344). Caught between cultures, Roz's experience is that of being a Displaced Person in her own country, where she decides to survive by adopting the immigrant's strategies of wariness and mimicry, even learning a new language: "She adds layers of language to herself, sticking them on, like posters on a fence" (345). With painful effort she transforms herself into an imitation of the Jewish princess she is supposed to be, adding for good measure her own interpretation to the performance. She becomes "smarter, funnier, and richer" than the other girls, for after all, she is "the joker" in the pack.

Even Roz's marriage to the man she loves does nothing to alleviate her sense of being an outsider; in fact, it exacerbates it, for the handsome Mitch Andrews, representative of old Toronto WASP society, is a continual reminder of her socially inferior background. Their courtship is a devastating satire on Toronto snobbery, with its hypocrisies of money and class: "Roz was new money, Mitch was old money; or he would have been old money if he'd had any money" (312). Though I do not propose to discuss sexual politics here nor the "holy hell with Mitch" (303) and his repeated infidelities, which is the subtext of their family life, it is perhaps worth noting that even after twenty years of marriage, the old class paradigms have not shifted at all. Confronted by her husband's air of social superiority, Roz still feels intimidated, remembering her own immigrant history: "Everyone she's descended from got kicked out of somewhere else, for being too poor or too politically uncouth or for having the wrong profile or accent or hair colour" (305).

However, despite her self-punishing love for Mitch, Roz is still her father's daughter, the inheritor of his business skills and his fortune, and his greatest admirer. Her father remains an ambiguous figure, a risk taker with a war history full of secrets. The uncles declare that he was "the best," but the best at what? Was he a hero (as Roz so much wants to believe), or was he a thief and a black marketeer? Was he perhaps both, as Uncle George suggests on his deathbed: "Your father was a crook. Don't get me wrong, he was a hero, too. . . . Only some wouldn't understand" (348–49). Of course it is through Roz's quest for her father's true story that Zenia first manages to seduce her with the claim that Roz's father saved her life during the war: "But this is what she's longed for always—an eyewitness, someone involved but impartial, who could assure her that her father really was what he was rumoured to be: a hero. Or a semi-hero; at any rate, more than a shady trader" (316).

In the version of her life story that Zenia tells Roz, Zenia comes of mixed Jewish and Roman Catholic parentage in Berlin. She is saved from the Holocaust by a forged passport Roz's father provides and brought to Canada as a child refugee, growing up in Waterloo, Ontario. Zenia's attack is characteristically double edged. On the one hand, her story speaks to Roz's deepest desire, for it is Roz's imagined tale of her father's heroism magnified and given back to her, while it is also a melodramatic reflection of her own mixed inheritance and sense of otherness: "She's not what she appears, a beautiful and successful career woman. . . . She's a waif, a homeless wandering waif" (365). On several occasions Roz wishes that she were Zenia, and at this early stage of her attack, Zenia grants her that illusion. However, Zenia's main function seems to be to confront Roz with her own limits of power: as a wife (Zenia seduces Mitch away from Roz), as a mother (Zenia claims to have seduced Roz's son, Larry), as a feminist (Zenia causes a debacle over *WiseWomanWorld*), as a businesswoman (Zenia defrauds Roz in several quite spectacular ways), and as a Canadian. Roz, like Tony, is both thrilled and reduced by Zenia's cosmopolitanism:

Zenia has been out in the world. The wide world, wider than Toronto: the deep world, deeper than the small pond where Roz is such a large and sheltered frog. Zenia makes Roz feel not only protected, but lax. (364)

Roz, however, refuses to be overawed by Zenia's contemptuous criticism of "gentle" Canada, deriving strength this time from her own immigrant history to defend the country adopted by her ancestors as a desirable safe haven: "However, *boring* has something to offer, these days" (367).

It is Roz who describes Zenia as the Other Woman; it is also Roz who describes her as the Robber Bride, in both names highlighting the soap opera or fairy-tale dimensions of Zenia's threats, and incidentally drawing attention to the artifice within constructions (and impositions) of identity. Roz, who has practiced her own identity performance for so long, putting on a clown face to cover up her distress, finds herself saddened at the scattering of Zenia's ashes, bereft of that shadowy other, but also delivered for the first time in her life from the "tumour" of her past. Free to reinvent herself, Roz does not have a new identity as she faces the future with openness: "Roz will finally be a widow. No. She'll be something beyond that. What? She will wait and see" (467).

When the three protagonists come together at the end for Zenia's "wake of sorts," it is Charis who is at the center of the group, and it is Charis who has foreseen Zenia's death. Though her life story as abused child and New Age eccentric would seem to be positioned "elsewhere" in any discourse of national identity, I believe that a case can be made for Charis as victim, which would relate her particular split subjectivity to Atwood's analysis of the Colonial Mentality. "Born to the wrong parents," beaten and sexually abused, the child Karen split herself in two in a desperately willed act of migration from herself: "Finally she changed into Charis, and vanished, and reappeared elsewhere, and she has been elsewhere ever since" (41). Such phenomena of self-alienation as the result of violently abusive social relations have been analyzed from a psychoanalytic perspective (Mycak, 230–38) and from a racial perspective (Bannerji, 99–103), though my concern here is with how Atwood translates that victimization into the representation of an emerging postcolonial mentality. Back in 1972, Atwood famously sketched out four Basic Victim Positions (*Survival,* 36–39), which she suggested could be applied "whether you are a victimized country, a victimized minority group, or a victimized individual." In many ways Charis's history might fit this model, though Atwood does mention that "there may be a Position 5, for mystics; I postulate it but will not explore it here, since mystics do not as a rule write books" (*Survival,* 39). I suspect that she is exploring Position 5 in Charis's case, though perhaps in order to expose its limited usefulness for repudiating the victim role.

Charis's meditative practices, her floating clothes, and her faith in herbal remedies are mildly satirized as ineffectual and unworldly, though her alternative lifestyle might be seen as a veil that hides a great deal of Charis from herself. Karen's body may have been "split open" to let Charis escape, but the traumatic childhood memories have not vanished; they are merely blocked off from consciousness, or as Charis herself realizes, "the lake was inside Charis really, so that's where Karen was too. Down deep" (265). It is Zenia who opens the way for the return of this abject othered self, forcing Charis (as she had forced Tony and Roz) to face the ghosts of her past; only in 1990, when Charis is already middle-aged, does her narrative of victimization end, in her final confrontation with Zenia. As Zenia plays her duplicitous tormenting games at their meeting in the Arnold Garden Hotel, "something breaks" inside Charis, and she is free for the first time to acknowledge the force of her rage and desire for revenge, which she had conscientiously displaced on to the dark Other Woman hidden inside her self. Now that rage is turned not against her shadow self, but against Zenia, in a truly schizophrenic struggle as Charis watches an irresistibly powerful Karen push Zenia out the window and over the balcony to her death. Perhaps this is a psychic drama, but it is also a moment of triumph for Charis, when she begins to recognize her own otherness and the ways in which she is like Zenia, "herself in the mirror, herself with power" (398). Only now can she truly forgive Zenia as she emerges from the shadows of her own past, ready to assume a new "creative non-victim" position (*Survival*, 38) to become somebody "who could achieve some kind of harmony with the world, which is a productive or creative harmony" (Gibson, 27).

In counterpoint to the story of Charis as victim stands the story of Shanita, Charis's employer at the shop called Radiance, who is herself one of Toronto's visible minorities. Through their conversations we catch a glimpse of that "everyday racism" experienced by nonwhite Canadians, which Bannerji records with such passionate anger and political awareness: "People coming into the store frequently ask Shanita where she's from. 'Right here,' she says, smiling her ultra-bright smile. 'I was born right in this very city!' . . . It's a question that bothers her a lot" (57). And when Charis fails to understand why, Shanita interprets with some impatience at her naivety: "What they mean is, when am I leaving." Shanita survives through her strategies of continual transformation, changing the name of her shop in response to the recession (Radiance is in the process of becoming Scrimpers), and teasingly reinventing the story of her origins: "Shanita has more grandmothers than anyone she knows. But sometimes she's part Ojib-way, or else part Mayan, and one day she was even Tibetan. She can be whatever she feels like, because who can tell?" (57) As someone who refuses to be a victim, Shanita understands how constructions of iden-tity are subject to change, depending on circumstances. Her dynamism offers a sharp critique of racial stereotypes, for though Shanita may look exotic and may even be psychic (as Charis believes), she is also a smart businesswoman, who in no way conforms to the image of East-ern mysticism or passive femininity. It is Charis, not Shanita, who "floats around in Radiance"; Shanita's gaze is level and Charis comes to see her position as one to be envied: "In her next life she's going to be a mixture, a blend, a vigorous hybrid like Shanita" (58).

So, to return to the question with which I began: "Who is a true Canadian?" Ironically, the only character in *The Robber Bride* to be explicitly classified as Canadian is Zenia, in the newspaper report of her first death in the Lebanon: "Canadian Killed in Terrorist Blast" (13). Zenia had at least three passports, though according to official records, "she was never even born" (416). Once again Zenia is the test case, and her nomadic existence highlights the fact that no single defi-nition of Canadian identity is possible. Through her, myths of origin are discredited, identities are reinvented, and her otherness finds its mirror reflection in the lives of the three Canadian-born protagonists. Her border crossings are a reminder of the international context with-in which Canada as a nation operates, a point that is elaborated more sharply with references to the recession and the Gulf War, an acknowl-edgement of how much the country is implicated in the forces of glob-al capitalism.[3] *The Robber Bride* is a ghost story, or rather a story about exorcizing ghosts, in an attempt at a realistic reappraisal of Canadianness in the 1990s and a more honest recognition of the dif-ferences concealed within constructions of personal and national iden-tity. Tony's final question addresses Zenia's status as the Other Woman, opening up the question of difference to a further stage in the debate: "Was she in any way like us? thinks Tony. Or, to put it the other way around: Are we in any way like her?" (470)

NOTES

1. According to the 1996 census, nine out of ten immigrants live in Canada's three largest cities, as do 86 percent of visible minorities. These figures are taken from R. Pen-dakur and J. Hennerbry, ed., *Multicultural Canada: A Demographic Overview* (20–27).

2. This interpretation of a second othering was sparked by a comment in Barbara Godard's "Canadian? Literary? Theory?" on questions of exclusion within Canadian narratives of national identity (22). Donna L. Potts's article, which I encountered after I had completed mine, asks similar questions, though she interprets the same textual evidence slightly differently. Linking Atwood's feminism and her nationalism, Potts emphasizes Zenia's foreignness and her role as sacrificial victim in an argument focused on Canadian women's emergence from the colonial mentality.

3. Stephen Morton's 1999 article engages with some of the identity questions that I raise here, though in the context of Atwood's articulation of Toronto within the contemporary globalized space of late capitalism.

. . . .

Humanizing the Fox: Atwood's Poetic Tricksters and *Morning in the Burned House*

KATHRYN VAN SPANCKEREN

Ethnographic approaches centering on the wily trickster recommend themselves in dealing with the complex, dynamic subversions in Atwood's newest work. Recent studies, such as Lewis Hyde's thought-provoking *Trickster Makes This World* (1998) and Hynes and Doty's collection, *Mythical Trickster Figures* (1993), investigate the amoral, creative energies that propel tricksters to transgress and redefine boundaries, and to shift shape. In the case of Atwood, a mistress of reversals and inversions, it is helpful to temper the ethnographic approach with the structural awareness of Tzvetan Todorov in *The Fantastic* (1973) and of Eric Rabkin in *The Fantastic in Literature* (1976). Rabkin's binary model of fantasy as a subversive "reversal" of convention and authority, usefully extended by scholars such as Christine Brooke-Rose (1981) and Rosemary Jackson (1981), sheds light on the trickster's complex rhetorical strategies and ability to deconstruct.

There is not space here to do justice to these approaches; essentially, as Elizabeth Ammons states tersely in her in introduction to essays collected in Ammons and White-Parks's *Tricksterism in Turn-of-the-Century American Literature* (1994), "Trickster disrupts" (xii). The shape-shifting trickster's sheer creative energy fuels its Protean resistance to formulations of all kinds. There is danger in any critical attempt to theorize tricksterism, since its essence is disruption.

Attempts to codify trickster narratives threaten to co-opt the trickster, to beat the joke-teller to the punch line. Accordingly, close readings of texts inhabited by tricksters are particularly illuminating, since they help us appreciate the tricks at close hand. It is well to remember that a trickster is a trickster only insofar as the tricks work, and that they may work on the reader as well as on other characters. W. R. Irwin's *The Game of the Impossible* (1977) convincingly demonstrates the essential "conspiratorial bond" that ties the reader to the fantasy or trick; the "conspiratorial bond" amounts to coercion in what I have elsewhere called Atwood's "trickster texts" such as "Rape Fantasies" and "Siren Song" (Van Spanckeren, 77–83).

Trickster texts—works that implicate and trick the reader—have long been a hallmark of Atwood's writing. In trickster texts Atwood plays on the reader's preconceptions, often exposing assumptions about power. Trickster texts are effective insofar as they manipulate the reader. They are witty and thought-provoking, and generally they are short enough to "trick" the reader in one reading. Atwood's novels are too long and complex to do so, though they use trickster themes extensively, as Karen Stein notes in *Margaret Atwood Revisited,* which devotes a chapter to "Victims, Tricksters, and Scheherazades: The Later Novels." The present essay investigates the trickster in Atwood's poetry, particularly her recent work. Her subversion of convention is nowhere better revealed than in her poetry, in which she is free to play with language, the primary tool of the trickster. The fox, the quintessential Western trickster figure and often a stand-in for Atwood herself, reveals the development of tricksterism in Atwood's poetry and sheds particular light on her recent volume, *Morning in the Burned House* (1995).

The fox as a trickster appears frequently in world mythology. According to Conner, Sparks, and Sparks (1997), in Japan the fox is *kitsune,* a great magician and shape-shifting trickster deity of the Shinto religion (203), while in China it is Hu Hsien, a dangerous shape-shifter who seduces humans and drains them of vital essence (179–80). In the West, Reynard (or, in French, Renart) is the trickster hero of medieval European fable, beast epic, and anti-clerical satire (Bercovich, 287–92). Through craft the subversive Reynard triumphs over the authorities and outwits Isengrim, the brutal, dull wolf. Reynard was not worshipped but, as Cox demonstrates throughout *The Feast of Fools,* the fox played a prominent role in that important medieval festival replete with theological overtones. Though Reynard purportedly commits rape and robbery, he is portrayed as an attractive, charming outlaw. Along with the Native American raven and coyote, the fox of most contemporary literature is an amoral, greedy trickster who is weak and defenseless and must rely on his wits.

Atwood's fox, like most foxes in literature from Aesop on, is a blithe opportunist, an unsentimental realist who knows the good guy does not always win out in the end. More than raven or coyote, the stylish, elegant fox suggests an entrepreneurial instinct for survival. Atwood's is an unscrupulous, wisecracking, twentieth-century, capital- istic beast that prospers by cashing in on others' errors. While foxy tricks may be essential for survival, too easy a reliance on tricks— deceptions, rhetorical techniques (including dramatic monologues), and deconstructions—undermine a work's emotional depth. Atwood is increasingly taming the trickster, using it as an element in a larger, more humane vision.

Atwood's title poem from the early volume, *The Animals in That Country* (1968), contrasts the realm of art ("that country") with reali- ty ("this country") through treatments of animals. In art, the cat, fox, and bull carry human hopes and fears and have "the faces of people." If they die, it is to some imaginative purpose: the fox is "run/ to earth, the huntsmen/ standing around him, fixed/ in their tapestry of man- ners." In modern life ("this country") the animals are drained of numi- nousness. They have "the faces of animals" and their "eyes/flash once in car headlights/ and are gone." They suggest the extinction of inner life and loss of vision: "they have the faces of no-one" (*SP*, 48–49).[1]

In her early work, Atwood connects art and its tricks with life. A life without make-believe and art is a dead life. In "Dreams of the Ani- mals," from PU (1970), wild animals project themselves into their own dream worlds—"birds dream of territories/enclosed by singing." But captive animals are (like) captive minds. The "caged armadillo/ near the train/ station" runs in obsessive figure-eights and "no longer dreams/ but is insane when waking." The crested iguana in the pet-shop window rules over "its kingdom of water-dish and sawdust." The trickster fox in captivity would even kill its own young out of desperation: "The silver fox in the roadside zoo/ dreams of digging out/ and of baby foxes, their necks bitten" (SP 124). We are what we dream, or so the early Atwood would argue; keeping our imaginations alive is a life-and-death struggle. We are surrounded by hostile environmental, political and economic forces that threaten us with abusive families, criminal insanity, and saw- dust. Like weak but crafty foxes, we must use our wits to survive.

Atwood realizes the pitfall of tricksterism—too much technical bedazzlement, too little emotional substance, and a desperate capacity for cruelty—quite early. In fact, the attempt to contain her art becomes one of her familiar topoi. At first, she attempts to overcome trickster-ism by more trickery, generally involving viewpoint and speaker. She will use a mask to voice her own feelings as a creator, and then inveigh against the mask's creations. In "Speeches for Dr. Frankenstein," from *The Animals in That Country* (1968), her persona Dr. Frankenstein addresses his monster: "Reflection, you have stolen/ everything you needed:/ my joy," and also, significantly, " my ability/ to suffer." He blames the monster for being a trickster and usurping his own emo-tional life: "You have transmuted/ yourself to me: I am/ a vestige, I am numb" (*SP*, 67).

Atwood uses this strategy of projection in later volumes as well. In "The Wereman," from *The Journals of Susanna Moodie* (1970), the speaker, a mask for Atwood, fears that her trickster husband will return and change her with a "fox eye" or "owl eye" (*SP*, 85). In the first of the "Circe Mud" monologues in *You Are Happy* (1974), she rejects the nonhuman trickster, writing, "Men with the heads of eagles/no longer interest me/ or pig-men, or those who can fly." "All those [legendary figures, tricksters like Odysseus] I could create, man-ufacture/ or find easily." Instead, the speaker searches for "the others,/ the ones left over, the ones who have escaped from these/ mythologies with barely their lives." These vulnerable survivors have "real faces and hands, they think/ they are / wrong somehow, they would rather be trees." This seems to be a moving poem, but yet this is Circe speaking in a dramatic monologue. We cannot trust her unstable narrative, for she is a compulsive trickster and mythmaker. As if to confirm our sus-picions, the next poem describes the dead men, who have turned into mute "drying skeletons" of animals, lying around her. She denies responsibility. "It was not my fault . . . these animals dying/of thirst because they could not speak" (*SP*, 202–3).

Atwood tries to bid farewell to mythic structures in *You Are Happy*'s concluding valedictory poem, "Book of Ancestors":

> So much for the gods and their
> static demands . our demands, former
> demands, death patterns
> obscure as fragments of an
> archeology, these frescoes
> on a crumbling temple
> wall we look at now and can scarcely
> piece together. . . .(*SP*, 239)

The poet declares that "history/ is over, we take place" and looks forward to a personal present, "your spine, my arms around/ you, palm above the heart." The meaning is clear enough: the past is static; the ways we were seem mythic, and our former selves assume the status of "gods" to us, inhabiting a crumbling and inadequate precinct we must escape from to save our emotional lives. Yet the declaration is not totally convincing. The elaborate fantasy metaphors out of *She* (archeology, frescoes, crumbling temple wall) remain artificial. They do not move as, say, Shakespeare's shipwrecked old Prospero does, when he vows to sink his book, or (to look at a more recent example) as the rags and bones do in "The Circus Animals' Desertion," where Yeats forswears the glamour of "circus animals" that were "all on show/ Those stilted boys, that burnished chariot,/ Lion and woman and the Lord knows what." The great legends had ended up tricking him: they "took all my love,/ And not those things that they were emblems of." Yeats's great poem abjures the fantastic animals and the metaphors. Instead, the old poet becomes vulnerable, alone, mortal among us, surrounded by outworn containers (poetic forms): "Now that my ladder's gone/ I must lie down where all the ladders start,/ In the foul rag-and-bone shop of the heart" (336). Human love, whether present or remembered, is what lasts. But the quality of that love is indicated in the state of the animals and how they are rendered.

Atwood's acclaimed book of poetry, *Morning in the Burned House*, is a *memento mori,* a skull on the desk, a look at death from a thousand angles. It traces a hard-won movement from a fox-like, self-oriented mode to a more human vision. This distinguished volume, the first since the publication of *Selected Poems II* in 1987, breaks new ground in its use of autobiographical material.

The book is vintage Atwood, deepening earlier themes, but with a major difference. *Morning in the Burned House* makes a claim to emotional authenticity, containing as it does a sequence of elegiac poems on the death of Atwood's father. The tragic note dominates this book, dwarfing themes of the male/female relationship prominent in her earlier books such as *Power Politics.* "You grow out/ of sex like a shrunk dress/ into your common senses," she writes in "Miss July Grows Older"; "after a while these flesh arpeggios get boring,/ like Bach over and over;/ too much of one kind of glory" (KVS 7). There is more to this older, wiser speaker than meets the eye: "Don't confuse me with my hen-leg elbows:/ what you get is no longer/ what you see" (23).[2] Taking the place of the love/sex poems are the darkly stained, moving elegiac poems about her father. The new book also develops a poignant setting that earlier poems had touched on, the burned house of "The Small Cabin," from *Procedures for Underground* (120). *Morning in the Burned House* has five parts recalling earlier phases of Atwood's work. The personal subjects, impatient colloquial diction, and witty irony of the first part remind one of Atwood's early poems from *The Circle Game* and *The Animals in That Country*. Part 2 consists of dramatic monologues spoken by women of myth, legend, or popular culture (Daphne and Laura, Helen of Troy, Sekhmet the Sphinx, Ava Gardner). It recapitulates earlier themes of identity seen, for example, in "Songs for Dr. Frankenstein" and "The Reincarnation of Captain Cook," from *The Animals in That Country*, and in *You Are Happy*'s songs of the animals and Circe/Mud poems. The wide-ranging third part takes up real forms of death seen in cancer ("Cell"), the poisoning of the environment ("Frogless"), species death in the biosphere and in language ("Marsh Languages"), and political violence ("Owl Burning"). "Down," reminiscent of the title poem of *Procedures for Underground*, reworks the descent-to-death theme. This third part reveals Atwood's concern for the environment throughout her works, including the novels (*Surfacing* and *Handmaid's Tale* especially) and short story collections such as *Wilderness Tips*. The powerful long poem in part 3, "Half Hanged Mary," recalls *The Journals of Susannah Moodie* in its chronological construction and transformation from realistic woman protagonist to mythical figure (in this case a witch). It evokes a consciousness mysteriously continuing after death, as in *Moodie*'s final poem, "A Bus along St. Clair: December": "I am the old woman/ sitting across from you on the bus,/ her shoulders drawn up like a shawl"(116). "A Pink Hotel in California," concluding part 3, introduces the father and the lakeside cabin where the speaker's family stayed in 1943. It also recalls World War II and the war-oriented words the speaker, a child at the time, was learning: "smoke, gun, boots," and (ominously) "oven," leading by a chain of associations to key terms in the rest of the book: "The fire. The scattered ashes" (77).

Part 4 represents Atwood's effort to deal with mortality and vulnerability. Atwood handles death by recourse to traditional images of nature and themes of rebirth, but their consolation is hard-won. The father endures the loss of his mental faculties in a nursing home where "Rage occurs,/ followed by supper" ("King Lear in Respite Care," 86). Empathizing, the speaker alternates between memories and dreams. "A Visit" mourns "the days/ when you could walk on water./ When you could walk" (88). The father's loss of recent memory is imagined as a wave that washes him back to 1947: "suddenly whole beaches/ were simply gone" ("Wave," 83). Over the course of part 4 the scene shifts to the family's forest cabin by Lake Superior, a cabin that burned long ago.

Part 5 takes place after the death, in the consciousness of the bereaved poet who at first subsists in a realm leached of meaning or moorings. In a moving sequence of mourning (a pun on the "morning" of the book's title), death accompanies the speaker abroad ("Vermilion Flycatcher, San Pedro River, Arizona"), yet waits back at home on return, "in the center of your room" ("The Moment," 109). Death even lurks at the moment of waking: "You wake up filled with dread" ("Up," 110). Home, ownership, identity, even one's work—in this case, the poet's words—are revealed as the mind's tricks, empty constructs over which the self has no final control. Death will transform all of them utterly ("Girl without Hands," "The Signer").

Tracing the use of viewpoint, one sees a sequence. The autobiographical "you" (occasionally "I") in the first part becomes "I" in the dramatic monologues of the second part. The third, environmental part uses a mixture of viewpoints, while the poems about the death of the father in part 4 are uttered by an unobtrusive speaker who avoids "I." In the fifth part speakers change place. The only consistently first-person poems are in the second part which explores the gendered female self, dramatized in a series of angry, dismissive tricksters who win their contests against males but remain isolated. The rest of the volume seeks ways to overcome such isolation. The viewpoint becomes more complex as it explores death. In the later poems there is a muted, newly humbled speaking voice tempered by tragedy that explores reversals of viewpoint in nature and physics (solstices, black holes) and discovers in destruction and transformation a hope for some sort of survival.

Together the poems show a progression from emotional death in the self (part one) and in tricksters involved in various survival strategies (part 2). There is no escaping death, which is considered in its complexity and variety in the world (part 3). By the end of part 3, the reader feels the might and terror of death, and the absence of meaning in the universe. The impressive long poem "Half-Hanged Mary" powerfully evokes cruelty and the human face of death. The reader sees no way out of the impasse of death. Unlike Hester Prynne, after all her suffering Mary remains emotionally dead and cut off from others. Paradoxically, it is death itself that provides a path. The self's grief at the parent's death (part 4) creates vulnerability, a chink in the emotional armor. The self begins to dream, vivid dreams that obviously come from the depths of the soul. After the death (part 5) the child/speaker/self who survives, like Hansel and Gretel, has accessed a rich sense of life informed by the mystery of death. The meaning of survival is shifted. It no longer means theft, but rather gift—of voice, dream, and self.

The movement from theft to gift, from a trickster's psychology of survival to a new mutuality, may be seen in the changing treatment of the fox and related figures such as the cat from part 1 to part 5. The first section contains a quasi-narrative sequence of seven poems investigating the aging self, threatened by emotional emptiness. The first poem takes place in a hellish zone of isolation due to overwork and stress ("no time off"):

> You come back into the room
> where you've been living
> all along. You say:
> What's been going on
> while I was away? ("You Come Back," 3)

The speaker has been sleepwalking, merely going through the motions of family life. Survival has been achieved at the cost of love. Later in the volume, the death of the father reminds us that we live this way at our peril. If one could come back from the dead, one would wish for more vital connection with our loved ones.

The rest of part 1, like a book of photographs, depicts a speaker resembling Atwood as she grows from childhood to maturity and old age. "A Sad Child" deconstructs sibling rivalry as a threat to the self. After the rude discovery that *I am not the favorite child,*" the poem concludes tartly, "My darling, when it comes/ right down to it / and the light fails and the fog rolls in" at the moment of death, "none of us is;/ or else we all are." (5) "In The Secular Night" compares night babysitting at age sixteen to trying to write in the middle of the night. Both are times of intense solitude. Fox-like, the speaker explains it's "necessary to reserve a secret vice" (6)—cigarettes at age sixteen, and baby lima beans forty years later. "Waiting" takes a large cue from Elizabeth Bishop's late poem "In the Waiting Room," for it evokes an epiphany in childhood, among lampshades and periodicals and news of disasters, when the self first realizes that it will someday be old and die. "February" is a comic fulcrum: the book shifts into the adult present and takes up the low theme of a cat who "settles/ on my chest, breathing his breath/ of burped-up meat and musty sofas, / purring like a washboard" (11). (Atwood's cats and foxes are often interchangeable; the title of *Cat's Eye* suggests a trickster's double vision.)[3] This cat commands comical ways of telling "whether or not I'm dead./ If I'm not, he wants to be scratched; if I am/ he'll think of something" (11). The speaker is as crafty and greedy as the cat: "I think dire thoughts, and lust for French fries/with a splash of vinegar" (12). This poem comically anticipates the volume's elegies, which try to work through sorrow:

> Cat, enough of your greedy whining
> And your small pink bumhole.
> Off my face! You're the life principle,
> more or less, so get going
> on a little optimism around here.
> Get rid of death. Celebrate increase. Make it be spring. (12)

Spring appears with a vengeance in "Asparagus," with all its unwieldy props: sunburn, falling tree pollen, crumbs, and infatuation. The speaker's lunch companion complains that he is in love with two women. The older speaker imagines herself as a fox-like wise woman: "I could wrinkle up my eyelids,/ look wise. I could get a pet lizard" (13). She greets his unruly spring with recognition—"messy love is better than none" and feels "wonder/ or is it envy" (14). Despite the asparagus of the title, spring still is not here, for the empty-hearted speaker at least.

Existence is a matter of survival. At least so the fox would argue, as she makes off with yet another fat domestic fowl. Atwood explicitly puts this opportunistic argument into the fox's mouth in "Red Fox," the last poem in the first section, and by implication the last stage of the author's career. "Red Fox" takes place in winter, the icy season reflecting the speaker's paralyzing alienation and cynicism. The speaker watches a fox, a "lean vixen," cross the "sheer glare" of an iced-over pond. The fox's ribs show, and its "sly trickster's eyes" are full of "longing and desperation" while its "skinny feet" are "adept at lies" (16). The speaker considers survival, concluding that in an extremity we would sacrifice others, even our own children, to save ourselves: Hansel and Gretel "were dumped in the forest/ because their parents were starving" (17). The poem continues,

> *Sauve qui peut.* To survive
> we'd all turn thief
>
> and rascal, or so says the fox. (17)

The stanza break underscores the ambiguity of who is speaking, speaker or fox: *sauve qui peut* is the speaker's idea, attributed belatedly to the fox with whom the speaker obviously identifies. Meanwhile the fox has saved her skin and rejoices in

> . . . her coat of an elegant scoundrel,
> her white knife of a smile,
> who knows just where she's going:
>
> to steal something
> that doesn't belong to her—
> some chicken, or one more chance,
> or other life. (17)

The last line twists the knife: the poem has made us like and even identify with this murderous fox. This is a trickster text that draws one in without one's being aware. The ending reminds us that we are imaginatively inhabiting a killer. The poem's art involves us in an ethical dilemma. Perhaps the reader believes she would sacrifice for her child. If so, the end of the poem makes us question our authenticity and the strength of our love. We also must consider how many ways there are to steal another's life. Not all of those ways involve physical killing.

But to be fully human and feel emotionally alive, should one focus on survival? Is life about success, new strategies for the theft of hens, the technology of survival? And what survival does one want, given that life must end—the survival of mere flesh, wavering and pitiful without mind and awareness, like the dying father in the book? Or do we want something more? The challenge, for Atwood's poems, as for her red fox, is to address real issues and dare vulnerability. The red fox survives, but always alone in her early poetry and in the first part of *Morning in the Burned House*. It is a perennial outsider, looking on and scheming, so focused on survival that she loses her soul and participates in cruelty. By the end of the volume, Atwood's fox has changed and become much more vulnerable.

The second part of *Morning in the Burned House* confirms the need for vulnerability. Its biting, hardboiled dramatic monologues explore manipulative, deathly relations between the sexes from the points of view of various female tricksters. This part recalls the Circe series from the view of an older Circe. It begins with "Miss July Grows Older" in Miss July's voice: "How much longer can I get away/with being so fucking cute?" and recalls that "men were a skill" for her in her youth, "something I did well," but which she has "grown out of" (21–23). Manet's Olympia, the subject of the second poem, looks out at "You, Monsieur Voyeur" and tells this "you" or reader to "Get stuffed" (25). "Daphne, Laura and So Forth" portrays the fate of women harassed by men. Safely transformed into trees, they have lost their voices and even the desire for articulation: "Why talk when you can whisper?/ Rustle, like dried leaves./ Under the bed." Only tricks, strategies for survival, remain interesting for them: I'm working on/these ideas of my own/ venom, a web, a hat,/ some last resort" (26–27). "Cressida to Troilus" ends with a cursed offering ("Have some more body") to the insensitive Troilus: "Drink and eat./ You'll just make yourself sick. Sicker./ You won't be cured" (28–29).

Only Ava Gardner, speaking from the dead and longing for "the flesh, the flesh" and "the joy" (32), is vulnerable. She softens us up for the next poem, "Helen of Troy Does Counter Dancing," a classic trickster text modeled on Atwood's "Siren Song" from *You Are Happy*. The reader/voyeur is first flattered and drawn in ("Not that anyone here/ but you would understand") and quickly victimized: "Try me./ This is a torch song./ Touch me and you'll burn" (33–36). "A Man Looks" continues the theme of voyeurism; a maimed man attempts sex with a patient woman; "he's nothing to her but luggage/she needs to haul from room to room,/ or a sick dog to be kind to." Realizing he is not desired, the man thinks, "*I am angry*" and then "*I will die soon*" (37–38).

The last poem of the sequence returns to the trickster, this time seen as a gigantic cat, the sphinx, in "Sekhmet, the Lion-Headed Goddess of War, Violent Storms, Pestilence, and Recovery from Illness, Contemplates the Desert in the Metropolitan Museum of Art." This humorous sphinx thinks that tombs look like "dunces' hats." Devoid of feeling, she says "if it's selfless/ love you're looking for,/ you've got the wrong goddess." "I just sit where I'm put, composed/ of stone and wishful thinking," she explains. The wish is "that the deity who kills for pleasure/ will also heal," and be a "kind lion" who

> will come with bandages in her mouth
> and the soft body of a woman,
> and lick you clean of fever,
> and pick your soul up gently by the nape of the neck
> and caress you into darkness and paradise. (40–41)

Part 3 considers death in its effect on the environment. "Marsh Languages" mourns the loss of biodiversity and the dying of languages, the loss of "sibilants and gutturals" (54). It ends with a horrific vision of English as a survivor's tongue, a colonial world language, and of all human languages threatened by an unfeeling binary computer code. The section includes "Half-Hanged Mary" (58–69), the striking sequence told from the viewpoint of Atwood's ancestor hanged (but not killed) for being a witch in seventeenth-century New England. This poem introduces the possibility of survival in a state of madness, anticipating the father's mental lapses in part 4. The cost of such a survival—alienated, isolated—is too great. Ironically, Mary becomes a sort of witch or trickster; her neck is saved at the cost of her humanity: "My audience is God,/ because who the hell else could understand me?/ Who else has been dead twice?" (69).

Part 4 evokes the father's dying. The father takes on aspects of a trickster. In "King Lear in Respite Care" he will "have to be sly and stubborn/ and not let on" that he's trapped in "snow, or possibly/wallpaper" (85). The father keeps to himself, like the fox: "who knows what he knows?/ Many things, but where he is/ Isn't among them" (85).

Like a sorcerer, he sees things that others don't: "better to watch the fireplace/ which is now a beach" in "A Visit" (89). Dreams of seeking for the father in water (diving into a lake) and fire (in the burned cabin) herald the death in "Two Dreams." In "Two Dreams, 2," the speaker and her sister compare dreams of unfinished tasks concerning the dying father. Death is two-sided and involves imaginative transformation and empathy. In a brilliant reversal of viewpoint Atwood shows how dying is known to us through our grief: "from under the water/ they clutch at us, they clutch at us,/ we won't let go" (100). The dying father has already let go. He is imagined embarking on a solitary dream journey upriver into a wilderness underworld in "The Ottawa River by Night."

Part 5 takes place after the death. It begins by another river, in a dry wasteland. In "Vermilion Flycatcher, San Pedro River, Arizona" only a tiny trickling desert river remains after a recent flash flood that has left wreckage, "trash caught overhead in the trees" (107). Recently submerged, this spot is envisioned as the locus of death (envisioned as immersion in "Wave" from part 4). The speaker, standing in trash, recalls Yeats's speaker in "Circus Animals' Desertion." Sekhmet and company are notably absent. Instead there is a small, but real, bird, a blood-red Vermilion Flycatcher (whose name suggests corpses). It has been attracted by the dense weeds and sings despite or because of death, imagined as an indeterminate

> man with brown
> or white skin lying reversed
> in the vanished water, a spear
> or bullet in his back. (107)

The speaker imagines the deer drawn at dusk to "cross and drink/and be ambushed." The red bird, like a singer/poet, continues singing, as if magically: "how he conjures." Like the inscrutable dying father, the bird remains mysterious. Atwood refrains from anthropomorphizing this bird. In her early poems, she would have told us what the bird was dreaming, but this is a real bird—specified as to species—not a trickster or mouthpiece in a dramatic monologue. With its mate, it sings, but not in human language. The birds are part of nature:

> He and his other-coloured mate
> ignore everything but their own rapture.
> Who knows what they remember?
> Birds never dream, being their own.
> Dreams, I mean. (108)

Listening to the bird-poet, the speaker grasps that she, too, is mortal. She reminds herself and us: "As for you, the river/ that isn't there is the same one/ you could drown in, face down" (107–108). The poem "Up," about depression, reintroduces the bird: "You wake up filled with dread" and though "morning light sifts through the window" and "there is birdsong," still "you can't get out of bed" (110). The poem ends with a koan-like question that points up the need to work through grief by accepting responsibility. Trickster-like, Atwood poses it as a joke ("here's a good one"):

> you're lying on your deathbed.
> You have one hour to live.
> Who is it, exactly, you have needed
> all these years to forgive? (111)

One must cease to be a victim (to use *Survival*'s terminology) without becoming a hollow-hearted victimizer like the fox, cat, or sphinx.

Atwood's "The Signer" imagines an interpreter using sign language who is standing behind the speaking poet. This poem elides Atwood as a poet-singer with the singing Vermilion Flycatcher. The poem captures the vulnerability inherent in creating poetry that will be interpreted or misinterpreted. Like the forest after a burn, the place (poem) will become unrecognizable. The interpreter is a numinous presence suggesting death and the future: "Unable to see her, I speak/ in a kind of blindness, not knowing/ what dance is being made of me (114). Death will erase and collapse everything; it is "the place where all the languages/ will be finalized and/ one; and the hands also" (114–15).

In "Statuary" the dead, memorialized in statuary (themselves art works, like poems), speak to the living and begin to exchange places with them. The poem's ending is a poetic tour de force, pulling the statues into the rubbish heap reminiscent of that in Yeats's "Circus Animals' Desertion." It uses viewpoint so fluidly that *I* and *you,* subject and object, are reversed and then become indistinguishable in the vortex of existence inflected by death. Death is envisioned as a black hole. An entropic existence that erases distinction lies on the other side of reality defined as time—on the other side of the black hole. Atwood whirls her viewpoint around like a vortex or knothole in time to recreate entropic erasure. A lengthy quotation is necessary to show the syntax's shape-shiftings:

> You won't be content until we're toppled,
> like you, by frost-heave or vandals, and lie melting
> in the uncut grass, like you. In the tall weeds. In the
>   young trees.
> Until we're rubble. Like you. Until we're pebbles
> on the shore of a vast lake that doesn't (like you)
>   exist yet.
> Until we're liquid, like you; like the small whirlpools
> an oar makes drawn slowly through water,
> those darkly shining swirls the shape of a galaxy,
> those knotholes the world turns itself
> inside out through
> for us, for a moment, the nothingness
> that by its moving
> edges defines time. That lets us see down
> and into. That lets us fly
> and embody, like you. Until we are like you. (119)

The leap to the burned house at the end of the volume is made possible by the beautiful long poem that precedes it, "Shapechangers in Winter." In this poem, Atwood uses animal imagery in the service of the vulnerable and human. She rejects the trickster fox. In the first section the speaker majestically locates us in space through guided imagery. From her bedroom in a snowstorm, the poet imagines her house from the attic to the cellar, and below that the earth and bones of ancestors, down to the earth's core. From there she imagines the land and oceans and animal species and wavelengths of human emotion, "hatred and love infra/ red, compassion fleshtone, prayer ultra-/ violet." Beyond these waves lie peace and war, and air, and stars. "That's where/we are" (122). The poem gracefully speaks for all life on earth, as well as for the speaker.

In section two of "Shapechangers in Winter" Atwood's speaker—who seems close to Atwood here—bids farewell to her fox, her favorite animal, which she sees as an outgrown aspect of herself. "Some centuries ago," when they "lived at the edge of the forest," "on nights like this" her mate would have put on his "pelt of a bear," and

> I would have chosen fox;
> I liked the jokes,
> The doubling back on my tracks,
> And, let's face it, the theft. (122)

A thief "doubles back on his tracks" and hides his crime from his victims, just as a fox doubles back to trick its hunters. The fox's humor, duplicity, and unapologetic lust for thievery retain their appeal for her. Like Offred in *The Handmaid's Tale* (108), whose survival hinges on her ability to trick the Commander, this speaker *likes* theft. She recalls her youth as a time of "many forms" when she and her mate were "all sleight-of-hand illusion." Animal images proliferate: "Once we were lithe as pythons, quick/ and silvery as herring, and we still are, momentarily,/ except our knees hurt." Now they "huddle" under a quilt ("the shed feathers of duck and goose"), staying out of the wind by keeping "still,/ like trout in a current" (122–23).

Age has transformed the speaker and her beloved back into humans hastening toward inorganic death. They have had to drop their tricksters' disguises, imaged as other-worldly animal skins, snaky or fish-like scales.[4] "Every cell/ in our bodies has renewed itself/ since then, there's not much left, my love/ of the originals." They are, instead, "footprints/ becoming limestone" or "coal becoming diamond," less

> flexible, but more condensed;
> and no more scales or aliases,
> at least on the outside. (123)

Atwood's speaker has been unable to maintain her fox shape under the press of tragedy, age and time. Moreover, she sees that she does not need it—"we've accumulated, /despite ourselves, other disguises." The new disguises (hair like a "bramble bush," failing eyesight) are part of the human condition. By this point the tragic and sobering fact of the father's death has worked itself into the newly sensitive language. The poem gently reminds us that we are all shape-shifters, moving through our lives and our changing bodily states. Atwood tames the trickster in this poem, the penultimate in her book, and uses the trope of shape-shifting to profound and moving effect. "The eye problem: too close, too far, you're a blur./ I used to say I'd know you anywhere,/ But it's getting harder" (124).

Section three of "Shapechangers in Winter" occurs at the solstice, when the sun seems to stand still at the cusp of seasons and where the "past/ lets go of and becomes the future."

> The walls of the house fold themselves down,
> and the house turns
> itself inside out, as a tulip does
> in its last full-blown moment, and our candle
> flares up and goes out, and the only common
> sense that remains to us is touch. (124)

Life is like a house or body that deconstructs, a mortal trick which we will not survive. Only human feeling, our "common sense" that "touches" us (the selves, the *you* and *I* blur here) remains when all is dark.

"Shapechangers in Winter" ends with beautiful, simple language, musical internal rhyme, and a new vulnerability seen in the gentle conversational tone that carries the speaker's genuine commitment to the individual beloved. The title is ironic—aging and changes in appearance are a form of shape-shifting—yet also deeply meant. Love is not a matter of evasions and disguises. The disguises come naturally enough, and the ultimate one will be death, imagined here as ultimate entropy or nuclear winter. The "trick is just to hold on/ through all appearances; and so we do." *I do*—words rhyming with the marriage vow unify the flowing passage: "and yes, I know it's you;/ and that is what we will come to." The poem ends on an affirmation. When "candles are no longer any use to us/ and the visibility is zero: *Yes./ It's still you. It's still you*" (124–25).

At the end of the volume the painful loss of the father is accepted in a meditation on the way nature reforests after a burn. In "A Fire

Place," the fourth poem from the end, the speaker remembers revisiting the place in the forest where the family's cabin had burned. When she had visited the charred site as a child, poplar, purple fireweed, and blueberries grew on the ashes; now "that bright random clearing/ or burn, or meadow" is gone and a new forest is growing. Only humans "can regret/ the perishing of the burned place./ Only we could call it a wound" (116–17). Nature is revealed as the great shape-shifter, the ultimate artist/trickster who cannot reverse time or restore individual life, but can console if we will become emotionally open.

The final, title poem, "Morning in the Burned House," like a coda, takes place in death, in the burned cabin; only here can regeneration occur. The poem is spoken by a longing, vulnerable voice that is simultaneously the poet as child and as aging adult; there is no need to imagine a trickster, because the consciousness of the aged and dying is double, half in the present and half in the past. The speaker is alone and simultaneously near imagined loved ones. Though everything "in this house has long been over/ including the body I had then/ including the body I have now," the speaker still sits "at this morning table, alone and happy," her "bare child's feet on the scorched floorboards," wearing "burning clothes, the thin green shorts" like a nature sprite or phoenix, cheerful amid destruction in her "grubby yellow T-shirt/ holding my cindery, non-existent,/ radiant flesh. Incandescent" (127).

The book's last poem links loss of consciousness with larger cultural losses—nuclear war, Hiroshima's burned spots in which large vivid flowers grow. All is "over." Still, like the Vermilion Flycatcher, or like the birds in so many elegies (Whitman's "When Lilacs Last in the Dooryard Bloom'd," Keat's "Ode to a Nightingale"), the poet sings despite death and celebrates " radiant flesh." The diction determinedly adheres to convincing incidental details, the child's bare feet, "thin green shorts" and the "grubby yellow T-shirt," because they are *not* the stuff of trickery or fantasy costumes. Rather, they are the very essence of grubby, vulnerable humanity.. The book's title assumes new meaning. We witness an elegiac new "morning" within "mourning," the long-anticipated advent of spring, precisely in the locus of death, the "burned house." We are what we most love; trickster fox has been left behind for human child. We celebrate the mortal body, both in ash (ashes to ashes) and "incandescent" flame.

Though seemingly unrelated and in various distinctive forms, the poems of *Morning in the Burned House* all touch on aspects of dying, imagined as various forms of loss (of oneself, a cabin, the past), moving from self to others to the world. When it finally comes, the death of the father seems naturally to grow out of what has come before. The book is masterfully structured as an elegiac sequence leading from the tragedy and horror of death through grieving to the consolation that art (poetry), nature, and contemplation of the cosmos offer. Atwood's subject, the death of a parent, is one of the most moving topics a poet may address. In this anti-heroic age of serial marriage and serial divorce, it may be our most tragic topic, after the death of a child. It is not surprising that Atwood would plumb new depths in her tricksters and trickster texts for the occasion.[5]

M. L. Rosenthal and Sally Gall suggest in *The Modern Poetic Sequence* (1983) that the poetic sequence is the "decisive form toward which all the developments of modern poetry have tended," one that "fulfills the need for encompassment of disparate and often powerfully opposed tonalities and energies" (3). It is clear that in constructing the elegaic sequence *Morning in the Burned House,* Atwood combines many such opposed tonalities and viewpoints. In the face of death, she finds the artistic resources effectively to humanize the fox. Like Yeats, in her late work Atwood sees in the trickster a profound humanity.

NOTES

The author thanks the University of Tampa for the Dana Summer Grant which supported the research and writing of this essay.

1. This and all subsequent references to poems by Atwood in the first section of this essay are to the Canadian edition of her *Selected Poems,* here abbreviated as *SP.*

2. This and subsequent unattributed page references to poems by Atwood in the second section of this paper are to the Houghton Mifflin edition of *Morning in the Burned House.*

3. The cat and fox are interchangeable protagonists in some of the same folktales, such as "Puss in Boots" and "The Fox-Matchmaker," Aarne Thompson 545B, where the fox features in most Asian versions, and the cat appears in more of the European versions. Some scholars have argued that Puss in Boots was originally a fox. (Kaplanoglou, 57–61).

4. Atwood uses magic birds and serpents, as well as foxes and cats, frequently throughout her work. In mythology around the world, birds and snakes (denizens of other realms, air and earth) are frequently associated with the shaman, and also with tricksters as totemic animals, as Beidelman points out. See Sharon Wilson's useful appendices on Atwood's folk tale types and folk motifs on pp. 314–46, especially "Animals" pp. 326–27, in *Margaret Atwood's Fairy-Tale Sexual Politics* (1993).

5. The death of a parent presents a particular challenge to women poets of Atwood's generation, the first beneficiaries of birth control and abortion rights and the first to have been able confidently to pursue writing along with parenthood. It will be interesting to see whether their elegies for parents will address death in ways earlier women (celibate, gay, or without children) did not. Atwood's volume bears

comparison with Sharon Olds's *The Father* (1992), in which Olds memorializes her father's death, and Heather McHugh's rich poetic sequence "Not a Prayer," about the death of her mother-in-law, which begins the poems in *The Father of the Predicaments* (1999). All three poetic sequences set the death in a framework interweaving present and past time. More than the others, Atwood see the dying parent as a trickster, psychopomp, or guide to the next world.

Quilting as Narrative Art:
Metafictional Construction in *Alias Grace*

SHARON R. WILSON

Alias Grace (1996) may appear to be a new direction for Margaret Atwood. The novel is based on considerable research of a real, uneducated Irish woman, Grace Marks, and a famous nineteenth-century crime she supposedly committed with one lover, James McDermott, against her Scottish master and lover, Thomas Kinnear, who represents his class with the aristocracy of social advantage and educational opportunity that continues in Canada (Margaret Atwood Papers, *AG*, Kinnear research). The novel also appears to take seriously topics and genres, including double personalities, sex scandals, and murder mysteries, previously exposed to parody. Because of this, it seems less experimental, less postmodern, than *The Handmaid's Tale* and *The Robber Bride*. Occasionally, since "Grace was the O. J. Simpson of her time" and may have resembled O. J. in feeling "battered" and minimizing the gravity of the crime (Wiley, 2; Atwood Papers, *AG*, Psychiatry notes), its story even seems to resort to the "parlour theatrics" and kind of melodrama (Joan Thomas, C10) associated with contemporary TV trials, throw-away mystery paperbacks, and popular histories, including one of her nineteenth-century sources, Susanna Moodie's *Life in the Clearings*. As Stein points out, the novel makes use of genres in which Atwood has written before, including the Jamesian ghost story, detective thriller, Gothic tale, autobiography, and Scheherazade story, but still uses what Stein considers a nineteenth-century style, including social realism, comedy of manners, epistolary form, Gothic fiction, and even a ballad (103). Since *The Blind Assassin* (2000) arises from what Atwood calls the same "UR Manuscript," *The Angel of Bad Judgment* (Margaret Atwood Papers), the two novels indicate a paradoxical but not uncommon direction for a postmodern writer: increasing documentation that compounds textual gaps and coexists with growing magical realism; in the case of *Alias Grace,* blood-red flowers that appear on the ground and in the cell of Grace's prison. *Alias Grace* is again a feminist, postmodern, and postcolonial metafiction.

Feminist fiction, grounded in a belief that change is possible, analyzes gender as socially constructed. As a tool of feminist critique, feminist metafiction can reveal the conventionality of the codes of fiction, how they have been constructed, and how they can be changed (Greene, 4). Feminist intertextual revisions, sometimes involving direct reader address and always revealing the ideologically determined discourses encoded in traditional tales, also frequently have a "metanarrative function" (Cranny-Francis, 85, 89, 94). In opposition to Jean-François Lyotard's philosophical usage, where "metanarrative" often refers to totalizing or legitimating master discourses, such as science (xxiii–xxiv), "metanarrative" here simply refers to narrative about narrative, as one of its varieties, metafiction, is fiction about fiction (Holman and Harmon, 297). Although postmodern metanarrative, including antinarrative, resembles Lyotard's questioning or deligitimating discourse (37, 79), it marks a fundamental historical and cultural break with modernism (Jameson, xvi). Despite some attempts to label Canadian fiction, including *Alias Grace,* as essentially realistic and transitional or "intramodern" (Kirtz, "Facts"; "The Past"), postmodernism is no less evident in Canadian than in U.S., Latin American, New Zealand, or Asian fiction; and characteristics of Canadian postmodernism (See Hutcheon, *Canadian Postmodern,* 1–25; "Circling," 168–69) even largely define international conceptions. Like the metafictions of Louise Erdrich, Rosario Ferre, and Keri Hulme, *Alias Grace* uses postmodern techniques such as self-reflexiveness and intertextuality to foreground issues of class, sexual politics, and other political issues, including those of the postcolonial condition.

The novel is based in part on Susanna Moodie's *Life in the Clearings,* designed to reconfirm English attitudes about the "uncivilized" life in Canada. It is also set immediately following the nearly successful Mackenzie Rebellion, widely supported by the Canadian poor, and during a period of large-scale Irish emigration. Thus, the novel is not only centered in nineteenth-century colonial attitudes about Canada, the lower classes, and the Irish, shared by many Anglo-Canadians as well as by the English; it also critiques these attitudes.

Alias Grace is about history, money, class, gender, ethnicity, psychoanalysis, legend, and myth. It is also about spiritualism, magic acts, master-servant narratives, misreading (Atwood letter to Ellen [Seligman], 17 March 1996), and all fictions, including Atwood's, Canada's, and our own. Resembling folklore itself (March, n.1), it deconstructs not only orally transmitted and published stories that we may assume are facts, but also national and social myth, gender roles, constructions of personal identity, and readers' expectations of novels and reality. Both Simon and Grace, "the artful minx, with her blandishments!" continually call attention to Grace's narrative-while-quilting as a "story." Not only Grace's attorney, MacKenzie, but Atwood notes that "butter wouldn't melt in [Grace's] mouth," and Grace knows how to arrange herself as well as her narrative to attract interest (Atwood letter to Edna Slater, 3 Sept. 1996). Once again, Atwood's use of intertexts, and, ironically, even her "Author's Afterword," foreground the novel's focus on fiction making. In this novel, however, Atwood uses the unique image of quilting to represent the piecing together of different stories into a new pattern, in this case a pattern that questions master patterns and, by implication, all patterns. In addition to marking and naming each of the fifteen sections that correspond to quilt squares, these metaquilts comment on themselves, the women who make them, any variation from traditional patterns, and the stories they depict. Thus, the quilt patterns and section titles highlight the metafictionality of *Alias Grace* and themselves function as postmodern metafiction.

Characteristically, Atwood's afterword begins with an assumption of clear boundaries between fiction and reality: "*Alias Grace* is a work of fiction, although it is based on reality." She notes the appeal of the Kinnear-Montgomery murder story and Grace's ability to "polarize opinion." Suggesting some of the reasons why this historical incident is significant, Atwood notes that "Attitudes towards [Grace] reflected contemporary ambiguity about the nature of women": Grace was simultaneously a female fiend, a temptress, the real instigator and murderer, and a silenced, unwilling victim (461). Again appropriate to Atwood's purposes, Grace gave three different accounts of the Montgomery murder and James McDermott gave two. The novel also quotes from Susanna Moodie's *Life in the Clearings* (1853), a central but third-hand source for information about the murder, and the one on which Atwood based her earlier CBC television play *The Servant*

Girl (1974). As Atwood points out, Moodie's book was influenced by Dickens's *Oliver Twist,* and anything based exclusively on it "cannot now be taken as definitive" (467). Atwood also referred to Canadian, U.S., and British newspapers; penitentiary, asylum, emigration, and medical records; letters from doctors who examined Grace; letters from clergymen and others who circulated petitions on Grace's behalf; the published confessions of Marks and McDermott; song lyrics; maps of Canada; photographs of Ireland; and research on Spiritualism, Mesmerism, mental illness, including "dissociation of personality" (dedoublement), the Mackenzie Rebellion, and psychology (See Acknowledgments; Atwood Papers, *AG*). In addition, she consulted quite a few other literary, historical, and medical accounts of the period, including *Letters of a Lifetime; History of Toronto and County of York, Ontario; Beeton's Book of Household Management* (467); Kiracofe's *The American Quilt; Cyclopedia of Fraternities;* Laver's *Costume and Fashion; The Collected Letters of Thomas and Jane Welsh Carlyle;* and the works of Emily Dickinson, Emily Brontë, Christina Rossetti, Charles Dickens, and Robert and Elizabeth Barrett Browning (Atwood Papers, *AG*). The afterword ends by stating what we have already observed, that "the written accounts are so contradictory that few facts emerge as unequivocally 'known'. . . . Where mere hints and outright gaps exist in the records, I have felt free to invent" (461, 465). Frequently, Atwood again does so by embedding literary, folklore, and other popular culture intertexts, including fairy-tale, mythic, and biblical stories and popular songs. Although she notes that "People want an outcome / They want a guilty person / They want to know who did it / They don't like not knowing," she chooses not to provide closure either to the relationship between Grace and Simon or the extent of Grace's involvement in the murders (Atwood Papers, *AG* Notes to 1995, 14 Aug.; Letter to Ellen, 17 Mar. 1996). Paradoxically, what most attracts readers, including those in her friend's book club where Atwood discussed this novel, are the gaps that remain in the novel, gaps that the reader is delighted to fill.

At the end of the novel, when Grace is married and possibly pregnant, she uses pieces of Mary Whitney's white petticoat, her faded yellow prison nightgown, and Nancy's pink-and-white flowered dress to make three of the triangles of a Tree of Paradise quilt, the first she has ever made for herself (459–60). Because traditional quilts are generally composed of fabrics actually used by the maker's family and friends, quilts are literally pieces of lives, as this one is.[1] Fabrics from pants, blouses, and dresses worn in the past and associated with random, daily events, sometimes significant (such as weddings, birthings, and funerals), are brought together to form a pattern. Fragments are ordered into a whole; bits of the past become useful parts of the present, available to provide warmth and comfort in illness and in daily life and to remind the users of their personal, familial, communal, ethnic, racial, and even national pasts.

Quilting styles and names vary according to regions, periods, and countries of origin, and quilts frequently tell stories. Probably originating in Asia and as old as the Egyptians (*Quilt History*), quilts have shown mythic, folkloric, biblical, and historic stories, including Tristan and Iseult, the Seven Deadly Sins, and Arthurian ones (*Quilt History*/Page.html). Quilt block names, thus, are rooted in history and may show biblical influence, as with Jacob's Ladder. Other names, a kind of "folkloric poetry" that was rightfully whatever the maker chose (Bacon, 70, 72), might come from trades and occupations, nature, square dancing, or politics (*Quilt Block Names*) or be inspired by familiar objects, humor, pathos, tragedy, or sentimental meaning (Bacon, 70, 72).

Significantly for Atwood's purposes, quilters have traditionally been women. As literary works, including Glaspell's play *Trifles* and short story "A Jury of Her Peers," Alice Walker's short story "Everyday Lives" and novel *The Color Purple*, and Molly Newman and Barbara Damashek's play *Quilters,* indicate (See also *Poetry and Prose Page*), quilts are pieces of women's lives and expressions of women's feelings. In addition, quilting has usually been a social activity, a means for women to be with other women in a socially approved activity and a means for them to exchange family stories and vent anger or frustration with the "male world" from which women have been excluded (See also Rogerson, 11). Where other arts have been unavailable to subordinated women whose primary role was defined as nurturer and who could not always afford such supplies as paints and canvas, quilting has been a vehicle for breaking silence and speaking. Quilting helped establish and maintain a separate women's culture with its own codes of language and manners prevalent in both the United States and Canada in the nineteenth century. Thus, quilting is an appropriate vehicle for retelling a nineteenth-century woman's story. In *Alias Grace,* Atwood alludes to these quilt patterns: the Log Cabin, Job's Tears, Old Maid's Puzzle, Tree of Life, Tree of Temptation, Pine Tree, Jacob's Ladder, Broken Plate, Flower Basket, Wild Goose Chase, Nine Patch, Memorial Quilt, Attic Windows, and Wheel of Mystery. In addition, she uses Jagged Edge, Rocky Road, Puss in the Corner, Young

Man's Fancy, Broken Dishes, Secret Drawer, Snake Fence, Fox and Geese, Hearts and Gizzards, Lady of the Lake, Falling Timbers, Solomon's Temple, Pandora's Box, the Letter X, and Tree of Paradise patterns as section titles.

In *Alias Grace,* Grace quilts in the sewing room at the governor's mansion where she works during the day while serving her prison sentence for the murders. As she quilts, she tells her story to an American psychoanalyst, Simon Jordan, a character Atwood invented for the novel, who is seen mostly through his objects and his position, as his father was.[2] As he writes down in a notebook what Grace says, she feels that he is drawing her or drawing on her skin and that she is splitting open like a ripe peach (69). He also records his own dreams, which suggest the locked boxes or fenced interiors he wants to open in Grace. Like other men of his period and profession, including Freud, Simon subscribes to the double standard and the angel/whore split and resents his loss of status and independence of action due to loss of the mills.[3] As in *The Robber Bride,* characters' dreams, such as those about corridors, drowning, and severed hands, seem to interpenetrate and comment on one another and on everyone's repressions, projections, and fragmentation. Letters Simon writes and receives (including to or from Dr. Workman and Bannerling; his mother, Mrs. William Jordan; his friend Dr. Edward Murchie; and clergy) and his interior monologues comment on, and are pieced into, Grace's narrative. Grace's interior monologue similarly comments on Simon, his expectations, his creation of story, her efforts to offer or deny him what he wants, and the psychologically revealing associations, visions, and dreams she rarely tells Jordan but tries to decipher herself. She also makes private metafictional comments to the reader about the story she tells and the memory— yet another story—she gradually constructs and unravels. Thus, Grace, a superior seamstress, presents the reader with blocks for a many-layered story quilt complete with border design and padding. As readers "progress" through the book, they must quilt the pieces, creating their own patterns and watching them deconstruct as they are constructed.

Grace uses the conversational style characteristic of folktales, frequently emphasizes the oral quality of her tale, and accompanies it with the folk activity of quilting. Atwood characteristically disarms the reader with allusions to nursery rhymes such as "Simple Simon" and "Little Jack Horner"; myths and folk tales about Perseus, Saint George, Ulysses and the Sirens, the Lorelei, mermaids, Pan, Pandora, Ariadne, Scheherazade, Eurydice, the Pied Piper of Hamlin [Hameln], "Fitcher's Bird," and "The Girl without Hands"; the Apocrypha story about Susanna and the Elders; literary and opera "myth" such as *The Lady of the Lake, The Faerie Queen, Heart of Darkness,* her own poem, "Five Poems for Grandmothers" (*THP*), and the opera *Sonnambulla*; and biblical stories about the Trees of Knowledge and Paradise, the Tower of Babel, Jacob and Esau, Solomon, Lot's wife, Jeremiah, Job, Simon Peter, Rachel, and Jonah. She even rewards the apparent murderess and her readers with a romantic fairy-tale resolution. But if Grace is a Scheherazade telling her story to entertain a doctor more associated, in her experience, with death than life, she is well aware of quilting's subversive potential. We should be as well.

Atwood admits that her pattern "got bigger than I intended it to be. . . . I think originally there were only nine quilt-pattern titles, and then I just needed more. I needed to have more to cover the actual story as it unfolded" (Wiley, 4). Each section features an illustration of the quilt pattern under the title and, on one or more pages, section epigraphs, usually consisting of quotations from historical documents paired with literary ones from the period. Together they ironically or humorously foreground the section content. Although section and quilt titles changed some as the novel developed, passages or events often ironically name both title and quilt.

Appropriately, the quilt marking the novel's first section, which is also its only chapter, is a "Jagged Edge" pattern that pictures a literal jagged edge, nicely opposing the closing "Tree of Paradise." It is accompanied with a quotation from Susanna Moodie's *Life in the Clearings* that ironically alludes to "the superior moral training of the feebler sex" but states Moodie's great interest in seeing "the celebrated murderess" Grace Marks (3). Grace, a model prisoner who has already been "shut up" for eight years for the murder of Thomas Kinnear, begins her story with the spots of dark red that appear in the prison-yard gravel, swell, burst, and then fall back to the ground as she walks. Grace associates these peonies, "glossy like satin," with the white ones in Mr. Kinnear's garden when she first saw Nancy. On that day, Nancy wore the pale dress with pink rosebuds that Grace wears not only when she is trying to escape, but also when she is on trial for the murder. They also contrast with the white ones she gathered for Mary Whitney's funeral, before she ever saw Nancy or Kinnear. Blood-red flowers, similar to those associated with violence and passion in Atwood's *Fitcher's Bird* watercolor (Wilson, *Margaret Atwood's Fairy-Tale Politics,* plate 3), *The Handmaid's Tale,* and "Bad News" (*GB*) subliminally haunt both Grace and the reader throughout the book, revealing Grace's unconscious preoccupation with blood, the murders it signifies, and dead characters alive within her. These red peonies thus introduce what Atwood refers to as the "is-it-alive-or-dead-or-both motif" later imaged in the decapitated chicken running around Kinnear's yard. As Atwood points out to one of her editors, Grace has a temper, life experience, and submerged rage: She is "very preoccupied with laundering" (Letters to Edna Slater, 3 Sept. 1996; Ellen, 17 Mar. 1996). These spots of color, both memories and anger she tries to repress, thus become a recurrent, subversive part of the pattern that constitutes this book-as-quilt.

Section 2, "Rocky Road," a variation of the well-known Jacob's Ladder pattern and one of several road designs, including Road to Tennessee or Kansas or the White House, is again brief and one of several "X" quilt patterns. It provides background on the crime and shows the "rocks" that Grace's friend Jeremiah predicts in her future, including the "rocky road" to and within prison. For the reader, it illuminates the "rocky road" to "solving" the book's mystery. At one point, the quilt pattern marking this section was "Wheel of Mystery."[4] The warning epigraphs from the *Toronto Mirror* about McDermott's execution and the Kingston Penitentiary punishment book about punishments for particular offenses, such as bread and water for staring and being inattentive at breakfast, contrast with the flattering pictures of Marks and McDermott and the poem celebrating their fame.

Section 3, "Puss in the Corner," a quilt design that is similar to Thirteen Squares and does *not* feature a cat, presents Grace as the sly puss, invisible to others and possibly invisible to herself. Like section 4, "Young Man's Fancy," section 3 presents "Ourself behind ourself, concealed" (46).[5] Susanna Moodie's description of Grace is matched with a passage from Emily Brontë's "The Prisoner." The "soft and mild" face of Brontë's captive contrasts with her announcement that she won't be held for long (19). In the governor's parlor with her hands folded "the proper way although I have no gloves," Grace thinks about "jellyfish ladies," who are mostly water and whose legs are penned in by wire crinoline cages. As a young girl, she remembers never having enough room and being told not to be too intelligent (33, 22–23). But here and elsewhere she counters such thoughts with the imagined comments, which she always labels "crude" or "coarse," of her dead friend, Mary Whitney. "As Mary Whitney said" increasingly signifies a less socialized, freer, irreverent, and possibly revengeful aspect of Grace that she seems to repress. Expressing relief that she was "not present" to see Nancy's rotting body, she says that "There are some things that should be forgotten by everyone, and never spoken of again." Beginning to see the red flowers again, this time growing on the wall of her cell, she notes that "when you go mad you don't go any other place, you stay where you are. And somebody else comes in" (26, 33). This section ends with Grace pressing to her forehead an apple she associates with the Tree of Knowledge.

Section 4, the "Young Man's Fancy" quilt pattern, identifies individual constructions of Grace, especially Dr. Jordan's romantic "fancy." It begins with the Dickinson epigraph from "One need not be a Chamber—to be Haunted": "Ourself behind ourself, concealed." Moodie's description of Grace in the asylum and a quotation from Dr. Workman, one of Grace's real doctors, follow. Unlike Dr. Bannerling, who favors cupping and bleeding to reduce the animal spirits of the insane, and Dr. Jerome Dupont—named after the chemical company (Letter to Ellen, 11 Mar. 1996) but really Jeremiah Pontelli, Grace's trickster peddler—Dr. Workman feels blindfolded in attempting to cure problems of the human psyche. Ironically, Simon—the doctor who sets out to see all but resembles his namesake, the apostle Simon Peter—is blind in a more general way. The section ends in the "quicksand" of Simon's sexual as much as medical frustration with Grace, who is "a hard nut to crack"; with his landlady, who waylays him; and with Lydia, who captures him on a "tongue-coloured setee" (54, 90). Feeling like the voyeur he is as he watches Grace threading a needle, he finally glimpses "the puss in the corner": He imagines Grace "washing herself with her tongue, like a cat" (91).

Sections 5, "Broken Dishes"; 6, "Secret Drawer"; and 7, "Snake Fence," again underline the sense in which we hide ourselves from ourselves. Section 5's title refers not only to the quilt pattern and to the actual broken dishes it suggests, in this section the teapot that Grace's Aunt Pauline gives her mother and that breaks on the journey from Ireland to Canada, but to the scraps and pieces, as of a broken plate or the book's mysteries, "that would seem to belong to another plate altogether; and then there are the empty spaces, where you cannot fit anything in" (103). Although "Secret Drawer" was once intended for section 7, with the "Snake Fence" pattern for section 6 (Atwood Papers, *AG*), it appropriately depicts the mind as a forbidden room. When Simon dreams of opening a door at the end of a Bluebeardian secret corridor, the sea rushes out and immediately closes over his head, suggesting lost memories rising to the surface. When he dreams that his father's dead hand is coming back to life, instead of exploring the implications for his identity, he rationalizes that his dream is really Grace's story (139–41). Although "Pandora's Box" is the title quilt of section 13, Grace works on a "Pandora's Box" quilt in this section and remembers all the beautiful quilts, including a "Wild Goose Chase," she saw at Mrs. Alderman Parkinson's house. She notes that in the "Attic Windows" pattern, from one point of view the boxes may seem open, and from another, closed (162). We get a peek inside the secret drawer or box when Grace faints after she hears the dead Mary's voice say, "Let me in." Later she does not remember worrying that Grace is lost and has gone into the lake, marking her first bout of amnesia (180). But if the Pandora's box of Grace's psyche—or, for that matter, of Simon's—is fully opened, what will we see inside? In section 7, after hearing about the ghost of Mary Whitney, Simon feels as if he has been closed in a dark room or come from an abattoir. This section's title, "Snake Fence," literally refers to the snake fence on which McDermott displays his agility and the period of harmony before the murder when Grace wishes nothing would ever change. Although this quilt pattern does actually depict "snakes," subliminally, it suggests the hidden snake in the Garden of Eden and anticipates the snakes Grace will hide in the Tree of Paradise quilt she makes after she marries the man who helped convict her, Jamie Walsh.

Many of the quilt titles and sections draw attention to the sexual politics Grace finds intrinsic in the display of quilts. In section 6 she sees quilts as flags of war, placed on the tops of beds as warnings of "the many dangerous things that may take place in a bed" (161). Section 8, "Fox and Geese," announces a chase. In addition to readers, chasers include prison keepers; ironically, they consider women edible but think that they should have been born without mouths, their only useful areas being below the waist (240). Lydia moons after Simon; Nancy, who has had one illegitimate baby, is pregnant with her master's child; Jamie makes Grace a May Queen; and Grace dreams of a man caressing her. The chapter ends with the possibility that Grace has been embellishing her story to please her audience, thus leading Simon and us on a wild goose chase. Section 9, "Hearts and Gizzards," prefaced with McDermott's grizzly description of choking and dismembering Nancy, juxtaposes a gruesome depiction of the crime, which McDermott says he committed to have Grace, with the humorous telling of Simon's romantic entanglements. In some of these he ironically feels snarled as in a spider's web (293), imprisoned, when he really only wants to be Grace's heroic rescuer (322).

Section 10 (X), "Lady of the Lake," like 14, "The Letter X" quilt pattern, marks two "Xs" in the text and foregrounds how quilt illustrations may self-reflexively mirror literature (Scott's *Lady of the Lake* and the lady in the lake of Arthurian romance), incidents in the text we are reading (Grace in the lake), and even names in the text (the steamer "Lady of the Lake," in which Grace and McDermott flee). Although Grace finds no lady and no lake in the quilt, she thinks that the boat was named for the poem and the quilt for the boat so that things do make sense "and have a design to them" (340). Similar to its treatment of other images of grand order and design, however, the book immediately undercuts this clarity, as the water seems to erase Grace's footsteps and all her traces, as if Grace Marks leaves "no marks." Even more disconcerting for readers who wish, like Dr. Jordan, to hold on to the image of her that Grace constructs, is her calm satisfaction with being erased: "It is almost the same as being innocent" (342).

Similarly, section 11, "Falling Timbers," a variation of the World's Puzzle, Solomon's Puzzle, and Drunkard's Path designs (Lithgow, 59), highlights the puzzles and falls in this section. It may also ironically suggest the timbers of the popular pioneer Log Cabin design, which, with the associated Pine Tree pattern, came to symbolize the American colonies' fight for freedom against oppression (Lithgow, 59). Not only are the timbers here falling, but the Log Cabin design itself is missing from the quilt-pattern section titles. Although Grace says that every young woman should have a Log Cabin quilt—to her, symbolizing home and hearth—and makes one for another young woman, the Log Cabin quilt she later sleeps under in marriage is both second-hand and potentially unlucky (Rogerson, 17). "Falling Timbers" also parallels Simon's fall with that of Grace and James McDermott and continues the self-reflexive emphasis that makes the novel metafiction. When Simon is not listening to Grace's consciously enhanced tale of capture (353), he sleeps with a "respectable woman," his opium-taking landlady. When Grace was preparing for trial, she received literary advice about recounting the story of the crime—"to tell a story that would hang together, and that had some chance of being believed"—and she apparently practices her skill with the stories she tells Jordan, readers (357), and possibly herself. What she dreads most about the possibility of being hanged is being "cut up into pieces, and bits and fragments" (358), unlike the "whole cloth" she wants to offer Jordan (353). Simon concludes that Grace's "strongest prison is of her own construction." Ironically, this quilt section ends as the previous one does: Like Grace, he wants to be anonymous and "lose himself completely" (366).

In section 12, "Solomon's Temple," another design without any apparent Solomon or temple, Simon definitively proves himself devoid of Solomon's wisdom. After hearing that Grace's attorney, Kenneth MacKenzie, thinks Grace is guilty of helping to kill Nancy, Simon recognizes that Grace is the only woman he wishes to marry. The section ends with his ludicrously whispering "murderess" while thinking of hothouse gardenias.

In section 13, "Pandora's Box," the "box" of Grace's psyche and what she has not remembered about the murders is opened during hypnotism, but Simon also faces the "Pandora's box" possibilities of his own actions as he is invited to murder his landlady's husband and contemplates murdering the landlady. In addition, as in other Atwood texts, when what was closed is opened, we face our inabilities to distinguish truth or reality from fiction. Illustrating the death-in-life motif, the Mary Whitney voice admits that she, not Grace, helped kill Nancy, thus solving the mystery of the book. But is it solved, or do the windows, including the one from which Mary's soul supposedly could not escape, again only appear to be open from one angle? The Mary personality also tells Simon that "Curiosity killed the cat" (400). Since the hypnotist is Grace's friend Jeremiah the Peddler posing as Dr. DuPont, we may be seeing a parlor trick. Grace could be acting, as, for that matter, she might have been in claiming not to remember. On the other hand, a double personality offers an explanation of details, in both novel and historical crime, that seem to defy rationality. In both the actual crime and in Atwood's novel, the first murder victim is a reader, Thomas Kinnear, who is killed while reading a "Godey's Ladies'" book. Although he is not killed in the bedroom, the magazine is later discovered, blood-covered, in Nancy's bed (331). In opening the Pandora's box of the novel, it is wise to remember the parodic images of Atwood's earlier prose poem "Murder in the Dark," where the persona invites us to play games with the game: "You can say: the murderer is the writer, the detective is the reader, the victim is the book. Or perhaps, the murderer is the writer, the detective is the critic and the victim is the reader. . . . In any case," the persona says, "I have designs on you . . . by the rules of the game, I must always lie" (*MD*, 30).

Section 14, "The Letter X," a pattern that forms five more X's in the text, relies on the puns of which Atwood is so fond: After the initial quotations, including a letter by Elizabeth Barrett Browning, the section consists entirely of letters, some probably not delivered. These letters fill in what happens to Simon, who interestingly experiences the kind of amnesia he thinks Grace has, and Jeremiah, who, in another disguise, performs "The Future Told in Letters of Fire" at area theaters. Section 15, based on "The Tree of Paradise" quilt, which ironically appears to be falling, consists of another letter that fills in what happens to Grace. Whether or not the Tree of Life and the Tree of Knowledge are the same, as Grace believes, making not only the Fruit of Life and the Fruit of Good and Evil the same, but the consequences of eating them equivalent, she is released from prison and marries. In Atwood's fictionalization, her rescuer is Jamie Walsh, the flute-playing Pan Grace knew when she worked for Kinnear. Recognizing that this role as an object of pity "calls for a different arrangement of the face" than when she was an object of horror and fear (443), Grace rejects the plausibility of the "happy ending" "just like a book" that Janet and many readers would supply (445). Whether Atwood's happy ending is indeed happy, and whether *quilt* spells *guilt,* are again questions for each of us.

As *Alias Grace* is a construction based on "reality," so all our histories and conclusions are exposed as theories, speculations, the best we can do to build a structure over the abyss after the grounds of our being have been deconstructed (Derrida, 351–52). Although readers will endlessly debate whether Grace really helps kill Thomas Kinnear and Nancy Montgomery, whether she really has either amnesia or a double personality, and whether she has sex with Kinnear and James McDermott, again such questions are beside the point, either/ors that overlook the pluralism of both identity and truth. As Grace notes in her mental letter to Dr. Simon Jordan on the final page of the novel's final section, "The Tree of Paradise," and of her version of her story, she may have finally guessed—or, more likely, is posing—a riddle. She will put a "border of snakes intertwined" on the Tree of Paradise quilt she makes after marriage, rather than the conventional bridal quilt with flowers and vines symbolic of fruitfulness, love, and longevity (Atwood Papers, *AG*, Fashion Quilts; see also Rogerson, 20). Her border suggests the snakes of the Great Goddess and of Atwood's other trickster snake goddesses including Circe and Zenia (*YAH, RB*) as well as the Eve/snake of Eden and Atwood's *Double Persephone* covers (Wilson, *Margaret Atwood's Fairy-Tale Politics,* figures 3, 4). Although the snakes will look like vines or a cable pattern, "without a snake or two, the main part of the story would be missing." She is changing the pattern to suit her own ideas and telling no one else, because her interpretation of the story on which the pattern is based is "not the approved reading." Although the snakes could be phallic symbols, as Freud and Rogerson suggest (qtd. in Rogerson, 20), if the border encodes deceit and sexuality, we cannot exclude either this trickster storyteller or the sexist cultures that make killers of female snakes into mythic heroes (Wilson, *Margaret Atwood's Fairy-Tale Politics,* 17–19). "Like everything men write down, such as the newspapers, they [get] the main story right but some of the details wrong" (459–60).

Atwood, too, throws in a few embroidered snakes in her pretty pattern (460), thereby subverting our approved readings of quilts, literature, gender, culture, reality, and all master narratives. Grace is "alias Grace" because all of her, and our, identities are aliases, fictions. Where gaps exist in her or our life narratives, we too are "free to invent."

NOTES

Shorter versions of this article were presented in 1997 at the International Popular Culture Association meeting in Brisbane, Australia, the Association for Canadian Studies in the U.S. Conference in Minneapolis, and the Rocky Mountain Modern Language Association in Denver.

1. In Atwood novels, many characters are also mainly "in pieces." In *Surfacing,* David is a clumsily worked patchwork, and in *Alias Grace,* Rev. Verringer would have us avoid the horror of being mere patchworks, without a soul, if we are mainly our unconscious mind, i.e., what we repress or forget (406).

2. When questioned about why Simon is not described further, in reference to more than objects and position, Atwood jokes that "the higher your class, the less likely you are to be subject to the impertinence of description! (It's the beginning of surrealism, which substitutes objects for people.)" (Letter to Nan [Talese], Ellen [Seligman], Liz [Calder], Phoebe [Larmore], Vivienne [Schuster], 30 Jan. 1996.) She had hoped to have Workman play the Simon Jordan part until she discovered that Grace's stay in the asylum overlapped his tenure by only three weeks. Early drafts do refer to this character as William (Atwood Papers, *AG*).

3. In short, "he is not a 20th-Century Sensitive Guy" (Atwood letter to Ellen [Seligman], 3 Mar. 1996.)

4. Atwood Papers, *AG,* Ap. 1995 Holographs. Other quilt designs that Atwood considered were "Bear Paw" for section 8 and "Fool's Puzzle" for 9.

5. Atwood also considered a similar design with space instead of squares beside the diamond.

9

. . . .

A Left-Handed Story: *The Blind Assassin*

KAREN F. STEIN

Margaret Atwood's novel *The Blind Assassin,* winner of the prestigious Booker Prize, is a virtuoso performance, an intricate layering of texts and ironies. Constructed like a Russian wooden doll, the novel is a nested series of stories within stories; and like the nested dolls, one story hides another until it is opened to reveal another one surprisingly similar to it. The narrator of the framing novel, eighty-two-year-old Iris Chase Griffen, a clever and compelling storyteller, tells a story replete with Gothic motifs such as sacrificial maidens, powerful and predatory men, wars, betrayals, and conspiracies. She is driven to complete her memoirs despite her failing health in order to retell the story of her family—a tale of a fall from fortune, the tragic deaths of her parents, sister, husband, and daughter, and the alienation of her granddaughter. Story-telling is her way to re-envision, understand, and justify her life; to gain power; to avenge herself on those who have betrayed her; and to set her life in order. Just as the novel encompasses multiple narratives, it develops many by now familiar Atwood themes (for example, power and powerlessness, entrapment, and gender relationships) and includes several genres: science fiction, tragedy, realism, and Gothic.

Intertwined within Iris's story are several parallel narrative strands woven in varying gradations of emotional depth and veracity. Untangling these narrative strands and matching them with the framing story becomes a game in which the reader is invited to participate. A central interpolated narrative is the novel *The Blind Assassin,* purportedly the posthumously published novel written by Iris's sister, Laura Chase. This novel describes a love affair between an affluent young woman and a disreputable young man. In the course of this novel, the young man tells a science-fiction story about a blind assassin. By nesting three novels with the same name within each other, Atwood is pointing to the intricacies and ambiguities of the narrative art, a theme that has shaped much of her work. These three novels and a series of interpolated newspaper articles retell the same story in different ways. By this means, Atwood reflects upon the nature of fiction and of reading. Stories both conceal and reveal information, and, in consequence, readers interpret and reinterpret, finding new meanings and following different threads of plot or symbolism in each reading. To mitigate confusion here I shall refer to the science-fiction novel of the planet Zycron as *The Blind Assassin* 1, the "Laura Chase novel" of the two unnamed young lovers as *The Blind Assassin* 2, and the complete novel (also referred to as the framing novel) as *The Blind Assassin* 3.

The story *The Blind Assassin* 1 is the novel's symbolic center, for it brings to a focus the motifs of hiding, blindness, futile sacrifice, and silencing that reverberate through the book. The story mirrors the real worlds of Port Ticonderoga and Toronto that are also caught up in hypocrisy, class conflict, and economic injustice. Sacrifice has become an empty ritual in the city of Sakiel-Norn, just as the personal sacrifices of the men and women in Toronto are in vain. The sacrificial maidens of Sakiel-Norn are speechless, and the assassin is blind. In Canada, Norval Chase has lost an eye in the war, and his daughters, Iris and Laura, are both speechless and blind, each in her own way. Similarly, just as the storyteller of the science-fiction novel reinvents his stories, slanting them differently for different audiences, so too Iris reinvents and rewrites her fictions.

These novels depict complex amalgamations of passions, of love and hate, of secrets and silences. Imagery of burning and of Hell infiltrates the narrative. In telling these interwoven stories, Atwood pursues a larger project: The book lays bare the basis of narrative and adumbrates a social critique of the hypocrisy, injustice, classism, and sexism of the twentieth century. My purpose here is to elucidate how the Gothic structure, imagery, and narrative strategies provide the means to carry out this project.

GOTHIC NARRATIVE

Hiding and revealing are the hallmarks of Gothic fiction, which is built on conventions such as dreams, interrupted narration, imprisoning structures, disguises, exploration of secrets, mysterious pictures, signs, and secret or hidden rooms or other enclosures. Its narratives feature interruptions, layering of stories, and a difficulty in telling the story. Eve Sedgwick explains that "the novel's form . . . is likely to be discontinuous and involuted, perhaps incorporating tales within tales, changes of narrators, and such . . . devices as found manuscripts or interpolated histories" (9). Mysteries and puzzles abound. Sexual stereotyping is common, with women portrayed as fragile, passive, frightened, and in need of rescue, while men are active, dominating, assertive, and threatening.

Across the theoretical spectrum, feminist criticism views the Gothic novel as a story of gender role inequalities and their concomitant anxieties. In a Bakhtinian reading, Jacqueline Howard argues that Gothic fiction of the eighteenth and nineteenth centuries "reveals the contradictions and dilemmas posed by the privileging of moral and aesthetic sensibility in women" (141). She points to tensions between different discourses, a male discourse of power in contrast to a female discourse of moral superiority, but physical weakness and fragility. Thus, although women are seen as morally superior, they are "weak, delicate and disordered" (141). Coral Ann Howells writes that "to be angelic and robed in white is only the romantic side of eighteenth-century convention, the other side of which is the condemnation of woman to a passive role in which she can be sacrificed by society for sexual and economic interests" (Howells, *Love, Mystery and Misery,* 11). Kate Ellis's Marxist critique asserts that the Gothic reflects bourgeois anxiety about keeping women at home. According to Claire Kahane, the Gothic probes psychological issues raised for women by a society that has devalued caring, nurturing, and the maternal principle.

The Gothic plot is based on hiding and revealing, on secrecy and stealth, and similarly the narrative tends to be convoluted and mysterious. Typically the heroine is a motherless young woman struggling to find her way through the mazes of a hostile patriarchal society. She encounters secrets and solves mysteries as she seeks to escape from a series of perils, particularly from threatening older men.

The traditional female Gothic tale (for example, Ann Radcliffe, *The Mysteries of Udolpho,* 1794; or Charlotte Brontë, *Jane Eyre,* 1848) tells of a woman literally or figuratively imprisoned in a tower, a castle, or a cell, threatened in some mysterious way by an ambiguous older male figure who has power over her. Typically the tale ends when the young woman escapes from this man and becomes romantically attached to a younger man, usually her rescuer (although in some variants, the woman, like Jane Eyre, marries the suitably tamed older man). This Gothic plot replicates the "master narrative" of women's development in postindustrial society (Massé). The woman's story is a tale of leaving the parental home, the father's space, and learning to mute her self, to lose her subjectivity, to turn inward and focus on her feelings, to suppress her ego in the service of others, especially of a male authority figure, be he lover or husband. Such are the stories of Laura and Iris; but, as is often the case with Atwood, the plot takes a surprising twist, laying bare the contradictions and the social implications of the genre.

Atwood's earlier novel, *Lady Oracle*—full of plot devices such as disguises, ghostly appearances, doubled characters, mysteriously threatening men, and novels nested within novels—is a comic Gothic book. In contrast, *The Blind Assassin* is a tragic novel that uses Gothic plot devices and narrative strategies to tell Iris's story of two orphaned and silenced sisters. This novel delineates the falls of two great houses, the "old money" Chase family of Port Ticonderoga and the nouveau riche Griffen family of Toronto. The cycle of events is set in motion when Iris's father, Norval Chase, returns physically and psychically wounded from serving in World War I. A combination of evil, tragic flaws, and blindness leads to the collapse of the Chase and Griffen dynasties. By the end of the novel, the only family member left is Iris's wayward granddaughter, Sabrina, for whom Iris writes her memoir in the hope that knowledge of the family secrets her narrative reveals will free Sabrina and empower her to reshape her life.

Two important motifs of this novel are hiding/revealing, and speech/silence. The female protagonists vacillate between these poles as they struggle to discover how to live in a dangerous society. Iris's story focuses on her sister, Laura, who kills herself by driving off a bridge. As she endeavors to understand her sister's life more clearly, Iris must unravel clues. The narrative recapitulates her process of uncovering, discovering, as its layers of stories unfold to reveal hidden meanings. Strands of narrative are superimposed on each other, one thread running ahead of another, so that the reader must watch in fascination as the patterns of the stories shift like kaleidoscopic images. In the process of writing her memoir of Laura, Iris first conceals and then reveals her own story.

THE STORY OF SAKIEL-NORN

To unravel the intertwined strands of narrative in this complex novel, let us start with the central fiction, *The Blind Assassin* 1. Critics speak of it as a science-fiction novel, but although it is set on the planet Zycron it is really a Gothic adventure romance of conspiracy and intrigue, the story of a beautiful young woman silenced and intended for sacrifice. The tale evolves as an unnamed man tells stories to entertain his lover during their assignations. Blindness and betrayal are the keynotes of this novel. The exploitative and hypocritical Snilfards grow rich from selling the intricate carpets woven by young children of the working class. These children become blind from their labor and are then sold as sexual slaves; however, some of them escape and become highly skilled assassins. (And, as we shall see, this plot recapitulates a version of the stories of Laura and Iris.)

The spiritual values of Sakiel-Norn degenerate: Although once the Snilfards sacrificed their own children to gods they believed in, they now sacrifice slave girls instead, performing an empty ritual that has lost its meaning for them. The tongues of the sacrificial young women are cut so that they will not cry out and disturb the rites. The hero of this tale, one of the blind assassins, falls in love with and rescues the sacrificial maiden he had been hired to kill in a complicated palace plot.

But the love story of the blind assassin and the tongueless girl (*The Blind Assassin* 1) is never completed. When the lovers discuss the evolving story, the woman proposes a happy ending but the man rejects it. In fact, when under an assumed name he publishes a revised version of this story, he omits the love plot altogether and produces instead a fable about the overthrow of class distinctions as all of the city's inhabitants join forces to fight interplanetary invaders.

ANGELS AND DEVILS

As is the case in the tale of Sakiel-Norn, the plot of Iris's memoir also revolves around hiding and revealing, secrecy and silence, sacrifice and betrayal. In the Gothic tradition, sexuality is often the basis of these secrets. Women in that tradition are often portrayed as innocent and threatened by male sexuality, and to that end *The Blind Assassin* utilizes imagery of angels and devils, fire and ice to characterize women, men, and sexuality.

When Liliana Chase dies from a miscarriage in 1925, her nine-year-old daughter, Iris, overhears conversations that attribute her death to Norval's excessive sexual demands on his fragile wife. In this manner Iris learns the gender stereotypes of frail, sexless women and demanding, dangerous men. Reenie, the Chase family housekeeper, is a staunch believer in Victorian ideology, and therefore she teaches Laura and Iris that women should be "angels in the house": dependent, selfless, pure, and devoted to family. Liliana and Laura are presented as serious and chaste, and they are linked to imagery of Heaven and angels, water and ice. In contrast, men are expected to be independent, assertive, and active in the larger world of business. While two of the Chase women are compared to angels, the men in the novel are associated with diabolic imagery. Indeed, the three male figures—Norval, Alex, and Richard—are each shown to be sexually demanding and dangerous, and they are repeatedly depicted in imagery of fire and Hell.

The feminine angel imagery first appears when Iris visits the cemetery where the Chase family monument is adorned with two softly draped female stone angels, "white marble, Victorian, sentimental" (44), indicating women's role as pure, chaste, inert, lifeless.[1] When Laura is little, she believes the angels were meant to be her and Iris, although the more realistic Iris disagrees (45). As she grows up, Laura is indifferent to social conventions and her concern with heavenly matters is radically innocent and earnest. Throughout her life she questions the Bible, cutting out passages she finds unpalatable, wondering about "the seating arrangements in Heaven" (513), and getting expelled from school in part for asking "Does God lie?". She asserts that she does not wish to get married and explains that there are no marriages in Heaven. Moreover, she is ready to sacrifice herself for the sake of saving others. One review of her posthumously published novel even claims that she "writes like an angel."

Liliana is an "angel in the house," morally superior, self-sacrificing, but physically frail and weak. Reenie reverently describes her as an angel (69) and "a saint on earth" (142); Iris views her as "selfless" (73). Her first two appearances in the novel connect her with winter, whiteness and cold. The first is a photograph of her in a frozen scene. Pictured with a group of friends before she is married, she looks jaunty, adventuresome. In the second vignette she is at an ice skating party, where Norval Chase, who previously knelt to lace up her skates, proposes and she responds appropriately, in passivity and silence: "What did [she] do at this crucial moment? She studied the ice. She did not reply at once. This meant yes" (69). Iris's description of this scene both reiterates and subverts the angelic imagery of whiteness, purity, and passivity, for the ice's seemingly solid surface conceals depths of instability. Although the skaters' world seems firm, secure, pure, and innocent, something darker and more turbulent lurks beneath: "under their feet . . . the ice . . . white also, and under that the river water, with its eddies and undertows, dark but unseen. This was how I pictured that time . . . before Laura and I were born—so blank, so innocent, so solid to all appearances, but thin ice all the same. Beneath the surfaces of things was the unsaid, boiling slowly" (69).[2]

The marriage that results from this romantic proposal lives up to Iris's description of turbulence beneath a seemingly calm surface. Norval leaves for war almost immediately after the wedding, and by the time he returns he and his wife have already grown apart and become strangers to each other. A veteran scorched in the cauldron of battle, he has lost his innocence through experiences of war and sexual relations with other women. Although Liliana silently forgives him, it is with an air of martyrdom: "Breakfast in a haze of forgiveness, coffee with forgiveness, porridge with forgiveness. . . . He would have been helpless against it, for how can you repudiate something that is never spoken" (77).

In contrast to the white and frozen outdoor scene of the proposal, an apparently cozy domestic scene introduces disconcerting fire imagery.[3] Sitting near the fireplace with her parents in the morning room of their home, Avilion, in November 1919, the young Iris recites a poem about the letter F: "F is for Fire, / Good servant, bad master. . . ." The picture accompanying the poem shows a "leaping man covered in flames—wings of fire coming from his heels and shoulders" (81–82). Iris is "in love" with the man of fire because "the fire can't hurt him, nothing can hurt him," and she draws "extra flames" with her crayons (81–82). The invincible winged man of fire carries a weight of implied connotations including passion, rebellion, the devil, and dangerous sexuality. And in this family scene before the fireplace, Iris is attuned to her father's restlessness, his disillusionment with the home life he had previously desired.

Iris intuits correctly that just as the solid ice concealed the turbulent water below, the quiet domesticity is a fragile facade covering an uncomfortable relationship. Her mother (who, unbeknownst to Iris, is pregnant with Laura) "is recovering from a recent, mysterious illness, said to have something to do with her nerves" (80). Iris senses that her father feels "a certain nostalgia for the war" as he "stares into the flames, watching the fields and woods and houses and towns and men and brothers go up in smoke. . . . This is his home, this besieged castle; he is its werewolf" (82).

A more striking fiery image characterizes Norval when, years later, he dresses up as Santa Claus crowned with a wreath of burning candles. His costume terrifies Laura, for she confuses his costume with his ordinary self, and thinks that he is just pretending to be like other people most of the time, while "underneath he was burning up" (385).

Alex Thomas is also associated with fire imagery. A war orphan of unknown parentage, called by his adoptive father "a brand snatched from the burning" (215), Alex is a shadow figure, a demon lover, and later the author of the science-fiction novel *The Blind Assassin* 1. He is a union activist, and in 1934 he is sought by the police for allegedly setting Norval Chase's button factory on fire. Laura hides him, concealing him first in the cellar and then in the attic of Avilion. Iris, who is then eighteen and chafing at the restrictions of her narrow life in Port Ticonderoga, dreams of him in dreams that are suffused with subconscious erotic imagery. She imagines herself "fleeing with him . . . away from a burning building. . . . It was Avilion that was burning" (216–17). Despite her dreams, when he responds sexually she is "transfixed," motionless, and she flees down the stairs. She knows that to respond to his advances "would be dangerous, at least for me" (218). She does not reveal this event to Laura, and, consequently, Alex remains a charged secret between the sisters.

Laura's hiding of Alex is a reversal of a typical Gothic plot device, for more frequently an older man conceals a woman as prisoner under his control. In fact, both Iris and Laura will be trapped in the house of an older man when, in order to save his button factories and guarantee his daughters' financial security during the Depression, Norval gives Iris in marriage to the most diabolic of the novel's three men, the clothing manufacturer Richard Griffen.

Norval is blind to Richard's real nature, and Iris believes she has no other choice. Numbed by her father's suggestion, the eighteen-year-old Iris consents to marry a wealthy businessman twice her age whom she hardly knows, and thus she sacrifices herself for the good of her family. The scene in which Richard proposes to Iris is vastly different from Norval's proposal to Liliana. Commensurate with his large ambitions and inflated sense of himself, Richard has reserved a table in the Imperial Room of the Royal York Hotel in Toronto. The room is ornately decorated with chandeliers and maroon velvet drapes, and seems "leathery, ponderous, paunchy" to Iris. There is a smell of burning, of "hot metal and smoldering cloth" (227). Iris is silent and hears little of what Richard says. When she is married to him, she loses control of her life and becomes an appurtenance belonging to Richard, a beautifully groomed trophy wife. Much later, Iris remembers the four fireplaces in their house, and the "flames licking on flesh" (229).

But Richard is even more dramatically described with fire imagery that links him to the flaming man in the young Iris's picture book. Laura later sends Iris a coded message: a picture from Iris's wedding album that she has altered, tinting Richard's hands red and painting flames coming out of his head, "as if the skull itself were burning" (451). But, as we shall see, Iris is initially blind to the warning encoded in this picture.

Iris herself participates in both the fire and ice imagery. We have seen that she hopes to be invulnerable like the flaming man in her ABC book, and that she experiences erotic dreams in terms of burning. But she also participates in the imagery of ice and cold. For example, after she accepts Richard's proposal she describes her feelings of numbness and terror by invoking the imagery of Lucifer's fall from Heaven. She feels cold, and experiences herself as falling "endlessly down" because of her failure to believe in God (228). "The arctic waste of starched white bedsheet stretched out to infinity" and she thinks she can never "get back to where it was warm" (228). However, she is a realist, and believes that the marriage is her only alternative. Whereas Laura is linked to the angel imagery, Iris reminds her sister repeatedly in different contexts that "this isn't heaven." Although Iris at first behaves according to the stereotypes of femininity that reduce her to passivity and dependence, she is ultimately able to resist. The novel's association of angelic women with white and ice, and diabolic men with red and fire is elaborated in its concern with costume and disguise, appearance and reality.

COSTUME AND DISGUISE

Clothing, costume, and disguise are among the devices that people choose to hide or reveal themselves. For example, in *The Blind Assassin* 2, the unnamed woman ineffectively attempts to disguise herself on her forays into the working-class neighborhoods to meet her lover. Nevertheless, he is annoyed because, lacking the proper clothing, she remains overdressed. In *The Blind Assassin* 1, the male Snilfards of Sakiel-Norn wear thin platinum masks that disguise their emotions and the women cover their faces with silky veils, "since imperviousness and subterfuge were reserved for the nobility" (16).

Iris's memoir, *The Blind Assassin* 3, uses imagery of costume and disguise to indicate how mysterious and confusing men are to her and her sister. Their father, Norval Chase, a complex and enigmatic man, is a distant figure to his daughters, and his strangeness is conveyed in nonhuman imagery: metal, fire, animal, monster. When she is young, Iris thinks "his medals [are] like holes shot in the cloth [of his clothing], through which the dull gleam of his real, metal body can be seen" (76). He seems to be "a shambling monster with one eye, so sad" (78). When drunk he paces in the small tower room of Avilion, his "bad foot dragging . . . Light step, heavy step, like an animal with one foot in a trap" (78). His agitated pacing and his "bad foot" suggest Captain Ahab of Melville's *Moby-Dick*, another man turned into a haunted and obsessive figure by his encounter with evil.

Iris remarks that people like to wear costumes and uniforms "because you could pretend to be someone else" (332). Richard's sister, Winifred, who arranges costume balls for charities, such as the 1936 costume ball on the theme of Xanadu, notes that people are able to "be as revealing or concealing as [they] might wish," draping themselves in veils and scarves, or baring themselves in scanty costumes (333).

The clothing that people wear functions both to hide and to reveal their personalities and social status. The devious Winifred wears "green alligator shoes" and carries "a reptilian purse" (506). Laura, who tends to the ascetic, wears clothing that looks "less like something she'd chosen to put on than like something she'd been locked up in" (2). And when she drives off the bridge, she is wearing white gloves, an indication that her hands are clean.

In contrast to her sister, Iris wears elaborately tailored clothing that signals her wealth and status. Winifred picks out much of Iris's clothing, seeking to control her under the pretext of helping her dress appropriately for Richard's social milieu. Wearing these clothes signals Iris's submission to her sister-in-law and husband. Not surprisingly, her clothing hints at her vulnerability: When she and Richard go to Avilion for the first time after Norval's death, she is wearing an "eggshell linen suit" (312) and matching hat. Her hat gets broken, as is usually the fate of eggshells. The light-colored, expensive costume (and the attention she pays to it) seems inappropriate, because she has just been orphaned and because she and Richard are driving six hours on muddy roads. When they arrive at Avilion, Laura is waiting for them. She is barefoot and Iris wonders about this. I take it to be an indication of her unconventionality, her vulnerability, her fragility, and her lack of concern for social niceties and for material goods.

As Iris gains independence from Richard and begins to assert herself, her relationship to clothing changes. When she visits the head of Laura's school to deal with a complaint, Iris wears clothing intended to demonstrate her position as the bearer of Richard's power. She manipulates the costume and its symbolism for her own purposes. She elects to wear a hat with a "dead pheasant on it, or parts of one," and an "impressive" cashmere coat trimmed with wolverine (373). Her intent is to convey the impression that there are four eyes, rather than two, staring at the administrator.

BLINDNESS, SECRETS, DISGUISE, LIES, AND BETRAYAL

But more serious than the superficial disguise achieved by costume is the far more damaging disguise accomplished by lying.[4] Through misrepresentation, concealment, and outright prevarication, the characters in this novel hide information, thus contributing to the blindness of others. As signaled by its title, blindness is a central theme of the novel. But whereas the blind assassin of the science fiction novel has sharpened his other senses to compensate for his blindness, the characters in the framing novel remain blind and fail to see important clues. Norval Chase epitomizes blindness, for he returns from the war with one bad eye that he covers with a patch. Throughout the novel Iris, like the traditional Gothic heroine, misperceives or fails to see a great deal.

Richard strives to keep Iris blind to his misdeeds by concealing information or by lying. Although Norval thought he was "sound," Richard turns out to be sinister, or as Iris later puts it, "rodent-like." Soon after his marriage he reneges on the promise he made to Norval, for he closes the button factory and fires the workers. He conspires with his sister to keep Iris silent and uninformed, and he preys upon Laura, who is vulnerable because of her belief in the efficacy of personal sacrifice. As in Greek tragedies, the audience, having picked up the clues that Iris liberally sprinkles through her tale, watches in horror as the events unfold relentlessly.

Richard, a villain of Dickensian proportions, lies to and betrays Laura and Iris. His public version of events is colored by his determination to further his image of power and prominence. He is able to manipulate the newspapers to slant stories about his family in a more favorable light. In his private life, in order to dominate and control Iris, he lies and withholds information from her.[5] On his honeymoon trip with Iris, Richard tears up the telegrams informing them about the death of Iris's father. Several years later, to cover up the fact that Laura has become pregnant with Richard's child, Winifred and Richard concoct a story that Laura has had a mental breakdown. They ship her off to a shady abortion clinic-cum-sanitarium and prevent Iris from receiving her letters.

SACRIFICE

Sacrifice, as Howells indicates, is a component of Gothic fiction (Howells, *Love, Mystery and Misery,* 11), and it constitutes an important motif of this novel. Men are sacrificed to the evils of war and economic depression, while the Chase family women are willingly or unwillingly sacrificed for lost causes.

Both the inner and the framing novels comment on the tendency of patriarchal societies to sacrifice women. There is a history of female sacrifice in the Chase family. Iris's grandmother, Adelia Montfort, was married off to Benjamin Chase in order to ensure her financial security. And Iris's mother, Liliana, works as a volunteer for many good causes, sacrificing her health in the process, so that she dies when Iris is nine and Laura is six. Iris and Laura are silenced by their situations and sacrificed by their father, who mistakenly believes that Iris's marriage to Richard Griffen will insure their well-being.

Sacrifice is an ideal that many talk about but that Laura takes quite literally. As a child of six, when Laura asks what sacrifice means (in connection with soldiers said to have "willingly made the supreme sacrifice"), she is told: "They gave their lives to God, because that's what God wants. It's like Jesus, who died for all of our sins" (150). Consequently, Laura believes that she too can sacrifice herself and make pacts with God to save other people. When she is six she tries to drown herself in the belief that this will restore her dead mother to life (150–51). And as a young woman she erroneously believes that she can save Alex Thomas's life by consenting to Richard Griffen's sexual overtures. Richard leads her to believe that he will turn Alex in to the authorities for setting fire to the button factory. Later, she explains to Iris: "It was horrible, but I had to do it. I had to make the sacrifice . . . that's what I promised God. I knew if I did that, it would save Alex" (487). Laura's sacrifice is in vain, for Richard never knew where Alex was hiding. In any event Alex dies in World War II.

Laura kept the secret of Richard's sexual pursuit from Iris. Among the secrets and silences of the novel, this is perhaps the most egregious. Laura's silence combines with the deception practiced by Richard and Winifred to keep Iris from learning Laura's side of the story in time to save her.

But although Laura is silenced in life, she is given voice posthumously through Iris, who tells her story after her suicide. In fact, Iris offers two versions of Laura's story. The first version appears in the novel *The Blind Assassin* 2, purportedly written by Laura. This novel describes the trysts of two unnamed lovers who meet clandestinely in a series of shabby houses. Readers are led to believe that the woman in the story is Laura herself. But Iris tells an alternative (truer?) version in her unpublished memoir, the framing novel *The Blind Assassin* 3. We learn that the upper-class woman who visits a disreputable lover is Iris herself, and the lover is Alex Thomas. By presenting these two parallel versions, Atwood continues her project of laying bare both the complicated relationship between fact and fiction and the duplicitous nature of narrative itself.

NARRATIVE STRATEGIES

In *The Blind Assassin* 3, the story is frequently interrupted by interpolated sections from the "Laura Chase novel" or by newspaper clippings about the social milieu of the Griffen family. Iris's narration takes new turns, and similar stories are repeated by different narrators in different versions. Every character in the novel conceals information, and every character fabricates stories that shape the narration in significant ways. Laura never tells her story of Richard's sexual abuse directly; instead she leaves coded messages. Alex Thomas tells science fiction stories that encode his socialist messages about Canadian society during the Depression and his critique of the moneyed class. Richard Griffen and his sister, Winifred, falsify and censor the information that they convey or withhold. But Iris has her own secrets, too, and manages a satisfying revenge. Indeed, her stories (*The Blind Assassin* 2 and 3) are a means of finding her voice, speaking out after long silence. As often happens in Atwood's novels, the female storyteller comes to understand her life and to exercise power and control through telling her tale. Iris wields her story like a weapon, captivating her readers and gaining justification and revenge against her husband and sister-in-law.

In this book, each of the nested narratives works in its own way to hide and reveal, convey or conceal information, and each of the protagonists is silent or speaks—sometimes openly, more often in code— as she chooses how (or whether) to reveal her emotions, thoughts, and experiences. Thus the novel explores the ways that narrative works by secrecy and cunning, by concealing and revealing. For just as paintings contain white spaces that add depth and contrast to the colored parts, and music may have discords and rests that set off and enrich its harmony and melody, works of fiction both hide and reveal, provide and withhold information.

Each of the genres informing this novel—Gothic, memoir, science fiction and tragedy—relies heavily on hiding and revealing. The Gothic is grounded in secrets and coded knowledge. Memoir pretends to assert the truth, but it can only recount a selection of one person's memories long after the fact. Speculative science-fiction speaks in code, refiguring contemporary society into other times and places. Greek tragedy often derives its power from dramatic irony, as the characters struggle to learn what the audience already knows. Even realist fictions must speak in codes and symbols, and develop their themes by hints and allusions. By including these genres and emphasizing the subterfuge that underlies them, Atwood furthers her metafictive project of revealing the literary conventions that underlie fiction.[6] Moreover, the metafictive project also exposes the social conventions that undermine women's power and strive to silence their voices. According to Gayle Greene, metafiction is "a powerful tool of feminist critique, for to draw attention to the structures of fiction is also to draw attention to the conventionality of the codes that govern human behavior" (1–2).

We trust Iris's narration, although, as she admits, her view is very limited. In her story Richard Griffen remains a flat character, almost a caricature, a Dickensian villain. Whereas Offred, the narrator of Atwood's earlier novel *The Handmaid's Tale,* is able to speak of her oppressive Commander and his wife with sympathy and compassion, Iris never extends this generosity to Richard Griffen. We never see his viewpoint or learn of his early life.

The voice of the eighty-two-year-old Iris is bitter, cynical, wryly humorous, as she contemplates the indignities of her failing body or the deterioration of her family's former mansion. As a child she is stolid, practical, unquestioning. She discovers that the way to gain her mother's approbation is by obedience and silence. As a married woman, insecurity and her fear of her husband effectively silence her. She finds her voice when she leaves Richard and tells the stories of her life.

Laura is the most complex character in *The Blind Assassin* 3. She is always curious, always pressing to learn more, to seek the underlying meanings of what she hears. For Laura, every phrase, every idiom, every word in a poem is a code she must decipher. Innocent, guileless, direct, and almost painfully honest, she takes whatever she hears literally. She continually questions the Bible stories she has learned. She is expelled from a private school because of her unconventional behavior and partly for raising the question: "Does God lie?" She is aware of the perfidy and betrayal at the roots of Western institutions. Yet Laura remains silent about Richard's sexual abuse, because the pact she believes she has made with God demands secrecy. Her most powerful stories are told in code: She colors the faces of the black-and-white family portraits, and cuts passages out of the family Bible.

It is only after Laura's death that Iris learns the significance of the clues she has left (such as the altered wedding picture of Richard with red hands and a flaming skull) that point to Richard's sexual abuse. The final clue lies in the notebooks that she leaves in Iris's drawer the day she drives off the bridge. Through most of the novel we are led to believe Laura's notebooks contain the manuscript of her novel, *The Blind Assassin* 2. Instead, we learn at the end of Iris's memoir that they contain a list of dates, words, and a string of *X*s that form the encrypted revelation of Richard's rape, thus revealing to Iris what she has been too blind to perceive. Iris in fact had been writing the novel to commemorate and record for herself her own affair with Alex Thomas, an affair that she has concealed from both Richard and Laura. In attributing *The Blind Assassin* 2 to Laura, Iris simultaneously hides and reveals her own story. By publishing the novel she is able to proclaim the affair publicly, while shielding herself from blame. Moreover, she promotes the misconception in order to avenge herself against Richard for his betrayal. Presumably, knowledge of Iris's affair might anger Richard, but it would not drive him to kill himself. When he believes it is Laura's story, he kills himself. (Actually, Iris does not make clear the means of his death. The newspaper announces that he has a cerebral hemorrhage, but we are led to believe from Iris's hints that he kills himself.)

• • •

We have seen that the story of Sakiel-Norn is an allegory of the economic injustice, the intrigue and betrayal rampant in the social world of Toronto during the Depression. And Iris's memoir, *The Blind Assassin* 3, operates in a similar fashion, exposing the hypocrisy, the social and economic injustice and spiritual malaise of our world. Blindness, betrayal, sacrifice, and silence lie at the heart of all three stories.

Who, then, is the blind assassin? All of the characters share some of the responsibility for Laura's death. Laura's posthumous farewell message to Iris consists of a passage in her old notebooks, her schoolgirl translation of the conclusion to Book IV of Virgil's *Aeneid,* in which Dido, betrayed by Aeneas, kills herself (abetted by Iris). Thus, Laura indicts Iris as the assassin. And, in an interview Atwood refers to Iris as the blind assassin (Gussow, 2).

But there is another sinister assassin contained in Iris's novel: time itself. In each of the texts that comprise *The Blind Assassin* 3 there are frequent references to time, as for example, "time itself will devour all now alive" (129) in the science-fiction story. The aging Iris thinks about time: "When you're young . . . [y]ou move from now to now, crumpling time up in your hands, tossing it away" (396). Moreover, the title *The Blind Assassin* invites comparison to Emily Dickinson's "blonde assassin." In Dickinson's poem, the "blonde assassin" is the obliterating power of time, the frost that nips the unaware flower in the bud, "beheading" it. And it is partly to forestall time's power and its erosion of memory that Iris writes her first novel to commemorate her love affair. Her second novel aims to influence the future by revealing Sabrina's ancestry, thus giving her the possibility of a new story and a new future.

A secret of parentage often underlies the Gothic, and that is the case here. Finding one's true parent often resolves a mystery and leads to the resolution of the plot. In this novel there are two revelations of paternity: Laura reveals that Richard fathered the child she was compelled to abort. And in her memoir, Iris informs Sabrina that her grandfather was not Richard after all. As she addresses Sabrina at the end of her memoir, Iris explains: "Your real grandfather was Alex Thomas, and as to who his own father was, well, the sky's the limit. . . . Your legacy from him is the realm of infinite speculation. You're free to reinvent yourself at will" (513). By leaving the story for Sabrina, Iris hopes to give her the means of reinventing herself, creating a new identity, a new story.

The denouement of a Gothic fiction typically restores the entrapped heroine to a daylight world where all mysteries are resolved and a young lover supersedes the older man. In this novel, the young lover died in the war many years ago. Iris, now an older woman, clarifies the mysteries, for it turns out that she has held the key to a central secret. The last secret she reveals is the secret of her daughter's paternity, a secret Freudians believe is the original story, the secret at the core of all narrative, all quests for knowledge.

Given the Hell the novel describes, and the inevitability of death and destruction, can there be even a temporary stay against tragedy? I would argue that the novel contains celebration despite its grim tenor. Michelle A. Massé argues that there are ways for women to resist the Gothic. She explains that the "transition from blindness to insight can lead to purposive action through aggression or subversion" (264) and that another approach, the refusal "to accept the binary options of subordinated/oppressed," remains a utopian future possibility (240). I would argue that Iris approaches that utopian possibility. For after she makes "the transition from blindness to insight" with the discovery of Richard's perfidy, she immediately leaves his house and becomes self-supporting, selling antiques, starting with artifacts from the Chase family home. She proves an astute businesswoman. By engaging in business, she transforms herself from a sedate domestic object into an active participant in the world of work. By disposing of the family heirlooms, she indicates her rejection of a tradition that kept women subservient, passive "angels in the house." The angel in the house was supposed to dust and polish the family artifacts; Iris sells them. Thus, the objects that (like the submissive feminine angels in the house themselves) functioned as decorations and objects of conspicuous consumption become the means of her transformation. Through her purposive action she rejects the role of the subservient, dominated wife that had kept her enthralled, and becomes an active agent. Further, by telling the story of her affair and of Richard's misbehavior, she liberates herself from "the binary options of subordinated/oppressed" and has the last word.

Additionally, Iris undergoes another transformation, from being the object of discourse to becoming the subject. At one point Iris feels that she is the blank paper on which someone else is inscribing a story. She thinks of herself as "blank paper, on which—just discernible—there's the colorless imprint of a signature, not hers" (407). At another time she thinks: "I sometimes felt as if these marks on my body [Richard bruises her during sex] were a kind of code, which blossomed, then faded, like invisible ink held to a candle. But if they were a code, who held the key to it? I was sand, I was snow—written on, rewritten, smoothed over" (371). In each of these passages she is the vehicle for someone else's story. But in the end of the novel her story is the one that survives. At one point Iris wonders if she remembers accurately, then decides that her memory is true now because she is "the only survivor" (217–18). Her story is now the official one, and in telling it she registers her resistance to the Gothic plot, her transformation from silence to speech, from dominated wife to independent agent. Thus, amidst the despair and tragedy lies an affirmation of the powers of the imagination and the force of storytelling itself.

Additionally, despite the novel's tragic subject matter, celebration of the imagination and a recognition of the dangers and powers of stories pervades the novel. Alex's fictional hero, the blind assassin, lives by his wits, spinning fictions to save himself from death after the invading army catches him. Alex also lives by his wits, writing under assumed names the science-fiction stories that earn him a meager living while he remains underground, wanted by the police. Laura's coded journal explains her story to Iris. And by her fictions Iris seeks to justify her sister and herself and gain revenge. One of the novel's intertexts is Coleridge's poem "Kubla Khan: or, A Vision in a Dream." Laura questions Iris at some length about the artist/poet figure in the poem (334). Coleridge's incantatory lines here are a celebration of art and the imagination. The dangerous poet with flashing eyes and floating hair has seen a vision and translates it into song:

> And all should cry, Beware! Beware!
> His flashing eyes, his floating hair!
> Weave a circle around him thrice
> And close your eyes with holy dread,
> For he on honey-dew hath fed,
> And drunk the milk of Paradise.

Laura questions why others fear him. But storytellers are all dangerous people; their stories have power to save or destroy, to help or to harm. We need stories to comfort us and to make order out of our lives. For we live in a complex and ambiguous world. In Paradise or utopia there is no need for stories, for "Happiness is a garden walled with glass: there's no way in or out. In Paradise there are no stories, because there are no journeys" (518). But for us who inhabit the real world, stories are essential: "It's loss and regret and misery and yearning that drive the story forward, along its twisted road" (518). The stories we tell may be ambiguous, incomplete, an uncertain blend of truth and lies. Yet this is what gives them their power.

Laura imagines that Heaven is a place where everyone sits at a circular table, so that everyone is at someone's right hand (513). The more practical Iris often reminds her sister that we do not live in Heaven yet. Accordingly, because her story reveals the sinister aspects of life that we usually try to overlook or hide she names it a "left-handed book" (513).

In his *Republic* Plato calls poets liars and, consequently, banishes them from his ideal society. Margaret Atwood agrees that storytellers lie. In *Murder in the Dark*, she claims that writers are inveterate prevaricators. Indeed, her novel *The Blind Assassin* contains three interlocking novels narrated by characters who lie by omission or commission. Not only do the storytellers themselves lie, but the stories they narrate are about treachery, betrayal, guile, encryption, disguise, and downright falsehood. But, whereas Plato would cast storytellers out of his society, Atwood, recognizing that our world is a fallen one, invites them in.

NOTES

1. Atwood's use of two stone angels in the graveyard alludes to Margaret Laurence's *The Stone Angel* (1961), an important Canadian novel, narrated by another cantankerous old woman, Hagar Shipley.

2. The concept of apparent solidity overlaying a threatening depth is prominent in Atwood's first published book, *The Circle Game* (1966). One of its poems, "A Place: Fragments," reads "Watch that man / walking on cement as though on snowshoes: / senses the road / a muskeg, . . . or crust of ice that / easily might break" (89).

3. Fire imagery is prevalent in each of the narratives. For example, in Laura's novel the young woman tells her lover "you'll burn yourself up" (10). During the Depression, disaffected employees or union agitators set Norval Chase's button factory on fire and burn effigies of Chase and his daughters. The eighty-two-year-old Iris even quotes from Milton's *Paradise Lost* to describe a burger restaurant called The Fire Pit with references to Lucifer's fiery fall from Heaven (293–94).

4. Lying is, of course, a betrayal of trust, and reinforcing the idea of betrayal, the novel contains abundant intertextual references to other fictions on this theme. The décor of the Chase family home includes stained glass windows depicting Tristran and Iseult, legendary treacherous lovers (60–61). The Chase family house is named Avilion for the place where King Arthur went to die after he was betrayed. Repeated allusions to the Arthurian legend remind us of the perfidious lovers Guinivere and Launcelot. Several quotations from Milton's *Paradise Lost* allude to Lucifer's betrayal of God and of Adam and Eve. Taking her laundry down to the basement, the eighty-two-year-old Iris thinks of herself as Little Red Riding Hood, reminding us of sexual predation. Most ominously, Laura's posthumous farewell message to Iris consists of a passage in her old notebooks, her schoolgirl translation of the conclusion to Book IV of Virgil's *Aeneid,* in which Dido, betrayed by Aeneas, kills herself (abetted by Iris).

5. Several feminist theorists explore lying as a moral issue of particular relevance to women. For example, Adrienne Rich, in her essay "Women and Honor: Some Notes on Lying" (1975), writes: "Women have been driven mad, 'gaslighted,' for centuries by the refutation of our experience and our instincts in a culture which validates only male experience. The truth of our bodies and our minds has been mystified to us. We therefore have a primary obligation to each other: not to undermine each others' sense of reality for the sake of expediency" (190). bell hooks writes: "men use lying, and that includes withholding information, as a way to control and subordinate" (40).

6. As she does here, Atwood often writes metafiction, a project defined as fiction that "self-consciously examine[s] the nature of fiction itself" (Murfin and Ray, 210).

. . . .

Talking Back to Bluebeard:
Atwood's Fictional Storytellers

"A large invisible thumb descended from the sky and pressed down on" Margaret Atwood's head as she walked home from school one day, and "a poem formed" (Atwood, *This Magazine,* 43). In this tongue-in-cheek manner, Atwood explains her inauguration as a writer. Well, perhaps. Let's look at her assertion more closely later. By means of this fiction she authorizes herself as a storyteller. As we read her novels we find that many of her female characters are also writers and/or oral storytellers. Why so many storytellers? What invisible thumbs press down on their heads? (Atwood's, of course, but how does she explain that thumb imprint?) In many cases, a symbol marks the moment when the thumb presses, turning them into storytellers. Elsewhere I discuss the theme of Atwood's storytelling from a different perspective (*Margaret Atwood Revisited*). Here I am interested in what storytelling means to her female protagonists. How and why do they become storytellers? How do their stories function to resolve their conflicts?

Storytelling is a powerful tool that these protagonists employ to develop an understanding of and relationship to the world. By telling her story, a person composes and inscribes her social self. Justine Cassell argues that "storytelling [is] a place where one decides who to be—where one constructs a social self—and where a perspective is maintained on one's own life—where one resists the attempts by more powerful others to silence that perspective" (Cassell, "Storytelling as a Nexus of Change," 310). By telling their stories, Atwood's female protagonists come to terms with their personal histories, assert their perspectives, and resist the attempts of others to silence them.

Compared to other contemporary novels, a surprisingly large proportion of Atwood's fiction (especially the more recent works) is told through the protagonists' narration rather than by dramatization. Most of the action they describe has either already occurred or happens offstage. For example, most of *Alias Grace* takes place in dialogue and exchange of letters many years after the main plot actions, the murders of Thomas Kinnear and Nancy Montgomery, have taken place. *The Robber Bride* has almost no "on-stage" action at all in the narrative present; three women meet, eat, and repeat their stories of past betrayals, and witness a death that has occurred. In *The Handmaid's Tale* Offred describes her rather passive life after a violent revolution; she chiefly waits for others, thinks, or sleeps (excellent conditions for developing into a storyteller). Moreover, Atwood deliberately blurs temporal and spatial references so that the reader may confuse the narrative time and the diegetic present. We learn at the end of several novels that the present-tense narrative is inscribed retrospectively, and perhaps, as in the case of *The Handmaid's Tale,* has been edited and altered by others. *Bodily Harm,* a detective thriller replete with violence, politics, drugs, and revolution, is the most action-oriented of Atwood's novels. Yet all of this action has already happened offstage, for we learn that the narrative is recounted in a few hours as two women who share a prison cell tell each other their life stories, using the third-person present tense.[1]

Strikingly, when depicting such dramas of violence and struggle, these novels focus on the telling rather than the action. We may suspect that the narrative process is as important as the stories. There may be several reasons for this focus. One reason is that first-person narration allows the reader the possibility of greater empathy for the characters. Because we hear their thoughts and recognize their feelings, we come to understand them, to enter their worlds, and to appreciate their motives. Thus, the stranger becomes more familiar. Atwood writes: "If writing novels—and reading them—have any redeeming social value, it's probably that they force you to imagine what it's like to be somebody else. Which, increasingly, is something we all need to know" (*Second Words,* 430). Clearly Atwood does believe in the "redeeming social value" of novels, and her emphasis on storytelling calls attention to the teller's/novelist's role.

Another explanation is that Atwood wishes us to hear women's voices and women's stories, for they have often been unheard, silenced, or ignored. Women have, as Offred claims, lived on the margins rather than in the text. Thus, in *Bodily Harm* we hear the voice of a woman who would be a minor character in the margins of a detective thriller. In *Cat's Eye* we hear the portrait of an artist as a young (and middle-aged) woman. In *The Handmaid's Tale* we hear the voice of a woman bound into sexual slavery.

Women's voices may tell alternative versions of traditional stories or reveal hidden, dangerous knowledge. For example, whereas many of the classic utopian fictions present male narrators delightedly describing male-centered social orders, Offred recounts a woman's vastly different view of such a society. Thus, another reason for using women narrators may be the wish to deconstruct and rewrite traditional plots. In her novels of quest and adventure, Atwood rewrites typical action-driven, male-centered plots from a woman's point of view, thus developing new emphases and critiquing traditional stories. For example, in *Surfacing* a woman's quest for her mother takes on greater symbolic power than the more traditional male quest for the father (Grace, "In Search of Demeter," 43–44). Rather than accentuate external action, the more recent novels reveal the implications and consequences of action-driven plots, as when *Bodily Harm* uses thriller strategies to demonstrate "that the thriller style itself may be dangerous" because of its simplistic treatment of "international politics and male-female relationships" (Patton, 163).[2]

But Atwood also critiques traditional women's plots. *Lady Oracle* deconstructs the stereotypical woman's Gothic romance plot as its open-ended conclusion sets up a contrast between the reassuringly neat resolutions of the romance fantasies that Joan Foster writes and the messy, unresolved predicaments of Joan's life. A key issue in these reconfigured plots is the amount of power female protagonists obtain. And storytelling turns out to be crucial for gaining power.

BECOMING A STORYTELLER

The theme of power attained through storytelling is a central one in Atwood's recent novels and in her second collection of stories, *Bluebeard's Egg* (1983). In the early novels the female characters' voices are usually weak and uncertain, perhaps even mute. In the later novels their voices grow stronger, more confident. The stories in *Bluebeard's Egg* represent characters at different points on the storyteller continuum, ranging from the silent, almost paralyzed Alma ("The Salt Garden") to the assertive storyteller, the narrator's mother ("Significant Moments in the Life of My Mother"). Some of these storytellers are tricksters who use narrative self-consciously to draw us into their confidence (perhaps also to con us) and to control the outcomes. How do their lives lead them to become spinners of tales?

Unhappy childhoods frequently predispose the protagonists to become storytellers. As children they may feel alienated or isolated. Their families seem different from others. Their parents are often absent (*The Handmaid's Tale, The Robber Bride, Life before Man*), or family members may be abusive (*Lady Oracle, The Robber Bride*). To escape from their unpleasant situations, the protagonists take refuge in fantasies that may include wordplay, such as Tony Fremont's reverse code. Thus, when the thumb descends, the women are already primed to be receptive to the imperative of narration.

Many of the protagonists, such as Joan Foster (*Lady Oracle*) or Rennie Wilford (*Bodily Harm*) work as writers or symbol makers of one kind or another. Before the revolution that stripped all women of their jobs, Offred (*The Handmaid's Tale*) transcribed books onto computer disks. Artists such as the nameless narrator of *Surfacing* and Elaine Risley of *Cat's Eye* tell stories through visual symbols. And even more characters are storytellers, producers of oral narratives.

Starting in childhood and continuing into adulthood, the protagonists feel vulnerable and powerless; they see themselves as victims. Indeed, Atwood claims that a central theme of Canadian literature is victimization, and her texts generate their share of victims. But she asserts that characters may move out of the victim position through reflection, introspection, and personal transformation (*Survival*, 36–39). Although the most obvious and physically dangerous instances of victimization occur in the most politically oppressive societies, often the victimization happens more subtly as a result of social convention or the workings of sexual politics, and the protagonists may be unaware of or deny their victimization.

An important intertextual motif running through many of Atwood's novels, the tale-type of Bluebeard, illustrates the sexual politics of victimization and indicates how victims may use storytelling to gain power and become what Atwood terms "creative non-victims." Folktales frequently exist in several versions, and the Grimm brothers retell several related versions of the Bluebeard tale-type. In these tales of betrayal and murder, an evil man murders a series of young women until the clever heroine outwits him, saves herself, and brings about his death. "The Robber Bridegroom" version is the most relevant for my purposes here, for in this version the heroine achieves her escape through storytelling, by asserting her perspective and resisting the robber's attempt to silence (and murder!) her. In this version the villain's fiancée feels uneasy and does not trust her intended husband. Her suspicions prove to be well founded, for she discovers his penchant for murder and cannibalism. At the wedding feast, when urged to entertain the guests with a story, she divulges her secret knowledge under the pretense that she is telling a dream (Zipes, *The Complete Fairy Tales of the Brothers Grimm,* 153–57). Although she presents her information in the guise of fiction, she proves its accuracy by revealing a finger chopped off one of his victims. By means of this tale she saves her own life. This motif of telling a story in order to name and blame an evildoer recurs in different forms in Atwood's fiction as her protagonists face dangers and struggle—with varying degrees of success—to save themselves and to make their voices heard. Sharon Rose Wilson explicates the Bluebeard tales as stories about the woman married to Death in the form of a destructive man, or a culture that is "dead or death-worshipping" (Wilson, *Margaret Atwood's Fairy-Tale Sexual Politics,* 199). To avoid the trap of real or psychic death, women must use their "powers of imagination, cunning, voice or art" (Wilson, *Margaret Atwood's Fairy-Tale Sexual Politics,* 260). The successful storyteller saves herself and turns the tables on her victimizer.

Yet there are several paradoxes involved in achieving a voice. Nathalie Cooke notes the amalgam of power and powerlessness that characterizes many of these protagonists. Using the example of Atwood's Siren, who lures her victims to their death by proclaiming her helplessness ("Siren Song"), Cooke identifies in many of Atwood's women a "powerful voice that asserts its own powerlessness" (Cooke, "The Politics of Ventriloquism," 215). It is important to recognize that the power the protagonists gain does not inhere in their social or political positions; it derives from their own authorization and self-assertion, from their voices. Telling the story is the act that gives them power. The metaphorical thumbs that press on their heads and spur them to tell their stories come from their own insights or compulsions. If the Robber Bridegroom's fiancée did not tell her story, she would undoubtedly meet the same death as his other wives. If the Siren were silent, she would pose no threat to sailors. Clearly, finding a voice is part of the survival strategy, a means to gain power and control.

How, then, do the heroines find the voices to talk back to the Robber Bridegrooms and Bluebeards who seek to silence them? We can see

Atwood's protagonists move from silence and denial toward power and assertiveness as we read her fictions chronologically. In the early novels the characters' voices are weak and tentative. They feel discomfort but lack the vocabulary to address its causes. As we continue our readings, we see them gathering strength and becoming more self-assertive, better able to tell their stories and to resist oppressive individuals and an oppressive social order. This development parallels the evolution of feminist social and political analyses beginning in the late 1960s. When feminist theorists began to name and define oppressive conditions, many women gained the language and the courage to express their discomfort. Through naming and articulating their experiences, women achieve clarity and focus. This often leads them to take action. As women begin to name the problems, to identify the causes, they may begin to resist those who would silence them, to address personal and social issues, and thus to gain control and power.[3] This is the process of talking back to Bluebeard.

EARLY NOVELS

In Atwood's first two published novels, *The Edible Woman* (1969) and *Surfacing* (1972), the protagonists develop awareness of their victimization chiefly through symbols rather than words, largely because they lack the language for analysis. Atwood wrote *The Edible Woman* just as the second wave of the feminist movement was emerging, before it began to articulate its analyses of sexual power relations and of patriarchal oppression.[4] Betty Friedan's landmark book, *The Feminine Mystique,* appeared in 1963, just two years before Atwood composed *The Edible Woman.* Friedan describes the "problem without a name," the depression many women felt in those years. She attributes their malaise to their relative powerlessness and their restricted roles as 1950s and early '60s housewives. Kate Millett's more analytical *Sexual Politics* appeared in 1970, two years before *Surfacing* was published. Millett gave a name to "the problem" Friedan describes: sexism, sexual politics.

The Bluebeards confronting the heroines of Atwood's first two novels are their male friends and lovers. Both women are uncomfortable with the conventional courtship process as they struggle with stereotypes of passive women and assertive men. Although she attempts to fit the stereotypically passive feminine role, Marian McAlpin experiences the unnamed malaise that Friedan documents. She fears her fiancé wants to destroy her (*The Edible Woman*). By the novel's conclusion little has changed. Atwood comments in an interview with Linda Sandler that Marian ends where she began: *The Edible Woman* is "more pessimistic than *Surfacing*. . . The Edible Woman* is a circle and *Surfacing* is a spiral" (Sandler, 14). Interestingly, although both protagonists work as symbol makers, neither defines herself as a writer or an artist, as do some of the later protagonists.

Although Marian's job is to translate the obscure language of psychologists into common speech for consumer surveys, she is unable to translate into words her own fears that her fiancé is trying to destroy her. Instead, she becomes anorexic, enacting her resistance to the traditional female romance plot with her body rather than with language. Increasingly concerned over her fiancé's domination, Marian feels herself shrinking and acts out this fear by consuming less and less food. Afraid that she is becoming an object of consumption, she contrives to test her version of reality: "what she needed was something that avoided words . . . a test" (279). She bakes a cake in the form of a woman and offers it to her fiancé as a substitute. The symbolic cake thus speaks for her, exorcising her demon lover and becoming a festive symbol of Marian's self-assertion as she enjoys consuming the confection she has constructed.

Similarly, the unnamed narrator of *Surfacing* uses symbolic gestures (a dive, a ritual spirit quest, and a period of silence) rather than language to explore her predicament. The narrator's quest leads her from the sterile and stultifying world of the city to a green but threatened island and culminates in a vision of symbolic and silent connection with each of her parents. At the book's end she resolves to enter the world of language again, knowing that it will entail miscommunication, but accepting the risks.

The narrator of *Lady Oracle* (1976), Joan Foster, is a more slippery protagonist, a writer of Gothic romance fictions in which heroines are rescued from Bluebeard and married to Prince Charming. In her own life Joan is unable to manage this feat. Although she escapes from a series of Bluebeards (including her mother: women can also be oppressors), she has not yet found her Prince Charming. Yet she does have a knack for escaping from problems, and it appears that her lively imagination will keep producing new evasions.

Joan identifies the moment when she experiences the metaphorical thumb press, her transformation into a writer, as the moment when she moves into an ornate hotel. In that setting her fantasies of villains and heroines bloom (136). This moment also indicates her conflation of the fantasy romance world with the real, external world: Both her fictions and her life are built on disguise and trickery. At the novel's conclusion she wonders if such an identification with her Gothic romance novels is bad for her. Her fiction may also encourage her readers to embrace society's idealization of romance. Nevertheless, her writing provides her with the money to escape from threats against her life and to flee to Italy, where she narrates the story of her past escapades that comprises the novel. A self-confessed Houdini, Joan does not so much talk back to Bluebeard as evade him. While *Lady Oracle* is a comic novel with a focus on sexual politics, Atwood's next two novels are more serious explorations of human rights issues that raise questions about the individual's responsibility to bear witness and thus to expose Bluebeard publicly.

LATER NOVELS

Bodily Harm (1981) and *The Handmaid's Tale* (1985) examine institutional politics and human rights issues. The Bluebeards here are not only demon lovers as in the earlier novels; they are corrupt politicians, despotic rulers, political revolutionaries, men who love power and danger. The female protagonists here have little power; they are at the mercy of often corrupt male authorities. In response to these threats, they determine to bear witness to social evils, to expose the political dangers. And, by making their voices heard, they become somewhat more powerful themselves.

Bodily Harm speaks explicitly about the writer's duty to be a voice for social justice. The novel's protagonist, Rennie Wilford, ultimately decides to become an investigative reporter, to point the finger at Bluebeard. She has resisted this mandate, preferring her superficial role as a lifestyle reporter. But her trip to a West Indian nation seething with poverty, violence, and political turmoil convinces her of the necessity to become an investigative reporter and to speak out. For much of the novel she is surprisingly oblivious to the political dangers that surround her, and she seems almost willfully determined to remain a victim. It takes a metaphorical sledgehammer rather than a thumbprint to move her to a position of resistance. She is deliberately blind to much of the brutality, corruption, and abuse she sees. The turning point arrives when her cellmate, Lora, is brutally beaten, perhaps killed. Rennie grasps her hand and licks her wounds, allowing herself to feel more deeply than she has previously and to become "massively involved." She vows to write the story of what she has seen if she returns home alive.

In contrast to Rennie's prolonged reluctance to write the story of political corruption and violence, Offred in *The Handmaid's Tale* is eager to tell her story. She paints a dystopian picture of Gilead, a fundamentalist totalitarian regime that denies literacy to women and hangs its "political criminals" in public view. In Gilead, storytelling is a rebellious act, yet it may gain Offred's salvation. It is a way for her to "compose herself," to give coherence to her experiences. It enables her to keep memories of her friends and family alive. Moreover, telling her stories may empower her to create new possibilities and new selves, to inscribe her perspective, and to resist the attempts of more powerful people to silence her. Telling her story may also be a way to spread the word about Gilead to other countries, and thus bear witness to its destructiveness.

Among Gilead's crimes are its denial of reading and writing to women. The government attempts to enforce one story on its subjects; therefore it erases and rewrites history. Women are supposed to remain in their homes and be silent. Offred comments wryly that enforced silence doesn't seem to agree with the wife of her Commander, and she speculates that the Commander's life must be a silent one as well. In telling her story, especially in speaking of her desires, Offred inscribes a story that runs counter to the official narrative.

Storytelling becomes an absorbing project for Offred. It is important to her that there be a listener, a person who receives the story. She is ambivalent and wishes her tale were more coherent, less fragmented, less shameful. She wishes it were fiction, because "then I have control over the ending. Then there will be an ending, to the story, and real life will come after it. It isn't a story I'm telling. It's also a story I'm telling" (52).

As we read the book, Offred's present-tense narrative appears to be an inner monologue recounting her daily life. Yet in the epilogue, we learn that the tale is really a composed narrative, spoken into a tape recorder some time after the fact.[5] Indeed, as the narrative proceeds, Offred becomes increasingly conscious of herself as a narrator, sometimes worrying about how accurately she renders remembered events, sometimes proffering several versions of an incident (such as her initial tryst with Nick). Many scholars have examined Offred's narrative strategies. Lee Briscoe Thompson makes several interesting observations about Offred as author. She notes that the groups of young women being trained (reeducated) to be handmaids are required to inform on others or to testify against themselves. To comply with these demands they start to invent stories about themselves (59). Thus, ironically, the oppressive institutions of Gilead train Offred to become a better storyteller and to perfect her means of resistance. Thompson points out that Offred experiences "anxieties about artistic goals" (40).

In fact, the emphasis of the book shifts "from her longing to escape to her much more often mentioned anxiety to tell her story as accurately as possible" (59). She is becoming an author. As Hilde Staels explains: "Gilead censors the threatening force of creative self-expression. Yet Offred defies the strict rules of authoritative discourse by giving life to a silenced discourse" (459). Glenn Deer points to a paradox inherent in Offred's narration: "Atwood's text compels us to see her narrator in two ways that are not entirely congruent: as an innocent recorder and as a skilled, self-conscious rhetorician and storyteller" (226). Where Deer perceives this paradox as a flaw in the novel, I argue it is the key to Atwood's storytelling here.[6] For Offred's narration models that of the novelist, the professional storyteller. To achieve her aims the novelist must often appear to be the innocent recorder at the same time that she is the skilled rhetorician.[7] Therein lies her authorial power. Offred's narrative gains credibility from her status as "innocent recorder," innocent witness to the events she reports, but it gains in artistry and impact from her rhetorical skill.

In Atwood's next four novels, *Cat's Eye, The Robber Bride, Alias Grace,* and *The Blind Assassin,* her most accomplished storytellers appear to be innocent recorders, yet they use their rhetorical skills to achieve their goals: to trick others, to teach valuable lessons, to gain revenge for past slights, to heal themselves, to assert their perspectives, to resist those who would silence them, and to gain power. These are the tricksters, figures that Atwood associates with all writers ("Murder in the Dark," in Atwood, *Murder in the Dark*). The trickster has a long history in traditional folklores.[8] He or she typically teaches, tricks, and entertains using a combination of story, parody, gesture, and joke. Elaine Risley of *Cat's Eye* obtains revenge on her childhood tormentors by painting parodic portraits. Zenia in *The Robber Bride* is the consummate trickster, who cons her friends and steals their men. Grace Marks in *Alias Grace* uses her rhetorical skill to win a temporary respite from prison and to convince influential supporters that she is innocent. Iris Chase Griffen in *The Blind Assassin* exposes her husband's treachery through her storytelling.

All of the characters in *The Robber Bride* (1993) create fictions. They change their names to shed unhappy pasts and they create new life stories, new identities for themselves. Zenia is the most proficient of these storytellers. She has a story for every occasion, and she devises a new identity for every situation. Yet we never hear her stories directly; they come to us filtered through the narratives of the three other protagonists. As a result, she remains mysterious, a dark stranger, while the others sustain their roles of innocent recorders. She is the perceived enemy, a sexy Siren who lures men away from other women and then abandons them. Like the Siren in Atwood's poem, she gains her power by professing that she is powerless and asserting that her listener is powerful and unique; she asks for help that only the listener can provide. By means of her stories, she charms each of the characters in succession. She is the consummate trickster, a tale teller, and a liar. The novel's other women (Roz, Charis, and Tony) believe that she is evil. Yet her function is crucial. For through her fabrications, she rescues the good women from their Bluebeards; Roz's womanizing husband, Mitch; and Charis's freeloading lover, Billy. She is uncannily aware of the other characters' secret dreams and aspirations. In turn, in their mixture of fear and admiration for Zenia, they grow to understand that she represents unacknowledged parts of themselves, their desires for power, their secret wishes for revenge.

In her introduction to *The Robber Bride* Atwood explicitly links tricksters such as Zenia and novelists: "Zenia is, among other things, an illusionist. She tells stories so plausible that each of her listeners believes her. . . . but isn't this the goal of every novelist—to deceive? Doesn't every novelist play Zenia to every reader's willing dupe? We writers like to feel there is another kind of truth concealed in the stories we tell, though each of our stories is—we say so ourselves!—a pack of lies. And perhaps Zenia, too, arch-liar though she is, tells a form of truth" (4).

Grace Marks in *Alias Grace* is a similar trickster. She is apparently powerless, yet she contrives to liberate herself from prison through her carefully crafted storytelling. She gains a temporary furlough from prison in order to talk to Dr. Simon Jordan, a young physician who utilizes the new techniques of psychotherapy in hopes that by encouraging her storytelling he will elicit her suppressed memories of the events surrounding the Kinnear and Montgomery murders. Her stories are plausible, yet we never know whether or not they are true. She holds Jordan spellbound, yet she does not reveal the information he most wants to learn. Literally incarcerated (where other Atwood protagonists have been figuratively imprisoned in their own fears or in oppressive cultures), Grace Marks seems to be the most trapped of the women. She is imprisoned for a murder she may or may not have committed. Yet she uses her talents as a storyteller and her gift for role-playing (she is a "model prisoner") to win advocates who may use their influence to obtain her freedom. As her story unfolds in dialogue with Dr. Jordan, we are aware of her control of her narrative. She chooses her words carefully, deciding what to reveal and what to conceal. She tells a compelling story rich in details about her life, yet when she has finished, the crucial questions about her complicity in the murder remain unanswered.

Iris Chase Griffen tells her story in an intricately layered text that provides her the means of escaping from her abusive husband and avenging herself on him (see "Left-Handed Story" in this volume).

We have seen that the protagonists of Atwood's novels often gain power and escape the victim role through telling stories. We will now turn to her short story collection *Bluebeard's Egg*, for that is where Atwood sets forth a fictional representation of a family history shaping the narrator into a storyteller.

BLUEBEARD'S EGG

Although there are plenty of Bluebeards in this book, few of the women in this collection have developed into assertive storytellers. For example, in the title story, "Bluebeard's Egg," Sally abdicates her power and keeps silent because she focuses on her husband to her own exclusion. Afraid to confront him with her suspicions that he is unfaithful, Sally is voiceless and powerless, unable to talk back to Bluebeard, unable to write her own story. In another story, Loulou struggles against the linguistic artifice and arrogance of the male poets who freeload in her house ("Loulou, or, The Domestic Life of the Language").

"The Sin Eaters," a richly symbolic fiction about the healing power of storytelling, appears in the 1983 McClelland (Canadian) edition and the 1998 Anchor (U.S.) edition of the *Bluebeard's Egg* collection. The narrator of "The Sin Eaters" links storytelling with confession and redemption from sin. She laments the death of her therapist, Joseph, for he was the person to whom she told her stories. After his funeral the reader presumably becomes the listener to whom the narrator tells her story, and thus, by implication, serves as confessor and "sin eater" (Stein, *Revisited*, 132–33).

The first and last stories in this collection depict a consummate storyteller and indicate how the narrator's childhood prepared her to become a writer, to interpret that thumbprint as a poem. Her family's summers in the bush without the distractions of a city—movies, television, radio—encouraged her to read and sharpened her sense of observation and her imagination: "most of the time I lived a life of contemplation. Insofar as was possible I sneaked off into the woods to read books and evade tasks" (311).

The narrator's parents are skilled storytellers, as well as self-sufficient, imaginative, resourceful, and energetic people. The family depicted here avoids the conventional and limiting stereotypes of femininity: passivity, consumerism, narcissism, and powerlessness. In contrast to the dysfunctional families in much of Atwood's fiction, this family is supportive and creative; children and parents share stories and enjoy each other's company. When we look for a model of a creative nonvictim, the mother represented in these stories is Atwood's best example. She is a self-confident, vibrant, unconventional, and courageous woman.

The family stories in this collection are purportedly autobiographical fictions (Atwood interview with Lyons, 225).[9] Autobiography, of course, is always told in retrospect; it is filtered through memory, and is a construct, a choice, a selection, and therefore always to some degree fictional. The narrator speaks in the first person, in the role of innocent reporter, although she is a skilled rhetorician who shapes the narrative to achieve her purposes. She accentuates her mother's capability and energy in contrast to her own (self-proclaimed) incompetence and lethargy. Through her self-deprecation she invites the reader to identify with her and to share her admiration, even awe, of her resourceful and practical mother.

The narrator spent her childhood living alternately in the bush and the city. This connection to the bush is significant because in the Atwood canon the city is Bluebeard's domain and the bush is its antithesis. The bush is a green world of curves, of possibilities, of boundary crossings, whereas Bluebeard's territory is the gray urban world of straight lines and grids, of rules and fences. The city's linearity is stifling and deathlike; those who attempt to live by its codes suffer constraint, ennui, despair, and madness.[10] The city stands for a sterile and regimented rationality, the bush for imagination and the irrational. The bush is the site of spontaneity, of connection to a vibrant life force; it is the home of the trickster. Certainly the bush harbors dangers—treacherous terrain, extreme weather, and wild animals—but it is a world that allows greater freedom from conventions, that offers room for individuality, for recognition of mystery. In contrast, the culture of the city promotes rigidity, constraint, stultifying conventionality, and stereotyped sex and gender roles. In these texts Bluebeard lurks metaphorically as the deadening urban culture that some of the heroines, chiefly the mother of "Significant Moments," are able to resist.[11]

The first story in *Bluebeard's Egg,* "Significant Moments in the Life of My Mother," establishes the mother's childhood as the daughter of a highly respected country doctor. The narrator recognizes the conventional family power hierarchy but acknowledges the special insights and secret lore of women, thus preparing us for the stories to come. The grandfather was the patriarch, at the top of the household hierarchy, but the house's "secret life . . . was female" (4). The house itself is presented as a powerful repository of secrets, untold stories: "The house, and all the objects in it, crackled with static electricity; undertows washed through it, the air was heavy with things that were known but not spoken. Like a hollow log, a drum, a church, it amplified, so that conversations whispered in it sixty years ago can be half-heard even today" (4). In telling her stories, the mother gives form and voice to these echoes.

The narrator's mother here is an unconventional woman who, in marrying, opted for an adventurous life, joining as a full partner with her husband, who spent a large part of each year living in different areas of the bush, where he conducted entomological fieldwork. She worked with him each year to set up tents for the family to live in while they built a more permanent cabin in which she cooked, cleaned, and managed family life without electricity, telephone, or running water. She kept the children fed, entertained, and comfortable during the times when her husband's field trips took him away for days or weeks.

The narrator's mother is a gifted storyteller who acts out the parts and even provides the sound effects: "my mother's face turns to rubber. She takes all the parts, adds the sound effects, waves her hands around in the air. Her eyes gleam, sometimes a little wickedly, for although my mother is sweet and old and a lady, she avoids being a sweet old lady" (8). Moreover she has a keen sense of audience and tailors her tales to appeal to particular audiences. The darkest stories of emotional drama and tragedy she reserves for women, because she believes men would be too upset by them. From her the narrator learns to be a storyteller, to listen to women's voices, and to resist the bourgeois world of stultifying conventionality.[12]

The events identified as "significant moments" seem not very important: getting permission to get her hair cut, playing in a tree house. Yet, cumulatively, the anecdotes of the mother's childhood in the book's first story, and the incidents of her adult life in the closing story, "Unearthing Suite," are significant, for in the telling the mother builds connections with her daughter and creates a shared past. Moreover, she models the storyteller's art. Most significantly, her anecdotes describe her life journey, pointing out how she escaped a life of boring conventionality in a middle-class urban setting to become her own person, a creative nonvictim: "Her marriage was an escape from its alternatives. Instead of becoming the wife of some local small-town professional and settling down, in skirts and proper surroundings, to do charity work for the church as would have befitted her status, she married my father and took off down the St. John's river in a canoe. . . . She . . . must have felt that she had been rescued from a fate worse than death: antimacassars on the chairs" (312).

A contrasting pair of trivial incidents will illustrate this passage from repressed young woman to powerful, unconventional adult. In "Significant Moments" the mother tells of a youthful misadventure. As a student at Normal School (teacher's college), she participated in an amateur theater production. For the role, she brought a cat needed as a prop. She wrapped the cat in a burlap sack and carried it on her lap as she and a male friend drove to the theater. During the drive, the cat became frightened and peed, soaking the sack and her skirt. "We didn't talk about such things then," confesses the mother as she remembers how she stared ahead in embarrassment and horror. Unable to break the conventional silence surrounding such an incident, both she and her friend were embarrassed and uncomfortable (11). But she was eventually able to surmount such constraining conventions, chiefly by marrying her husband and taking up a life that the narrator describes as nomadic, alternating between city and bush.

The book closes with another trivial incident that dramatically contrasts with the earlier cat incident. At the book's close, the narrator explains how her mother, still active now at seventy-three, was "clambering nimbly about" on the steeply pitched roof of their house, sweeping off the leaves, when she found the droppings of a fisher (a rare, small furry mammal) on her roof. She sees the droppings as a sign of grace, "a miraculous token" (323). Happy to see them, she joyfully shares this information. In her role as storyteller the mother reads nature's signs and invests the incident with symbolic importance. She communicates her perspective to others who might have perceived the occurrence differently. To her husband, in contrast, the events are simply a fact of nature.

The embarrassing cat incident took place in a car, a constrained enclosed space identified with the urban world and its technology. In contrast, the inspiring fisher event occurs out of doors as the mother is climbing on the roof, symbolically on top of her house, restoring order. Whereas she was previously locked into urban conventions and forced to be uncomfortably silent about the cat urine, she now participates in the natural world and is free to be happily vocal about the fisher droppings. Of course, there is a historical factor operating here as well; taboos about what may be said in polite company have loosened. Nevertheless, the contrasting anecdotes work symbolically to make a point. The narrator's mother now successfully asserts her own perspective, lives the active and adventurous life she has chosen, resists the deadening social conventions that would try to constrain and silence her, and passes her legacy of independence, power, and storytelling to her daughter.

* * *

Clearly, for Atwood storytelling has value in itself. She believes narrative has moral authority and may teach as well as entertain:

> I believe that poetry is the heart of the language, the activity through which language is renewed and kept alive. I believe that fiction writing is the guardian of the moral and ethical sense of the community. Especially now that organized religion is scattered and in disarray, and politicians have, Lord knows, lost their credibility, fiction is one of the few forms left through which we may examine our society not in its particular but in its typical aspects; through which we can see ourselves and the ways in which we behave towards each other, through which we can see others and judge them and ourselves. (*Second Words*, 346)

She takes a strong moral stance, as evidenced by her essays on politics and human rights in *Second Words* and by her work on behalf of Amnesty International and PEN. Yet she conveys her position primarily in fiction and only secondarily in essays. For fiction is the medium of the illusionist, the trickster. As we have noted, the trickster employs story, parody, and joke. The novelist is simultaneously an illusionist, a seemingly innocent recorder, and a rhetorician. Accordingly, fiction may operate on many levels at once. It may both make assertions and question them; it may suggest many possibilities; it may be simultaneously serious and parodic or comic; and it may convey moral concerns as well as psychological and symbolic material. Atwood's fiction is many-layered, rich with allusion, and open-ended. Thus it remains open to multiple interpretations and to innuendo. Fiction allows the writer to present experience in all its complex richness.

As Atwood's successive narrators grow more self-aware, they approach the role of the trickster, the illusionist. They may develop narrative strategies to further their own storytelling goals, to move from victimization to positions of power. They may speak in the voice of the innocent recorder even as they employ their rhetorical skills to create complex and multifaceted fictions. In creating her female storytellers Atwood gives voice to the formerly silent, allowing them to express their encoded wisdom, their dangerous knowledge. She presents them as innocent reporters or even sometimes as airheads, but she empowers them to expose sexual politics and dangers to human rights, to resist those who would silence them, and to talk back to Bluebeard.

NOTES

I wish to thank Elena Gonzales, Karen Markin, Larry Rothstein, Linda Shamoon, Jon Sutinen, and Sharon Wilson for their suggestions and comments on successive drafts of this paper. Thanks also to Marta Dvorak and Lee Briscoe Thompson for their careful readings.

1. In fact, Lorna Irvine suggests that the novel's action may all take place in Rennie's imagination, as she lies anesthetized after surgery (Irvine, 96–99).

2. See also Grace Epstein's discussion of *Bodily Harm*.

3. Particularly in consciousness raising and in various forms of psychological therapy, storytelling is a recognized strategy for personal growth and awareness. Consciousness raising is a feminist strategy based on sharing stories as a means of gaining insight into oppressions and developing assertiveness; the process may lead to resistance. Traditional psychological therapies also use storytelling as a tool for analysis. In both of these models, telling stories in supportive environments enables the individual to understand uncomfortable situations and to gain self-awareness and empowerment. Muriel Rukeyser writes of the power of storytelling in her poem "Kathe Kollwitz": If even one woman were to tell her life story truthfully, "The world would split open."

4. Atwood writes of *The Edible Woman*:

> I myself see the book as protofeminist rather than feminist: there was no women's movement in sight when I was composing the book in 1965, and I'm not gifted with clairvoyance, though like many at the time I'd read Betty Friedan and Simone de Beauvoir beyond locked doors. . . . [M]y heroine's choices remain much the same at the end of the book as they are at the beginning: a career going nowhere, or marriage as an exit from it. . . It would be a mistake to assume that everything has changed. In fact, the tone of the book seems more contemporary now. (*Second Words*, 370)

5. Moreover, scholars who discover Offred's tapes over a hundred years later and piece the narrative together, perhaps inaccurately, have modified the text we read. This raises questions beyond the scope of this paper about who has final control of the text, the author or Bluebeard.

6. Nathalie Cooke responds to Deer's comment in a different way, identifying this narrative strategy as the confessional form (217).

7. Atwood expounds this paradox in *Murder in the Dark*. The writer must appear to be telling the truth but is really lying.

8. Atwood has long been interested in the trickster. She reviewed Lewis Hyde's study of the trickster figure for the *Los Angeles Times*. For a fuller discussion, see her review and Hyde's book, *Trickster Makes This World: Mischief, Myth and Art.*

9. Although Atwood describes both parents as gifted storytellers, the focus here is on her mother. Her relationship to her father is spelled out more fully in the fourth section of *Morning in the Burned House* and a portrait of him appears in *The Labrador Fiasco.*

10. This critique of the city is directly articulated in two poems: "The City Planners" and "Progressive Insanities of a Pioneer." Most of Atwood's novels, especially *Life before Man* and *Cat's Eye,* reiterate this city-bush dichotomy in one form or another.

11. Similarly, in *Cat's Eye* Bluebeard also represents the sexual politics of a death-worshipping culture. Probably because she has spent her earlier life living in the bush, Elaine Risley is finally able to resist her friends' attempts to enforce rigid social codes. By becoming a painter Elaine gains a measure of freedom, and in her paintings she both avenges herself on her childhood tormentors and heals her own pain.

12. Barbara Godard discusses this story from a somewhat different perspective. She reads the anecdotes as a way to build community. She analyzes the intertwining of the mother's and daughter's stories, and describes the levels of interpretation possible.

Works Cited

Aarne, Antti, and Stith Thompson. *The Types of the Folktale.* 2nd rev. ed. F. F. Communications, no. 184. Helsinki: Suomolainen Tideakatemia, Academia Scientiarum Fennica, 1961.

Allen, Robert, ed. *The Lyric Paragraph: A Collection of Canadian Prose Poems.* Montreal: DC Books, 1987.

Allen, R. E., ed. *The Concise Oxford Dictionary of Current English.* 8th ed. Oxford: Clarendon, 1990.

Ammons, Elizabeth, and Annette White-Parks. *Tricksterism in Turn-of-the-Century American Literature: A Multicultural Perspective.* Hanover, N.H.: UP of New England, 1994.

Atwood, Margaret. "Afternotes." In *Sudden Fiction International: Sixty Short-Short Stories.* Ed. Robert Shapard and James Thomas. New York: W. W. Norton, 1989. 298–99.

—. "Afterword" to *The Journals of Susanna Moodie.* Toronto: Oxford UP, 1970. 62–64.

—. *Alias Grace.* New York: Nan A. Talese, Doubleday, 1996.

—. *The Animals in That Country.* Toronto: Oxford UP, 1968.

—. *The Blind Assassin.* New York: Nan A. Talese, Doubleday, 2000.

—. *Bluebeard's Egg.* New York: Fawcett Crest, 1990.

—. *Bodily Harm.* New York: Bantam, 1983.

—. *Bones and Murder.* London: Virago, 1995.

—, [M.E.]. *Double Persephone.* 1st edition, Market Book Series. Toronto: Hawkshead Press, 1961.

—. *Cat's Eye.* Toronto: McClelland and Stewart, 1988.

Bibliography

—. Atwood, Margaret. *Cat's Eye*. New York: Doubleday, 1989.

—. *The Circle Game*. Toronto: Anansi, 1966.

—. *Eating Fire: Selected Poetry 1965–1995*. London: Virago, 1998.

—. *The Edible Woman*. New York: Bantam, 1991.

—. *Good Bones*. Toronto: Coach House, 1992.

—. *Good Bones*. London: Bloomsbury, 1992.

—. *Good Bones*. London: Virago, 1993.

—. *Good Bones*. "Afterword" by Rosemary Sullivan. Toronto: New Canadian Library, 1997.

—. *Good Bones and Simple Murders*. Large Print. Rockland, Mass.: Wheeler, 1995.

—. *Good Bones and Simple Murders*. New York: Nan A. Talese, Doubleday, 1994.

—. *The Handmaid's Tale*. Toronto: McClelland and Stewart, 1985.

—. *The Handmaid's Tale*. New York: Ballantine, 1987.

—. *Interlunar*. Toronto: Oxford UP, 1984.

—. *The Journals of Susanna Moodie*. Toronto: Oxford UP, 1970.

—. *Lady Oracle*. Toronto: Seal Books, 1977.

—. *Lady Oracle*. New York: Simon and Schuster, 1976.

Letters and faxes. Margaret Atwood Papers. Collection 200: *Good Bones, Good Bones and Simple Murders*. Thomas Fisher Rare Book Library, University of Toronto Libraries. Toronto, Canada.

—. Margaret Atwood Papers. Collection 200: *Good Bones, Good Bones and Simple Murders, Power Politics* Manuscripts; *Alias Grace* Research Notes, Notes, Correspondence, Manuscripts; Collection 335: *Good Bones*. Thomas Fisher Rare Book Library, University of Toronto Libraries. Toronto, Canada.

—. "Me, She, and It." Special Issue. "Who's Writing This: Notations on the Authorial I." Ed. Daniel Halpern. *Antaeus* 73/74 (spring 1994): 6–7.

—. *Morning in the Burned House*. Boston: Houghton Mifflin, 1995.

—. *Morning in the Burned House*. Toronto: McClelland and Stewart, 1995.

—. *Murder in the Dark: Short Fictions and Prose Poems*. London: Cape, 1984.

—. *Murder in the Dark: Short Fictions and Prose Poems*. Toronto: Coach House, 1983.

—. *Power Politics*. Toronto: Anansi, 1971.

—. *Procedures for Underground*. Toronto: Oxford UP, 1970.

—. Review of *Trickster Makes This World: Mischief, Myth and Art*, by Lewis Hyde. <www.web.net/owtoad/trickste.html>, accessed 19 July 2002.

—. Review of *Trickster Makes This World: Mischief, Myth and Art*, by Lewis Hyde. *Los Angeles Times*, 25 Jan. 1998: 7.

—. *The Robber Bride*. London: Bloomsbury, 1993.

—. *The Robber Bride*. New York: Nan A. Talese, Doubleday, 1993.

—-. *The Robber Bride*. London: Virago, 1994.

—-. *Second Words: Selected Critical Prose*. Boston: Beacon, 1984.

—-. *Second Words: Selected Critical Prose, 1960–1982*. Toronto: Anansi, 1982.

—-. *Selected Poems*. Toronto: Oxford UP, 1976.

—-. *Selected Poems 1965–1975*. Boston: Houghton Mifflin, 1976.

—-. *Selected Poems II: Poems Selected and New 1976–1986*. Toronto: Oxford UP, l986.

—-. *Selected Poems II: Poems Selected and New 1976–1986*. Boston: Houghton Mifflin, 1987.

—-. "Spotty-Handed Villainesses: Problems of Female Bad Behavior in the Creation of Literature." 4 Jan. 1996. <http://www.web.net/owtoad/vlness.html>, accessed 7 Aug. 2002.

—-. *Strange Things: The Malevolent North in Canadian Literature*. Oxford: Clarendon Press, 1995.

—-. *Surfacing*. New York: Ballantine Books, 1987.

—-. *Surfacing*. New York: Popular Library, l976.

—-. *Surfacing*. New York: Fawcett Crest, 1987.

—-. *Survival: A Thematic Guide to Canadian Literature*. Toronto: Anansi, 1972.

—-. "Survival, Then and Now." *Maclean's*, 1 July 1999: 54–58.

—-. "Three Chronicles: Epaulettes, Cold-blooded, Hardball." *This Magazine* 24.3 (Sept. 1990) 38–41.

—-. *True Stories*. Toronto: Oxford, 1981.

—-. *Wilderness Tips*. Toronto: McClelland and Stewart, l991.

—-. *Wilderness Tips*. New York: Doubleday, 1991.

—-. *Wilderness Tips*. London: Virago, 1992.

—-. *You Are Happy*. Toronto: Oxford UP, 1974.

—-. "Using Other People's Dreadful Childhoods." Interview with Bonnie Lyons, 13 Feb. 1987. *Margaret Atwood: Conversations*. Ed. Earl Ingersoll. Princeton, NJ: Ontario Review Press, 1990. 221–33.

—-. "While I Was Growing Up," *Chatelaine* May 1985: 93–94.

—-. "Why I Write Poetry," *This Magazine* 29 March–April 1996, 43.

Atwood, Margaret, and Victor-Lévy Beaulieu. *Two Solicitudes: Conversations*. Trans. Phyllis Aronoff and Howard Scott. Toronto: McClelland and Stewart, 1998.

Bacchilega, Cristina. *Postmodern Fairy Tales: Gender and Narrative Strategies*. Philadelphia: U of Pennsylvania P, 1997.

Bacon, Lenice Ingram. *American Patchwork Quilts*. New York: William Morrow, l973.

Bannerji, Himani. *Thinking Through: Essays on Feminism, Marxism, and Anti-Racism*. Toronto: Women's Press, 1995.

Barth, John. "Author's Note." *Lost in the Funhouse: Fiction for Print, Tape, Live Voice*. New York: Bantam, 1969. ix–xi.

Bibliography

Baudelaire, Charles. *The Flowers of Evil*. Selected and edited by Marthiel and Jackson Mathews. New York: New Directions, 1963.

Beidelman, T. O. "The Moral Imagination of the Kagaru: Some Thoughts on Tricksters, Translation and Comparative Analysis." In Hynes and Tody, eds., *Mythical Trickster Figures*. Tuscaloosa: University of Alabama Press, 1993: 174–92.

Berkovich, Sacvan. "Clerical Satire in *The Fox and the Wolf*." *Journal of English and Germanic Philology* 65 (1966): 287–94.

—. *Die Blumen des Bösen, Der Spleen von Paris* (French/German). Leipzig: Insel Verlag, 1973.

—. *The Parisian Prowler: Le Spleen de Paris; Petits Poèmes en prose*. Transl. by Edward K. Kaplan. Athens: U of Georgia P, 1989.

Baxter, Charles. Introduction. *Sudden Fiction International: Sixty Short-Short Stories*. Ed. Robert Shapard and James Thomas. New York: W. W. Norton, 1989. 17–25.

Becker, Susanne. "Celebrity, or a Disneyland of the Soul: Margaret Atwood and the Media." In Nischik (ed.), 2000. 28–40.

Beckett, Samuel. *Three Novels*: Molloy; Malone Dies; The Unnamable. Transl. from French. New York: Grove, 1965.

Bemrose, John. Review of *Good Bones*. *Maclean's* 105.40 (5 Oct. 1992): s10–s11.

Beran, Carol. "Images of Women's Power in Contemporary Canadian Fiction by Women." *Studies in Canadian Literature* 15.2 (1990): 55–76

Bercovich, Sacvan. "Clerical Satire in *The Fox and the Wolf*." *Journal of English and Germanic Philology* 65 (1966): 287–94.

Best Loved Nursery Rhymes and Songs. Ed. Augusta Baker. New York: Parents', 1974.

Bettelheim, Bruno. *The Uses of Enchantment: The Meaning and Importance of Fairy Tales*. New York: Vintage, 1977.

Bhabha, Homi K., ed. *Nation and Narration*. London: Routledge, 1990.

—. *The Location of Culture*. London: Routledge, 1994.

Birch, Dinah. "Post-Feminism." Review of *Cat's Eye* and *Interlunar*, by Margaret Atwood, *John Dollar*, by Marianne Wiggins, and *Broken Words*, by Helen Hodgman. *London Review of Books,* 19 January 1989: 3, 5.

Bishop, Elizabeth. *The Complete Poems, 1927–1979*. New York: Farrar, Straus and Giroux, 1979.

Blais, Marie-Claire. "The Forsaken." In *Stories by Canadian Women*. Toronto: Oxford UP, 1984.

Blott, Anne. "Journey to Light [*Interlunar*]." In *Critical Essays on Margaret Atwood*. Ed. Judith McCombs. Boston: G. K. Hall, 1988. 275–79.

Bouson, J. Brooks. *Brutal Choreographies: Oppositional Strategies and Narrative Design in the Novels of Margaret Atwood*. Amherst: Massachusetts UP, 1993.

Braidotti, Rosi. *Nomadic Subjects: Embodiment and Sexual Difference in Contemporary Feminist Theory.* New York: Columbia UP, 1994.

Brooke-Rose, Christine. *A Rhetoric of the Unreal: Studies in Narrative and Structure, Especially of the Fantastic.* Cambridge: Cambridge UP, 1981.

Brydon, Diana. "The White Inuit Speaks: Contamination as Literary Strategy." In *Past the Last Post: Theorizing Post-Colonialism and Post-Modernism.* Ed. Ian Adam and Helen Tiffin. Calgary: U of Calgary P, 1990. 191–203.

Buckner, Philip. "Portnoy's Complaint Revisited: Limited Identities and Canadian Nationalism." Paper delivered at Annual Canadian Studies Symposium, Birkbeck College, University of London, February 1998. To be published in *British Journal of Canadian Studies.*

Campbell, Susan. Review of *Good Bones and Simple Murders.* Fayette, NC, *Observer-Times.* 18 Dec. 1994.

Cassell, Justine. "Storytelling as a Nexus of Change in the Relationship between Gender and Technology: A Feminist Approach to Software Design." In *From Barbie to Mortal Kombat: Gender and Computer Games.* Ed. Justine Cassell and Henry Jenkins. Cambridge, MA: MIT Press, 1998. 298–326.

Clack, Beverley (ed.). *Misogyny in the Western Philosophical Tradition: A Reader.* Houndmills and London: Macmillan, 1999.

Coleridge, Samuel Taylor. "Kubla Khan." In *An Oxford Anthology of English Poetry.* Ed. Howard Foster Lowry and Willard Thorp. 2nd ed. New York: Oxford UP, 1956. 683–84.

Conner, Randy, David Hatfield Sparks, and Mariya Sparks. *Cassell's Encyclopedia of Queer Myth, Symbol and Spirit.* London: Cassell, 1997.

Cooke, Nathalie. "Lions, Tigers, and Pussycats: Margaret Atwood (Auto) Biographically." In Nischik (ed.), 2000. 15–27.

—. *Margaret Atwood: A Biography.* Toronto: ECW, 1998.

—. "The Politics of Ventriloquism: Margaret Atwood's Fictive Confessions." In York (ed.), 1995. 207–28.

Cox, Harvey. *The Feast of Fools: A Theological Essay on Festivity and Fantasy.* Cambridge: Harvard UP, 1969.

Cranny-Francis, Anne. *Feminist Fiction: Feminist Uses of Generic Fiction.* New York: St. Martin's Press, 1990.

Crew, Robert. "Good Bones on Which to Build." Review of *Good Bones* (play), adapted and directed by Neta Gordon, Helen Gardiner Phelan Playhouse. *Toronto Star,* 2 Sept. 1995.

Daemmrich, Horst S., and Ingrid. *Themes and Motifs in Western Literature: A Handbook.* Tübingen: Francke, 1987.

Davey, Frank. *Margaret Atwood: A Feminist Poetics.* Vancouver: Talonbooks, 1984.

—. *Post-National Arguments: The Politics of the Anglophone-Canadian Novel since 1967.* Toronto: U of Toronto P, 1993.

Davidson, Arnold E. *Seeing in the Dark: Margaret Atwood's* Cat's Eye. Toronto: ECW Press, 1997.

—. "Negotiating *Wilderness Tips.*" In *Approaches to Teaching Atwood's* The Handmaid's Tale *and Other Works.* Ed. Sharon R. Wilson, Thomas B. Friedman, and Shannon Hengen. New York: MLA, 1996. 180–86.

Deer, Glenn. "Rhetorical Strategies in *The Handmaid's Tale:* Dystopia and the Paradoxes of Power." *English Studies in Canada* 18.2 (June 1992): 215–33.

Delville, Michel. *The American Prose Poem: Poetic Form and the Boundaries of Genre.* Gainesville: UP of Florida, 1998.

—. "Murdering the Text: Genre and Gender Issues in Margaret Atwood's Short Short Fiction." In *The Contact and the Culmination: Essays in Honour of Hena Maes-Jelinek,* ed. Marc Delrez,Bénédicte Ledent, and Juliette Dor. Liège, Belgium: Liège Language and Literature, 1997. 57–67.

Derrida, Jacques. "The Principle of Reason: The University in the Eyes of Its Pupils." rpt. *Contemporary Literary Criticism: Literary and Cultural Studies,* ed. Robert Con Davis and Ronald Schleifer. 4th ed. New York: Longman, 1998. 345–63.

Dickinson, Emily. *The Complete Poems of Emily Dickinson* (1890). Ed. Thomas H. Johnson. Boston: Little, Brown, 1960.

Drobot, Eve. Review of *Good Bones,* by Margaret Atwood. *Globe and Mail* (Toronto), 19 Sept. 1992, p. C17.

Ellis, Kate Ferguson. *The Contested Castle: Gothic Novels and the Subversion of Domestic Ideology.* Urbana: U of Illinois P, 1989.

Epstein, Grace. "*Bodily Harm:* Female Containment and Abuse in the Romance Narrative." *Genders* 16 (spring 1993): 80–93.

Evans, Margery A. *Baudelaire and Intertextuality: Poetry at the Crossroads.* Cambridge: Cambridge UP, 1993.

Fowke, Edith. *Tales Told in Canada.* Toronto: Doubleday, 1986.

Frenzel, Elisabeth. *Motive der Weltliteratur.* 4., *überarbeitete und ergänzte Aufl.* Stuttgart: Kröner, 1992.

Friedan, Betty. *The Feminine Mystique.* New York: Norton, 1963.

French, William. "Atwood's Snappy Snippets Pack a Wallop." Review of *Murder in the Dark. The Globe and Mail,* 15 March 1983. n.p.

Funk and Wagnalls Standard Dictionary of Folklore, Mythology, and Legend. Ed. Maria Leach and Jerome Fried. San Francisco: Harper and Row, 1984.

Gadpaille, Michelle. *The Canadian Short Story.* Toronto: Oxford UP, 1988.

Gerlach, John. "The Margins of Narrative: The Very Short Story, the Prose

Poem, and the Lyric." *Short Story Theory at a Crossroads*. Ed. Susan Lohafer and Jo Ellyn Clarey. Baton Rouge: Louisiana State UP, 1989.

Gibson, Graeme. *Eleven Canadian Novelists*. Toronto: Anansi, 1973.

Godard, Barbara. "Canadian /Literary? Theory?" *Open Letter* 8. 3 (spring 1992):5–27.

—. "Palimpsest: Margaret Atwood's *Bluebeard's Egg*." *Recherches Anglaises et Nord-Américaines*. 20 (1987):51–60.

Grace, Sherrill E. "'Franklin Lives': Atwood's Northern Ghosts."In York (ed.), 1995. 146–66.

—. "In Search of Demeter: The Lost Silent Mother in *Surfacing*." In *Margaret Atwood: Vision and Forms*. Eds. Kathryn Van Spanckeren and Jan Garden Castro. Carbondale: Southern Illinois UP, 1988. 34–47.

—. "Surviving with Atwood." *Canadian Forum* 70 (Nov. 1991): 30–33.

Greene, Gayle. *Changing the Story: Feminist Fiction and the Tradition*. Bloomington: Indiana UP, 1991.

Gussow, Mel. "An Inner Eye That Sheds Light on Life's Mysteries." <http//www.nytimes.com/2000/10/10/arts/10ASSA.html> (October 10, 2000). Accessed 7 Aug. 2002.

Hall, Stuart. "Cultural Identity and Diaspora." In *Colonial Discourse and Post-Colonial Theory. A Reader*. Ed. P. Williams & L. Chrisman. New York & London: Harvester Wheatsheaf, 1993. 392–403.

Hammond, Karla. "A Margaret Atwood Interview with Karla Hammond." *Concerning Poetry* 12 (1979): 73–81.

Haraway, Donna. "Cyborgs at Large: Interview with Donna Haraway." By Constance Penley and Andrew Ross. *Social Text* 25.6 (1990): 8–23.

—. *Modest_Witness@Second_Millennium.FemaleMan_Meets_OncoMouse: Feminism and Technoscience*. New York: Routledge, 1997.

—. "Monkeys, Aliens, and Women: Love, Science, and Politics at the Intersection of Feminist Theory and Colonial Discourse."*Women's Studies International Forum* 12.3 (1989): 295–312.

—. "Overhauling the Meaning Machines: An interview with Donna Haraway." By Marcy Darnovsky." *Socialist Review* 21.2 (April–June 1991): 65–84.

—. *Primate Visions: Gender, Race, and Nature in the World of Modern Science*. New York: Routledge, 1989.

—. *Simians, Cyborgs, and Women: The Reinvention of Nature*. New York: Routledge, 1991.

Henderson, Joseph L. "Ancient Myths and Modern Man." *Man and His Symbols*. Ed. Carl G. Jung and M-L von Franz, Joseph L. Henderson, Jolande Jacobi, Aniela Jaffe. New York: Dell, 1975. 95–156.

Hengen, Shannon. *Margaret Atwood's Power: Mirrors, Reflections and Images in Select Fiction and Poetry*. Toronto: Second Story, 1993.

—. "Zenia's Foreignness." In York (ed.), 1995. 271–86.

Bibliography

Holman, C. Hugh, and William Harmon. *A Handbook to Literature.* 5th ed. New York: Macmillan, 1986.

hooks, bell. *All About Love: New Visions.* New York: Harper Collins, 2000.

Howard, Jacqueline. *Reading Gothic Fiction: A Bakhtinian Approach.* Oxford: Clarendon Press, 1994.

Howells, Coral Ann. "'It all depends on where you stand in relation to the forest': Atwood and the Wilderness from *Surfacing* to *Wilderness Tips.*" In York (ed.), 1995. 47–70.

—. *Love, Mystery and Misery: Feeling in Gothic Fiction.* London: Athlone Press, 1978.

—. *Margaret Atwood.* London: Macmillan, 1996.

—. "Morning in the Burned House: At Home in the Wilderness." *Margaret Atwood: The Shape-Shifter.* Ed. Coomi S. Vevaina and Coral Ann Howells. New Delhi, India: Creative Books, 1998. 135–45.

—. "Transgressing Genre: A Generic Appoach to Margaret Atwood's Novels." In Nischik (ed.), 2000. 139–56.

Hutcheon, Linda. *The Canadian Postmodern: A Study of Contemporary English-Canadian Fiction.* Toronto: Oxford UP, 1988.

—. "Circling the Downspout of Empire." In *Past the Last Post: Theorizing Post-Colonialism and Post-Modernism.* Ed. Ian Adam and Helen Tiffin. Calgary: U of Calgary P, 1990. 153–66.

—. Foreword. *Likely Stories: A Postmodern Sampler.* Ed. George Bowering and Linda Hutcheon. Toronto: Coach House, 1992.

—. *Splitting Images: Canadian Ironies.* Toronto: Oxford UP, 1991.

Hyde, Lewis. *Trickster Makes This World: Mischief, Myth and Art.* New York: Farrar, Strauss and Giroux, 1998.

Hynes, William J., and William G. Doty, eds. *Mythical Trickster Figures: Contours, Contexts, and Criticism.* Tuscaloosa: U of Alabama Press, 1993.

Ingersoll, Earl G., ed. *Margaret Atwood: Conversations.* Princeton, NJ: Ontario Review Press, 1990.

Irvine, Lorna. *Collecting Clues: Margaret Atwood's* Bodily Harm. Toronto: ECW Press, 1993.

—. "Murder and Mayhem: Margaret Atwood Deconstructs." *Contemporary Literature* 29.2 (summer 1988): 265–76.

Irwin, W. R. *The Game of the Impossible: A Rhetoric of Fantasy.* Urbana: U of Illinois P, 1977.

Jackson, Rosemary. *Fantasy: The Literature of Subversion.* New York: Methuen, 1981.

Jameson, Fredric. Foreword. *The Postmodern Condition: A Report on Knowledge/Jean-Francois Lyotard.* Trans. Geoff Bennington and Brian Massumi. Volume 10, Theory and History of Literature. Minneapolis: U of Minnesota P, 1993. vii–xxi.

Kahane, Claire. "The Gothic Mirror." In *The (M)other Tongue: Essays in Feminist Psychoanalytic Interpretation*. Ed. Shirley Nelson Garner, Claire Kahane, and Madelon Springnether. Ithaca: Cornell UP, 1985. 334–51.

Kaplanoglu, Marianthi. "AT545B 'Puss in Boots' and 'The Fox-Matchmaker': From the Cental Asian to the European Tradition." *Folklore* (London) 100 (1999): 57–62.

Kirtz, Mary. "'Facts Become Art through Love': Narrative Structure in Marian Engel's *Bear*." *American Review of Canadian Studies* (autumn 1992): 351–62.

—. "'The past belongs to us because we are the ones who need it:' *(Alias) Grace* Notes." 1997 ACSUS Paper, Minneapolis.

Kirtz, Mary K. "Canadian Literary Cultures Observed: Carol Shields' *Small Ceremonies* and Margaret Atwood's *Lady Oracle*." In *Canada Observed: Perspectives from Abroad and from Within*. Eds. Jurgen Kleist and Shawn Huffman. New York: Lang, 2000. 175–83.

Kubler-Ross, Elisabeth. *On Death and Dying*. New York: Macmillan, 1969.

Kuester, Martin. "Atwood: Parodies from a Feminist Point of View." Chap. 5 in Kuester, *Framing Truths: Parodic Structures in Contemporary English-Canadian Historical Novels*. Toronto: U of Toronto P, 1992. 124–47.

Laframboise, Jana. "Laurentian University Students Meet Margaret Atwood." Laurentian University Student Newspaper, 2 Dec. 1999.

Lakoff, George, and Mark Johnson. *Metaphors We Live By*. Chicago: The U of Chicago P, 1980.

Larmore, Phoebe. Letters to Margaret Atwood and her staff. Collections 200 and 335. "Good Bones and Simple Murders" and "Good Bones." Margaret Atwood Papers, Thomas Fisher Rare Book Library. University of Toronto Libraries. Toronto, Canada.

Laurence, Margaret. *The Stone Angel*. Toronto: McClelland and Stewart, 1961.

LeBihan, Jill. "*The Handmaid's Tale, Cat's Eye*, and *Interlunar*: Margaret Atwood's Feminist (?) Futures (?.)." In *Narrative Strategies in Canadian Literature*. Ed. Coral Ann Howells and Lynette Hunter. Buckingham, UK: Open UP, 1991. 93–107.

Lee, Hermione. "Writers in Conversation: Margaret Atwood." Interview, VHS Video film. Roland Collection No. 43, 52 minutes, Color. Northbrook, IL.

Letters. See Margaret Atwood Papers.

Lithgow, Marilyn. *Quiltmaking and Quiltmakers*. New York: Funk and Wagnalls, 1974.

Locus Index to Science Fiction. Description *Good Bones and Small Murders*, by Margaret Atwood. <www.locusmag.com/index//631.html#A268>.

Bibliography

Lyotard, Jean-François. *The Postmodern Condition: A Report on Knowledge.* Trans. Geoff Bennington and Brian Massumi. Volume 10, *Theory and History of Literature.* Minneapolis: U of Minnesota P, 1993.

Lypchuk, Donna. "Boning Up on Atwood: at a Recent Nightclub Reading, 'Peggy' Was in Her Element." Book Review. *Good Bones,* by Margaret Atwood. <http://www.eye.net/eye/issue/issue_10.01.92/ARTS/bo1001a.htm>. Accessed 25 July 2002.

MacDonald, George. "The Imagination, Its Functions and Its Culture." In *The Imagination and Other Essays.* Boston: Lothrop, l883.

McHugh, Heather. *The Father of the Predicaments.* Hanover, NH: Wesleyan UP, 1999.

MacLennan, Hugh. *On Being a Maritime Writer.* Sackville, New Brunswick: Mt. Allison UP, 1984.

Mandel, Eli. "Atwood's Poetic Politics." In *Margaret Atwood: Language, Text, and System.* Ed. Sherrill E. Grace and Lorraine Weir. Vancouver: U of British Columbia P, 1983. 53–66.

March, Cristie. "Crimson Silks and New Potatoes: The Heteroglossic Power of the Object: Atwood's *Alias Grace.*" *Studies in Canadian Literature* 22.2 (1997): 66–82.

Marchand, Philip. Review of *Good Bones. Toronto Star,* 25 Sept. 1992. Margaret Atwood Papers.

Marvell, Andrew. "To His Coy Mistress." In *An Oxford Anthology of English Poetry.* 2nd ed. Ed. Howard Forster Lowry and Willard Thorp. New York: Oxford UP, 1956. 326–27.

Massé, Michelle A. *In the Name of Love: Women, Masochism, and the Gothic.* Ithaca: Cornell UP, 1992.

McCombs, Judith. "Contrary Re-memberings: The Creating Self and Feminism in *Cat's Eye.*" *Canadian Literature* 129 (1991): 9–23.

Merivale, Patricia. "From 'Bad News' to 'Good Bones': Margaret Atwood's Gendering of Art and Elegy." In York (ed.), 1995. 253–70.

—. "'Hypocrite Lecteuse! Ma Semblable! Ma Soeur!': On Teaching *Murder in the Dark.*" In Sharon Wilson, Thomas Friedman, Shannon Hengen (eds.), *Teaching* The Handmaid's Tale *and Other Texts.* New York: MLA, 1996. 99–106.

Meyer, Michael. *The Bedford Introduction to Reading, Thinking, and Writing Literature.* 4th ed. Boston: St. Martin's, 1996. 792.

Monroe, Jonathan. *A Poverty of Objects: The Prose Poem and Politics of Genre.* Ithaca: Cornell UP, 1987.

Morton, Stephen. "Postcolonial Gothic and the New World Disorder: Crossing Boundaries of Space/Time in Margaret Atwood's *The Robber Bride.*" *British Journal of Canadian Studies* 14.1 (1999): 99–114.

Moodie, Susanna. *Life in the Clearings versus the Bush.* 1853. Toronto: New Canadian Library, l989.

Mukherjee, Arun. *Postcolonialism: My Living.* Toronto: TSAR, 1998.

Murfin, Ross, and Supryia M. Ray. *The Bedford Glossary of Critical and Literary Terms.* Boston: Bedford Books, 1997.

Mycak, Sonia. *In Search of the Split Subject: Psychoanalysis, Phenomenology, and the Novels of Margaret Atwood.* Toronto: ECW, 1996.

Myers, George Jr., ed. *Epiphanies: The Prose Poem Now.* Westerville, OH: Cumberland, 1987.

Neuman, Shirley, and Smaro Kambourali, ed. *Amazing Space: Writing Canadian Women Writing.* Edmonton: Longspoon/Newest, 1986.

Nicholson, Colin. "Living on the Edges: Constructions of Post-Colonial Subjectivity in Atwood's Early Poetry." *Margaret Atwood: Writing and Subjectivity.* Ed. Colin Nicholson. New York: St. Martin's, 1994. 11–50.

Nischik, Reingard M., ed. *Margaret Atwood: Works and Impact.* ESALC. Rochester, N.Y.: Camden House, 2000.

—-. "Von guten Knochen und Mord im Dunkeln: Margaret Atwoods inverse Poetik intertextueller Winzigkeit." *Germanisch-Romanische Monatsschrift* 52, no. 3 (2002): 401–16.

Norfolk, Lawrence W. "Do they travel?" Review of *Interlunar. TLS* 18–24 August 1989: 903.

The Norton Anthology of Poetry: Shorter Edition. Ed. Arthur M. Eastman et al. New York: Norton, 1970.

Olds, Sharon. *The Father.* New York: Knopf, 1992, 1995.

Ondaatje, Michael *In the Skin of a Lion.* New York: Knopf, 1987.

Patton, Marilyn. "Tourists and Terrorists: The Creation of *Bodily Harm.*" *Papers on Language and Literature* 28.2 (spring 1992): 150–73.

Pendakur, R., and J. Hennebry, eds. *Multicultural Canada: A Demographic Overview.* Ottawa: Department of Canadian Heritage, 1998.

Poetry and Prose Page. <http://www.quilt.com/History/ PoetryAndProsePage. html>. Accessed 6 Aug. 2002.

Potts, Donna L. "The White Goddess Displaced: National/Sexual Parallels in Atwood's *The Robber Bride.*" *Literature of Region and Nation: Proceedings of the 6th International Region and Nation Conference, University of New Brunswick in Saint John, Saint John, New Brunswick, Canada, 2–7 August 1996.* Vol. 2. Ed. Winnifred M. Bogaards. Saint John: University of New Brunswick in Saint John, 1998. 230–38.

Prickett, Stephen. *Victorian Fantasy.* Bloomington: Indiana UP, l979.

Quilt Block Names. <http://www.quilt.com/History/ BlockNames.html>. Accessed 6 Aug. 2002.

Quilt History. <http.//204.249.244.10/QuiltHistory/Page.html>.

Rabkin, Eric S. *The Fantastic in Literature.* Princeton: Princeton UP, 1976.

Relke, Diana M. A. "Myths of Nature and the Poetry of Canadian Women: An Alternative Reading of Literary History." *New Literature Review* 23 (1992): 31–49.

Bibliography

Review of *Good Bones and Simple Murders,* by Margaret Atwood. *Kirkus.* 1 Oct.1994. <www.amazon.com/exec/obidos/ts/book-reviews/0385471106/103-9666739-8059815>. Accessed 7 Aug. 2002.

Review of *Good Bones and Simple Murders,* by Margaret Atwood. <www.theatlantic.com/unbound/aandc/brfrevs/brv9501.htm>. Accessed 7 Aug. 2002.

Rich, Adrienne. *On Lies, Secrets and Silence: Selected Prose 1966–1978.* New York: W. W. Norton, 1979.

Roberts, Diane. "Fiction from Abroad." Review of *Swimming the Channel,* by Jull Neville, *Good Bones and Simple Murders,* by Margaret Atwood, *Green River Rising,* by Tim Willocks. *The Atlanta Journal-Constitution.* 29 Jan. 1995. Arts: 10.

Rogerson, Margaret. "Reading the Patchworks in *Alias Grace.*" *The Journal of Commonwealth Literature* 33.1 (1998): 5–22.

Rosenthal, M. L., and Sally M. Gall. *The Modern Poetic Sequence: The Genius of Modern Poetry.* New York: Oxford UP, 1983.

Rukeyser, Muriel. "Kathe Kollwitz," *The Collected Poems of Muriel Rukeyser.* New York: McGraw-Hill, 1982. 482.

Sandler, Linda. "Interview with Margaret Atwood." *Malahat Review* 41 (January 1977): 7–27.

Schoemperlen, Diane. *In the Language of Love.* Toronto: Harper Collins, 1994.

Seaman, Donna. Review of *Good Bones and Simple Murders,* by Margaret Atwood. *Booklist.* 1 Nov. 1994. <www.amazon.com/exec /obidos/ts/book-reviews/0385471106/103-9666739-8059815>. Accessed 7 Aug. 2002.

Sedgwick, Eve Kosofsky. *The Coherence of Gothic Conventions.* New York: Methuen, 1986.

Shakespeare, William. *The Merchant of Venice. Shakespeare: The Complete Works.* Ed. G. B. Harrison. New York: Harcourt, 1952. 583–612.

Shapard, Robert, and James Thomas, ed. *Sudden Fiction International: Sixty Short-Short Stories.* New York: W. W. Norton, 1989.

Sharpe, Martha. "Margaret Atwood and Julia Kristeva: Space-Time, the Dissident Woman Artist, and the Pursuit of Female Solidarity in *Cat's Eye.*" *Essays on Canadian Writing* 50 (1993): 174–89.

Spriet, Pierre. "Margaret Atwood's Post-modernism in *Murder in the Dark.*" *Commonwealth Essays and Studies* 11. 2 (spring 1989): 24–30.

Staels, Hilde. "Margaret Atwood's *The Handmaid's Tale:* Resistance through Narrating." *English Studies* 1995, 5: 455–67.

Staines, David. *Beyond the Provinces: Literary Canada at Century's End.* Toronto: U of Toronto P, 1995.

Steele, James. "The Literary Criticism of Margaret Atwood." *In Our Own House: Social Perspectives on Canadian Literature.* Ed. Paul Capon. Toronto: McClelland, 1978. 73–81.

Stein, Karen F. *Margaret Atwood Revisited*. Twayne's World Authors Series No. 887, ed. Robert Locker. New York: Twayne, 1999.

Sturgess, Charlotte. "Margaret Atwood's Short Fiction." In Nischik (ed.) 2000. 87–96.

Sullivan, Rosemary. "Afterword." Toronto: New Canadian Library, 1997. 113–17.

—. *The Red Shoes: Margaret Atwood Starting Out*. Toronto: Harper Flamingo, l998.

Talese, Nan. Letters to Margaret Atwood and her staff. Collections 200 and 335. "Good Bones and Simple Murders" and "Good Bones." Margaret Atwood Papers, Thomas Fisher Rare Book Library.

Thomas, Dylan. *The Collected Poems of Dylan Thomas*. New York: New Directions, 1957.

Thomas, James. "Introduction." In *Flash Fiction: Very Short Stories,* ed. James Thomas, Denise Thomas, and Tom Hazuka. New York: W. W. Norton, 1992. 11–14.

Thomas, James, Denise Thomas, and Tom Hazuka, eds. *Flash Fiction: Very Short Stories*. New York: W. W. Norton, 1992.

Thomas, Joan. "Atwood Jogs a Murderous Memory." Review of *Alias Grace* by Margaret Atwood. *The Globe and Mail*. 7 Sept. 1996: *Books,* C10.

Thompson, Lee Briscoe. *Scarlet Letters: Margaret Atwood's* The Handmaid's Tale. Toronto: ECW Press, 1997.

Thompson, Stith. *Motif-Index of Folk Literature*. Revised and Enlarged Edition. Six Volumes. Bloomington: Indiana UP, 1955.

Thoreau, Henry David. *Walden*. 1854. Rpt. *The Harper American Literature*. Ed. Donald McQuade et al. New York: Harper, 1987. 1242–1414.

Todorov, Tzetvan. *The Fantastic: A Structural Approach to a Literary Genre*. Trans. Richard Howard. Ithaca, N.Y.: Cornell UP, l973.

Tostevin, Lola Lemire. *'Sophie*. Toronto: Coach House, 1988.

Van Herk, Aritha. "The Art of Blackmail." *Canadian Literature* 100 (spring 1984): 329–32.

Van Spanckeren, Kathryn. "The Trickster Text: Teaching Atwood's Works in Creative Writing Classrooms." In Sharon Wilson, Thomas Friedman, and Shannon Hengen, eds. *Approaches to Teaching* The Handmaid's Tale *and Other Works*. New York: MLA, l996. 77 –83.

Verduyn, Christl. "*Murder in the Dark*: Fiction/Theory by Margaret Atwood." *Canadian Fiction Magazine*. Feminist Fiction/Theory Issue. 57 (1986): 124–31.

Wagner-Martin, Linda. "'Giving Way to Bedrock': Atwood's Later Poems." In York (ed.), 1995. 71–88.

Wigston, Nancy. Review of *Good Bones*, by Margaret Atwood. *Quill and Quire* 58.10 (Oct. 1992): 21.

Wiley, David. "Natural Born Quilter." *A & E.* 23 Jan. 1997. <http://www.daily.umn.edu/ae/Print/1997/03/csgrace.html>. Accessed 6 Aug. 2002.

Wilson, Sharon Rose. *Margaret Atwood's Fairy-Tale Sexual Politics.* Jackson: UP of Mississippi, 1993.

——. *Margaret Atwood's Fairy-Tale Sexual Politics.* Toronto: ECW Press, 1993.

Wilson, Sharon R. "Camera Images in Margaret Atwood's Novels." *Margaret Atwood: Reflection and Reality.* Ed. Beatrice Mendez-Egle. Edinburg, Tex.: Pan American UP, 1987. 29–57.

——. "Deconstructing Text and Self: Mirroring in Atwood's *Surfacing* and Beckett's *Molloy.*" *Journal of Popular Literature* 3.1 (spring/summer 1987): 53–69.

——. "Mythological Intertexts in Margaret Atwood's Works." In Nischik (ed.), 2000. 203–16.

Wilson, Sharon R., Thomas B. Friedman, and Shannon Hengen, co-editors. *Approaches to Teaching* The Handmaid's Tale *and Other Works.* New York: MLA, 1996.

Woodcock, George. "Metamorphosis and Survival: Notes on the Recent Poetry of Margaret Atwood." *Margaret Atwood: Language, Text, and System.* 125–42. Reprinted in his *Northern Spring: The Flowering of Canadian Literature.* Vancouver, BC: Douglas and McIntyre, 1987. 266–84.

Yeats, William Butler. *Collected Poems.* New York: Macmillan, 1933 (1956).

York, Lorraine M., ed. *Various Atwoods: Essays on the Later Poems, Short Fiction, and Novels.* Concord, Ontario: Anansi, 1995.

Zimmerman, Barbara. "Shadow Play: Zenia, the Archetypal Feminine Shadow in Margaret Atwood's *The Robber Bride.*" *Pleiades* 15.2 (1995): 70–82.

Zipes, Jack, trans. *The Complete Fairy Tales of the Brothers Grimm.* New York: Bantam, 1987.

Notes on Contributors

Carol L. Beran is Professor of English at Saint Mary's College of California. She has published essays on works by many Canadian writers, including Margaret Atwood, Robert Kroetsch, Hugh MacLennan, Alice Munro, Michael Ondaatje, and Aritha Van Herk. Her book *Living over the Abyss* is about Atwood's *Life before Man*.

Shannon Hengen is Professor of English at Laurentian University in Canada. She has published articles on Atwood, H.D., comedy, Canadian theatre, and *Beowulf*. Books include *Margaret Atwood's Power, Comedy's Edge* (2 volumes); editor of *Performing Gender and Comedy: Theories, Texts, Contexts*; editor, with Sharon Wilson and Thomas Friedman, of *Approaches to Teaching Atwood's* The Handmaid's Tale *and Other Works*. From 1999 to 2000, Hengen was president of the Margaret Atwood Society.

Coral Ann Howells is Professor of English and Canadian Literature at the University of Reading, UK. She has written and lectured extensively on Canadian women's writing in Britain, Europe, North America, India, and Australia. Her books on Canadian literature include *Private and Fictional Words: Canadian Women Novelists of the 1970s and 80s*; *Narrative Strategies in Recent Canadian Literature* (coeditor Lynette Hunter); *Margaret Atwood*; and *Alice Munro*. She is currently working on the multicultural profile of Canadian women's fiction in English.

Mary K. Kirtz is Professor of English and Director of Canadian Studies at the University of Akron, Ohio. She has published articles on Atwood in *Approaches to Teaching Atwood's* The Handmaid's Tale *and Other Works* and *Margaret Atwood: Reflection and Reality* and on contemporary Canadian literature in numerous journals. She has been treasurer of the Margaret Atwood Society and won the Rufus Z. Smith Prize for distinguished articles in the *American Review of Canadian Studies,* 1991–1992.

Reingard M. Nischik is Professor of American Literature at the University of Constance, Germany. She has published articles on American, Canadian, and English literature and literary theory and books, including *Mentalstilistik: Ein Beitrag zu Stiltheorie und Narrativik, dargestellt am Erzählwerk Margaret Atwoods* (1991); ed. and intro. *Margaret Atwood, Polarities: Selected Stories* (1994); ed. and intro. *Margaret Atwood: Works and Impact* (2000); ed. with Robert Kroetch, *Gaining Ground: European Critics on Canadian Literature (1985); Short Short Stories Universal (1993);* ed. and intro. *Leidenschaften literarisch.* Nischik is editor of the book series European Studies in American Literature and Culture for Camden House and coeditor of the interdisciplinary journal *Zeitschrift fur Kanada-Studien.*

Karen F. Stein is Professor of English and Women's Studies and Chair at the University of Rhode Island. She has published articles on Atwood, drama, Toni Morrison, Janet Frame, Alice Walker Adrienne Rich, Margaret Laurence, Susan Glaspell, and films of the Frankenstein myth and *Margaret Atwood Revisited* (1999).

Kathryn Van Spanckeren is Professor of English at the University of Tampa and former president of the Margaret Atwood Society. In addition to numerous articles on Atwood and a history of American literature for non-Americans, she has edited *John Gardner: Critical Perspectives* and, with Jan Garden Castro, *Margaret Atwood: Vision and Forms.*

Sharon R. Wilson is Professor of English and Women's Studies at the University of Northern Colorado. Her published works include articles on Margaret Atwood, Doris Lessing, Jean Rhys, Samuel Beckett, E. R. Eddison, the film *Citizen Kane,* and the book *Margaret Atwood's Fairy-Tale Sexual Politics* (Jackson and Toronto: University Press of Mississippi and ECW, 1993). With Thomas B. Friedman and Shannon Hengen, she is coeditor of *Approaches to Teaching Atwood's* The Handmaid's Tale *and Other Works* (New York: MLA, 1996). She is currently working on *Contemporary Women's Metafiction.* Sharon Wilson began writing about Atwood in 1980; was founding copresident, with Arnold Davidson, of the Margaret Atwood Society in 1983; and has taught both graduate and undergraduate courses on Atwood and Canadian, U.S., British, and postcolonial literature.

Index

Index

Index

Index

Index

Index